The economics of price discrimination

The economics
of price discrimination

LOUIS PHLIPS

Center for Operations Research & Econometrics
Université Catholique de Louvain

CAMBRIDGE UNIVERSITY PRESS

Cambridge
London   New York   New Rochelle
Melbourne   Sydney

Published by the Press Syndicate of the University of Cambridge
The Pitt Building, Trumpington Street, Cambridge CB2 1RP
32 East 57th Street, New York, NY 10022, USA
296 Beaconsfield Parade, Middle Park, Melbourne 3206, Australia

© Cambridge University Press 1983

First published 1983

Printed in the United States of America

Library of Congress Cataloging in Publication Data
Phlips, Louis.
The economics of price discrimination.
Includes bibliographical references and index.
1. Price discrimination. I. Title.
HF5416.5.P46   1983   338.5′21   82–14625
ISBN 0 521 23994 X hard covers
ISBN 0 521 28394 9 paperback

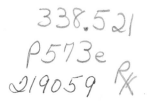

To
P.J.
V.M.
A.S.
S.J.C.
B.F.   At last!

Contents

Figures and tables

Figures

Tables

Preface

This book was written not only for students in applied price theory and industrial organization but also for lawyers, civil servants, and consultants who want to consider the economic rationale behind the legalistic scenery of the antitrust cases in which they are involved. In addition, I hope that businessmen will find a moment to read the pages that follow, to gain a better understanding of the practices that are the custom of their trade.

Readability has therefore been my first and main objective. Whenever possible, my reasoning is explained in plain words and is illustrated graphically; technicalities and mathematical niceties are avoided. In a few places, I must confess, some algebra does appear when the argument did not seem amenable to graphic demonstration. But even there it should be possible to read between the equations and to understand the point being made. For the same reason, each essay begins with an introductory chapter describing the business practices that are to be explained in succeeding chapters. The reader is asked to keep these examples in mind while reading the more theoretical developments and to refer to them constantly.

I am grateful to Sheila Verkaeren and her staff at CORE for cheerful and efficient secretarial assistance. I am particularly indebted to Simone Vincken, who typed and retyped the various drafts of the manuscript with the greatest care.

My intellectual debt to Mel Greenhut (Texas A & M University) should be obvious from the text. Henk Witlox, from the European Economic Communities in Brussels, convinced me of the necessity of studying price discrimination in 1976 and is thus directly responsible for the writing of this book (though he may not necessarily agree with the conclusions reached, of course).

Helpful suggestions and comments were made at various stages by Colin Day of Cambridge University Press, by two anonymous referees, and by L. Berlage, J. Drèze, J. Gabszewicz, R. Masson, S. Maynes, D. Neven, R. Schuler, Y. Shilony, F. Spinnewyn, V. Stevens, J. Thisse, and C. Zakaropoulou and are acknowledged with thanks.

De Haan, April 1982   L.P.

Preliminaries

It is tempting – and I shall not resist the temptation – to start with a plagiarism. Baumol and Bradford and their famous 1970 paper "Optimal Departures from Marginal Cost Pricing" are the victims. The need for the present book is a paradox, and this volume might be subtitled: *The Purloined Proposition; or, The Mystery of the Mislaid Maxim.* For the results that it describes have appeared many times in the literature and have been reported by most eminent economists in very prominent journals. Yet these results may well come as a surprise to many readers who will consider them to be at variance with ideas that they have long accepted. The proposition in question asserts that, *generally, discriminatory prices will be required for an optimal allocation of resources in real life situations.* The reason for the difficulty into which uniform pricing is likely to fall is that real life firms do have at least *some* monopoly power and can use marketing techniques to keep their markets separate, so that price discrimination is generally possible. This fact of life is not well known, nor is it widely recognized that there exists a highly sophisticated and well-developed – though recent – body of literature indicating what should be done in such circumstances.

The discussion of this book differs from the earlier writings in several ways. First, instead of considering regulatory public utility pricing, it explores parallel developments in the framework of a private economy with profit-maximizing firms. Second, it attempts a simplified exposition, which is, of course, possible only at a cost in terms of loss of generality. Third, it brings together, explicitly, all three strands of the discussion: the welfare theoretic, the regulatory, and the industrial organization contributions. Finally, as far as I know, it offers the first overview of the extensive literature that has grown up in the area.

Price discrimination and market failure

Welfare economics traditionally focuses on maximizing *aggregate* welfare measures such as the sum of producers' and consumers' surpluses. Recent discussions have centered on the question of whether *every* economic agent is *strictly* better or worse off when facing a particular price structure.

1

On the aggregate level, the standard welfare theorems leave no room for price discrimination. These aseptic theorems simply ignore the different elements of product differentiation (spatial and temporal elements, quality or taste differences, uncertainty) that make price discrimination possible and profitable and consider pairs of homogeneous "goods" between which the marginal rate of substitution has to be equal for all consumers and so on. The upshot is that any Pareto optimum is a competitive equilibrium and vice versa. It is an easy step, from here, to the stigmatization of price discrimination as "market failure." Part of the profession no doubt is "against" price discrimination (or at least some forms of it) for this very reason. A condemnation based on this sort of theorem seems totally unwarranted, given that the assumptions of product homogeneity and absence of monopoly power are totally unrealistic. The obvious next analytical step is to redefine the Pareto optimum (or the consumers' and producers' surpluses to be added up and maximized) in such a way that product differentiation is fully integrated in the analysis through an enlargement of the definition of an economic good.

In the case of a spatial economy, for example, different avenues – leading to the same conclusion – have been followed. Thisse (1975) examines the properties of the equilibrium prices of spatially differentiated goods and concludes that freight absorption (the most common form of price discrimination over space) is incompatible with a competitive equilibrium and therefore with a Pareto optimum. Mougeot (1975) redefines the optimum for an economy with a fixed location of economic agents, regional availabilities of given factors, and transportable resources and concludes that prices vary with location. However, for a given location he rediscovers all the properties of the nonspatial optimum, with the implication that all buyers served by a given firm must, at the optimum, pay the same net price (the delivered price minus the cost of transportation) equal to the marginal cost of production: Spatial price discrimination is not compatible with the optimum. Analogous results are available for the intertemporal optimum with and without uncertainty, as in the pioneering article by Malinvaud (1953). Competitive futures prices have to have rates of growth equal to the rate of interest, just as competitive delivered prices must fully reflect the cost of carriage.

A further step toward more realism is to admit that in real world situations, some form of monopoly power is unavoidable, if only because differences in location or in dates of delivery between competing firms imply that they have downward-sloping demand curves, not to mention objective or subjective quality differences in their products, hence the need for considering socially optimal pricing by a monopolist operating under a profit constraint. This is the public utility approach followed in the literature brilliantly summarized and expanded by Baumol and Bradford (1970). It leads us into the realm of *constrained* welfare maximization, or *second-best* optima, in contradistinction to the spatial or temporal optima just noted, which imply a redefinition of the problem (the conditions of the nonspatial and atemporal optimum being considered irrelevant in a spatial or temporal context). In the Baumol and Bradford approach, additional constraints are superimposed on a problem that remains basically the same.

The power to fix prices being granted, firms are now constrained to earn less than maximum profits, without being allowed to take losses. For one reason or another, firms in the Baumol–Bradford economy operate under what amounts to a fixed-profit constraint. They also market a number of goods. One way to describe this economy is to consider that all industry has been nationalized and that one giant multiproduct firm is dedicated to the maximization of social welfare. To do so, it maximizes aggregate social welfare

$$W = \mu S + \Pi$$

where Π is its profit function, S is the sum of consumers' surpluses, and μ is fixed at a value between zero and one. If μ were equal to one, we would have unconstrained welfare maximization (with or without product differentiation, depending upon the way in which revenue functions and reservation prices are specified). If μ were equal to zero, we would have full profit maximization.

Such constrained welfare maximization typically leads to the conclusion that prices that deviate in a systematic manner from marginal costs will be required for an optimal allocation of resources, even in the absence of externalities. In particular, each price is to be set so that its percentage deviation from marginal costs will be required for an optimal allocation of resources, even in the absence of externalities. That is, each price is to be set so that its percentage deviation from marginal cost is inversely proportional to the item's price elasticity of demand. Baumol and Bradford comment as follows:

> According to this result, the social welfare will be served most effectively not by setting prices equal or even proportionate to marginal costs, but by causing unequal deviations in which items with elastic demands are priced at levels close to their marginal costs. The prices of items whose demands are inelastic diverge from their marginal costs by relatively wider margins.
>
> This result is surely not immediately acceptable through intuition. It strikes us as curious, if for no other reason, because it seems to say that

ordinary price discrimination might well set relative prices at least roughly in the manner required for maximal social welfare in the presence of a profit constraint. Since the objective of the analysis can be described as the determination of the optimally discriminatory set of prices needed to obtain the required profit, some degree of resemblance is perhaps to be expected. The case studied here is, thus, in a sense the obverse of the problem of profit maximizing price discrimination, and while the two solutions bear some qualitative resemblance, it can be shown that they may in fact differ substantially in quantity. [1970, p. 267]

Socially optimal prices thus *resemble* discriminatory prices set by a profit-maximizing monopolist, to the extent that the latter are lower for goods with elastic demands, whereas the former are closer to their marginal costs. The resemblance does not go far, certainly not far enough to justify profit-maximizing discriminatory prices from a social point of view.

On the other hand, the socially optimal prices derived are said to be optimally discriminatory prices. This statement is confusing and unwarranted when it is interpreted to mean that the optimal prices are those that a discriminating monopolist should fix. Indeed, Baumol and Bradford can do no more than pinpoint a qualitative resemblance of their optimal prices with discriminatory prices that is due to their common link with price elasticities. For their model does *not* incorporate the possibility of discriminating: Theirs is a model of multiple production, in which a firm produces several commodities, each having not only its own marginal revenue *but also its own marginal cost.* The price discrimination rule (that the marginal revenues of the different products must be equal to *the* – unique, common – marginal cost of production) thus cannot appear in the model, and it is a misnomer to talk about "the optimally discriminatory set of prices." The difficulty is far more than a question of semantics. By concentrating on the profit constraint, Baumol and Bradford have lost sight of those elements of product differentiation that make price discrimination possible.

Whether or not the interpretation just discussed is correct, I want to adopt another, more stringent type of constrained welfare maximization, in which – although and notwithstanding the fact that μ is fixed between zero and one – the monopolist can still effectively price discriminate over time, space, quality, or whatever element of product differentiation happens to permit separation of the markets involved. This is the approach pioneered, as far as I know, by Spence (1980). Formally, it implies that, when the structure of the discriminatory prices can be determined, these prices are inserted in (i.e., used to specify) *both S* and Π before our equation is maximized. The objective of the analysis is then to compare the properties of the first-order conditions of this (doubly constrained, so to speak) maximum with those of simple profit maximization ($\mu=0$) and possibly with those of the unconstrained optimum ($\mu=1$). For me, the latter exercise makes sense only as a purely academic effort, in the pejorative sense of the adjective, to reestablish links with theories of "market failure." The former exercise aims at showing to what extent an uncontrolled monopolist will tend to deviate from the policy that would be optimal for a given social or political objective (i.e., μ with a value between zero and one) and under the given circumstances, that is, without erasing those indelible features (differences in location, time of delivery, incomes, tastes, know-how) that make economic life as it is and thus make price discrimination itself unerasable.

Such considerations raise the question of how to define price discrimination, to which I now turn.

How to define price discrimination

The more one thinks about price discrimination, the harder it is to define. A good definition should cover all possible cases, including the new forms of price discrimination that seem to appear in the literature every day. A good definition should also eliminate cases that at first appear to resemble price discrimination but later prove to be quite different when examined more closely. On both accounts the standard definition of price discrimination seems to perform badly.

Indeed, in my search for an acceptable definition, I invariably came upon the usual answer: There is price discrimination when the same commodity is sold at different prices to different consumers. Obviously this statement does not satisfy my two criteria. On the one hand, it would restrict the scope of this book to cases where *the same commodity* is sold, say an entrance ticket to Disneyland; on a particular day, senior citizens receive a discount, as do children and military personnel. Yet it seems obvious (at least to me) that differentiated products can also be sold at discriminatory prices. Discrimination is revealed, for example, when people flying tourist class discover that first-class passengers enjoy a service (perhaps champagne or caviar) that is much better than is justified by the difference between tourist and first-class fares, that is, the service has a higher "worth per dollar." Since the day I flew over the ocean first class – thanks to an error "made by the computer" – I have always felt discriminated against when sitting among my poor fellow tourist-class passengers!

On the other hand, when the same good is sold *at different prices to different consumers* there may be no discrimination at all. If the price difference fully reflects the difference in the cost of carrying the good from the seller's location to the buyers' location, then nobody would argue, I am sure, that a discriminatory practice is involved. Quite to the contrary, there would be price discrimination if the price differences did not fully reflect transport costs. In spatial economics, freight absorption is the classical example of price discrimination. Sales at uniform delivered prices – where all customers pay the same price regardless of their location – are treated as examples of indisputable discrimination that favors more distant customers "against" those who are located closer to the seller's plant.

The difficulty centers on the concept of a "commodity." If we want to arrive at a definition that is neither too narrow nor too broad, we cannot avoid discussing the meaning, from an economic point of view, of this term. A commodity, then, is a group of products or product class, that is, a group of goods possessing a particular set of characteristics (Lancaster 1979). Variations in the characteristic contents of products within the same group lead to what we call "product differentiation." Each variation gives a different "variety," such as different models of automobiles or radios.

For the purpose of our analysis of price discrimination, it is necessary to include the terms of sale in the list of characteristics to be considered. As Debreu emphasizes, "A good in one place and the same good in another place are *different* economic objects and it is vital to specify the place where the good is available" (1959, p. 33). Similarly, some automobile dealers may perform more service or may carry a larger range of varieties in stock. One implication is that there is almost never absolute homogeneity in the commodity.[1] Another implication is that some price dispersion is always to be expected in the market for a commodity (Stigler 1961, p. 214). There is no reason why such price dispersion should imply price discrimination. (Paradoxically, it is rather in the absence of price dispersion that one should suspect discrimination.)

If it is true that both product differentiation and price dispersion are to be expected in all commodity markets, price discrimination should be defined as implying that two varieties of a commodity are sold (by the same seller) to two buyers at different *net* prices, the net price being the price (paid by the buyer) corrected for the cost associated with the product differentiation.[2] The "standard" case, referred to above, where two identical varieties (entrance tickets to Disneyland) are being sold at the same moment at different prices, is then a very special case indeed (the exception rather than the rule!).

My criterion clearly refers to a cost associated with a change in the characteristics content of a product. Transportation and storage costs are examples that readily come to mind. Costs of product design and of changes in specifications and of services offered by distributors are perhaps less obvious examples. Given such costs, there is no price discrimination when these costs are fully reflected in the price differences, for example, when the difference between two "delivered prices" quoted at two different locations in space is equal to the transportation cost between these two locations, or when the difference between two future prices is equal to the storage cost incurred between the two dates of delivery, or when the price difference between two different specifications (models) is equal to the cost associated with the change in specification.

The reader will not fail to notice that cost increases are not fully reflected in prices as soon as a firm exercises some monopoly power, that is, as soon as its demand curve becomes downward sloping. It is well known, indeed, that a tax, for example one imposed on a commodity sold under monopolistic conditions, is only partially reflected in the price of a profit-maximizing firm. If this statement is true for a "simple" monopolist, who sells one product in one market at a single price, it must also be true for a firm selling several varieties in several markets at different prices. The latter will not fully reflect cost differences due to differentiation for the simple reason that the demand curves are downward sloping: The phenomenon is not tied to price discrimination as such, and its presence is not, therefore, a sufficient condition for price discrimination. But it is a necessary condition.

What *is* typical, for discrimination, is that prices reflect the opportunities for larger profits resulting from selling to *several* submarkets simultaneously, at different prices, while maximizing *overall* profits. This overall maximization – which implies that the firm takes several time periods, several regional markets, and several product models into account when deciding about the price for any of these in particular – generally operates like a filter, instituting a smoothing process, as compared with a pricing policy that would consider each period (or region or model) separately, and thus provides an additional reason for *net* prices to be different between these periods (or regions or models).

Admittedly the line of reasoning that I have just outlined implies that price discrimination is likely to be a rather ubiquitous phenomenon, as most firms probably sell several varieties in separate markets under monopolistic conditions. Discrimination might be as common in the marketplace as it is rare in economics textbooks. Am I stretching the concept too far? The answer to this question is a function of one's perception of product differentiation; it depends ultimately on how we define a commodity in an economically meaningful sense. The reader who responds irritably to definitions – as most economists, myself included, no doubt do – will want to base his or her judgment on an evaluation of the extent to which my analyses in the present book give a better insight into the way prices are actually determined in the real world.

Joint production

To invalidate the concept of price discrimination, it suffices to proclaim that two varieties (of a commodity) are in fact two different commodities with nothing in common (on the demand side). If these commodities result from a "joint" production process, then the theory of joint production is relevant. The latter theory thus offers an alternative analytical framework, and it is often not clear which framework is the one to use. Only a detailed analysis of a particular case will make clear whether a model of price discrimination is relevant or whether one should set up a model of joint production.

No doubt the debate between Taussig and Pigou about the theory of railway rates is the best example to refer to. "The Taussig–Pigou controversy centered, essentially, on the question of whether the observed pattern of multiple railway rates could best be explained by Marshallian joint supply (Taussig's position) or by the presence of common cost accompanied by the ability to discriminate between buyers (Pigou's position)" (Ekelund and Hulett 1973, p. 370). Taussig (1891) argued that the joint cost of carrying all passengers had to be allocated among the different classes of travelers according to their demand price, just as the rate at which sheep are slaughtered is established where the sum of the prices for wool and lamb or mutton is equal to the marginal cost of slaughtering. In his *Wealth and Welfare,* published in 1912, Pigou argued that transport services offered were *not* different and that Taussig was in error in identifying rail costs as preponderantly joint.

In *The Economics of Welfare,* published in 1920, Pigou called attention to the question of whether rail services are joint products in the sense that simple competition would produce a system of divergent prices. He argued that it would not. Under competitive conditions, equal prices would obtain for copper transport or coal transport or for all passenger transport. Differences in rates for bulk freight, or different passenger classes, are the result of efforts to collect consumer surplus, that is, to price discriminate.

Today a similar debate could easily center on the question of whether air fares are discriminatory or not. Differences between freight and passengers could, in my opinion, be explained by the theory of joint production, as an aircraft inevitably offers space for freight when carrying passengers (although the reverse is not true): Costs of air travel could be predominantly joint, as far as freight is concerned (and totally joint, as far as luggage is concerned). However, nothing obliges a carrier to offer a tourist and a first-class service, as is easily verified. Here, Pigou's thesis is clearly correct.

In his final word on the matter, Taussig (1933) identified a different kind of jointness, sometimes called "time jointness" or the "peak-load problem." Just as electric utilities have to make arrangements to satisfy demand on peak hours, and necessarily have excess capacity during off-peak hours, railroads will have to plan capacity with reference to rush-hour traffic. To invalidate the concept of price discrimination, it suffices again to proclaim[3] that service offered during rush hours is so inferior as to be a "different commodity" when compared with traveling conditions in the afternoon. The next step is often (and quite wrongly) to say that there is joint supply of these different products, offered in different markets. Again, a careful analysis, such as that in Steiner (1957), shows that the price discrimination model may be relevant to understand certain types of peak-load pricing. It will be necessary, though, to make clear which type of cost should be reflected in the price difference between peak and off-peak hours.

Uncertainty and the state of the world

Conditions of uncertainty have been introduced in economic theory through a redefinition of a commodity. In the work of Debreu (1959), "commodities are distinguished not only by physical and spatial characteristics, and by the date at which the commodity is made available, but also by the 'state of the world' in which it is found," to quote King (1978, p. 315). Our previous discussion suggests that this characteristic should have implications for the concept of price discrimination: A correct and complete characterization of a commodity should reveal which costs are to be taken into account. In the case of uncertainty, the question involves identifying the cost associated with differences in the state of the world, just as, over space, price differences are to be compared with the transport costs associated with differences in location.

Suppose, for the sake of concreteness, that Mr. X makes a reservation for a flight from Brussels to New York, three weeks from now, and pays his ticket at a Sabena desk. He thus claims to be guaranteed a seat on this flight, on a particular day, and Sabena receives a payment with certainty. Mr. Y also wants to fly from Brussels to New York, but does not care about the precise date. He is a student at an American university, has a room there, and is already preregistered for next term's courses; all he wants is to reach New York at the end of his vacation in Brussels. Mr. Y is therefore glad to discover the existence of standby fares such that he will fly on a certain date, if there are seats available. Otherwise he will fly with the next flight on which there is an extra seat available. Sabena (presumably) adjusted the capacity of its aircraft to the demand of people like Mr. *X,* who insist on being guaranteed a seat on a particular date.

Given the capacity of the aircraft, and the fact that it has to fly on schedule, possibly with empty seats, it seems natural – when there are unreserved seats available – to offer a seat to Mr. *Y* at a "bargain price." If the state of the world is such, from the point of view of Mr. *Y,* that there is an unreserved seat available, the cost of his occupying it should be very small indeed. And if, then, Mr. *Y* is charged a standby fare that is equal to this cost, and is thus much smaller than the fare that reflects the cost of providing seats to all Mr. *X*'s, no discrimination is involved. After all, *X* and *Y* are buying two very different varieties of the same commodity: The uncertainty about the day of departure of *Y*'s ticket is a source of differentiation, just as is a difference in comfort between tourist-class and first-class travel. If the associated cost difference is truly reflected in the fares, Sabena cannot be said to discriminate against Mr. *X.* It would be doing so, however, if Mr. *Y* were flown to New York free or at a fare less than the marginal cost of occupying a seat. Conversely, Mr. *Y* would be discriminated against if the difference in costs were, say, split, so that *Y* ended up paying more than this marginal cost. In principle this reasoning is rather clear. In practice, however, it might be very difficult to determine the marginal cost of an uncertain supply (here an additional seat): We will discuss this point later, together with the problem of ascertaining the marginal cost associated with an uncertain demand. Demand uncertainty indeed raises similar problems.

Suppose, for example, that Mr. *X* still buys his Sabena ticket three weeks in advance, whereas Mr. *Z* decides he will fly from Brussels to New York, three weeks from now, if his father (who is very sick) dies. Compared with Mr. *X,* Mr. *Z* makes planning difficult for Sabena. People like Mr. *Z* tend to appear half an hour before a flight's departure and to buy their ticket there and then, without previous reservation. If Mr. *Z* were charged the "regular" fare, whereas Mr. *X* paid the lower "Apex" fare, should Mr. *Z* feel discriminated against when he discovers this fact (perhaps while sitting next to Mr. *X* in the same aircraft on the same flight)? No, if the difference between the fares truly reflects the extra cost involved in making sure that people in a hurry will find a seat waiting for them. Again, Mr. *Z* and Mr. *X* have, in fact, bought two rather different varieties of the same commodity.

Imperfect information

The microeconomics of information is an outgrowth of the theory of uncertainty. The former is active where the latter is passive, in that more than mere adaptation to a state of ignorance is involved; one considers the gathering of more evidence prior to terminal action, to paraphrase Hirschleifer (1973, pp. 31–2).

The information available is often asymmetric in that one side of the market is better informed than the other. Where prices and qualities are concerned, sellers are often better informed than buyers, especially if they are also the producers of the commodity considered. Buyers may then wish to search for the better price or the better quality, and this search will involve some costs. These costs comprise at least the alternative cost of the time used in this search procedure but may also include expenses (travel costs, telephone calls, cost of catalogs). At any rate, the search costs are on the buyer's side and affect his or her reservation prices. There is no reason why they should be reflected in the seller's prices to the extent that the seller has no search activities. If, then, the seller manages to extract a higher price from customers with high search costs – typically richer people for whom time is money and who do not want to waste it in shopping tours – discrimination *is* involved.

It may happen that buyers are better informed than sellers, especially when buyers are not final consumers but industrial firms. They may, through a bargaining process with individual sellers, have a better idea about the level of prices in a market, the different prices offered by individual sellers, and particularly the price discounts that can be negotiated. Here the buyer is in a strong bargaining position. The asymmetry in information implies that sellers may be tempted to undercut each other, on the basis of information (possibly wrong) given by the buyers about their competitors' prices. As a reaction, sellers might then organize industrywide pricing schemes, such as delivered price systems, which make the market "transparent" for all parties involved (see Phlips 1964b). These schemes often involve *systematic* price discrimination, in that price differences are based on costs (of transportation) that are not the ones effectively incurred. For example, sellers agree that railway rates will be used to compute transport costs, even though goods are in fact carried by water or truck, or the transport costs will be computed as of the nearest "basing point," even though the goods are in fact produced elsewhere. In general, freight absorption or phantom freight will be the result, so that price discrimination is inherent in the scheme.

Three types of price discrimination

In *The Economics of Welfare,* Pigou (1920, pt. 2, chap. 17) presents what is perhaps still the most penetrating analysis of price discrimination available. After clarifying a number of issues, Pigou distinguishes three degrees of discriminating power, leading to three types of price discrimination. His distinction has proved very helpful and is still very much in use. I shall constantly refer to it throughout this book.

First-degree, or "perfect," discrimination "would involve the charge of a different price against all the different units of commodity, in such wise that the price exacted for each was equal to the demand price for it, and no consumers' surplus was left to the buyers" (p. 279). One way of visualizing this situation is to assume that all buyers are ready to buy one unit of commodity and that the seller manages to set a price equal to what is now called the buyer's "reservation price," that is, the highest price the buyer is ready to pay for one unit. Alternatively, assume that all buyers have exactly the same demand curve. Then first-degree discrimination "could be achieved by the simple device of refusing to sell in packets of less than the quantity which each consumer required per unit of time, and fixing the price per packet at such a rate as to make it worth the consumer's while, but only just worth his while, to purchase the packet" (p. 279). This device looks very much like what is now called "commodity bundling," each bundle being created so that it exactly fits *each* consumer's needs. Still another way of achieving the same result is to bargain separately with each individual buyer, but this method would involve "enormous costs and trouble" and "opens the way, not only to error, but also to the perversion of agents through bribery" (p. 280). Recent cases of bribery on an international scale in the aircraft industry – widely discussed in the newspapers – make one wonder whether Pigou was correct in stating that first-degree discrimination is of academic interest only and is not likely to be encountered in real life.

Second-degree discrimination obtains when a firm is able to make n separate prices such that all units with a reservation price greater than p_1 are sold at the price p_1, all with a reservation price less than p_1 and greater than p_2 at a price p_2, and so on. Here buyers are separated into n groups and there is one (identical) price per group. Some buyers have a consumers' surplus (those whose reservation price is higher than the price applicable to the group to which they belong). The situation is depicted in Figure P.1, where the shaded areas represent the consumers' surplus left to the buyers. (Each buyer is assumed to buy at most one unit.)

Notice that all buyers have the opportunity actually to buy if they want to: Each member of each group is offered a unit of the commodity at a price that is smaller or equal to his or her reservation price. First-, second-, and third-class railway tickets are good examples, since the assumption is made that everybody can afford traveling third class.

Third-degree discrimination does not look very different from second-degree discrimination, according to the following quotation from Pigou: "A third degree would obtain if the monopolist were able to distinguish

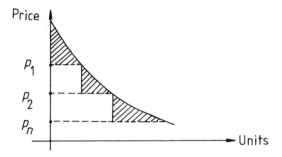

Figure P.1. Second-degree discrimination.

among his customers n different groups, separated from one another more or less by some practicable mark, and could charge a separate monopoly price to the members of each group" (p. 279). Yet Pigou insists: "This degree, it will be noticed, differs fundamentally from either of the preceding degrees, in that it may involve the refusal to satisfy, in one market, demands represented by demand prices in excess of some of those which, in another market, are satisfied" (p. 279).

An example taken from spatial pricing may help us understand what is typical of this third degree. Suppose a firm is selling in three geographically separated markets situated along a straight line (e.g., a road). Transportation cost per unit from one market to the next (and back) is $10. The firm charges the following delivered prices (i.e., prices valid at the point of delivery, transportation costs included):

first market	$90
second market	$95
third market	$100

A buyer located in the third market is ready to pay (has a demand price equal to) $99. This amount exceeds the prices charged in the two other markets, yet the person is put in the position of being unable to buy anywhere: not in the third market nor in the two other markets. (Indeed, going to the second market would imply paying $95 + $10 = $105, as the commodity must be transported back to the buyer's location. Going to the first market would lead to a price of $90 + $20 = $110.) The same is true for a buyer located in the second market with a demand price lower than $95, even if it is in excess of the delivered price ($90) in the first market. Price discrimination as discussed in the spatial economics literature is thus typically third degree. The same is true, a fortiori, for international discrimination ("dumping") based on the existence of import tariffs.

Discrimination plainly arises in the numerical example just discussed because the differences between the delivered prices are not equal to (in fact are less than) the transportation costs involved. As a result the net prices to the firm, after we have deducted the transportation costs involved in carrying the commodity to the three markets, are different. In that sense, the firm is charging different net prices to different customers.

Conditions for price discrimination

For price discrimination to be possible, markets must be separated. It is sometimes inferred from this rule that price discrimination is impossible when "demands" can be transferred from one market to the other. This hasty conclusion would be wrong, though: One must carefully distinguish between what Pigou calls the transferability of a unit of the commodity (the so-called arbitrage) between markets and the transferability of a unit of demand. To the extent that the former is present, the possibilities for discriminating are reduced; to the extent that the latter is present – given some nontransferability of the commodity – the seller may have to discriminate *more*.

Consider arbitrage, that is, the transferability of the *commodity,* first. Units of services applied directly to the person of the customer are entirely nontransferable: That is why physicians, lawyers, dentists, and so forth can charge different fees to richer and poorer clients. The same is true for services applied directly to commodities, such as transport services for particular types of commodities. In Pigou's words: "A railway's offer to charge one price for a ton-mile of transport services to copper merchants and a lower price to coal merchants cannot lead to any middleman device, because it is physically impossible to convert copper into coal for the purpose of transport and afterwards reconvert it" (1920, p. 276). Electricity and water supplies to private dwellings are other instances in point. Lesser degrees of nontransferability result from costs of transportation, tariff charges, or contracts that penalize resales. Price discrimination is possible here, but only to the extent that these costs are not fully reflected in the prices charged. In other words, these costs are upper bounds to the degree of price discrimination that is feasible.

To the extent that, in addition, *units of demand* are nontransferable, discrimination is more profitable. The highest nontransferability of demands occurs when the separation of the markets is based on personal characteristics such as the wealth of the purchasers: Rich people do not become poor for the sake of cheap doctoring. Other personal characteristics, such as differences in tastes or different rates of time preference, do not preclude transfers to cheaper markets. Here, the seller will have to create nontransferability by attaching special trademarks, special brands, or special types of packing to different varieties of the commodity and by undertaking advertising campaigns. In particular, the seller may have to increase the quality difference between high-priced and low-priced products to make sure that customers who can afford to pay the higher price do not switch to cheaper brands. In this sense, transferability of units of demand may be said to lead to more discrimination. The same is true with respect to spatial or intertemporal price discrimination. To avoid spatial or intertemporal shifts in demand (e.g., if buyers have their own transportation equipment or can easily store the commodity), sellers may have to announce more uniform delivered prices or more stable future prices than if demands were not transferable. Again, the degree of discrimination may be said to be higher, as transport or storage costs are absorbed to a greater extent.

In most cases, some transferability of demands remains. That is one reason why self-selecting devices are so common. Their purpose is to make the customers choose for themselves the markets into which they want to transfer their demands and the extent to which they want to do so. In the quality domain, concertgoers are given the opportunity to subscribe to a concert series at a lower price per unit, but they may also buy separate tickets for particular performances. In the time domain, customers with a low time preference (for whom the cost of search is low) are offered sales at the end of the season. Over space, the technique of freight absorption, to which I just referred, seems capable of eliminating completely whatever transferability might exist, so that there would be no point in giving the customers a choice between buying at a free-on-board-mill (fob-mill) price or at a delivered price. (To the extent that such choices are operational, delivered prices would have to be equal to the fob-mill price plus full transportation cost, and no discrimination would be involved.)

Another reason why self-selecting devices are so common is that they provide a simple and cheap way of identifying different groups of customers when this identification is not given exogenously. Gathering information to identify customers is costly, so that a device that leads customers to identify themselves (and their reservation prices) is welcome. A self-selection process is involved in the subscription to a concert series or in other forms of commodity bundling. Similarly, nonlinear pricing techniques such as two-part tariffs (a fixed entrance fee plus a constant price per unit) and block tariffs (marginal prices different for successively large demands, or "blocks") cause the consumers to reveal how much they want to consume and what average price they want to pay.

Perfect discrimination implies complete nontransferability of both the units of commodity and the units of demand, as well as complete information on the reservation prices per unit. Complete information in turn requires information on the states of nature, if the reservation prices depend on uncertain events. In practice, therefore, discrimination is likely to be imperfect, either because some degree of transferability is present, as stressed by Pigou, or because information is imperfect, as emphasized by Leland and Meyer (1976), or both. Third-degree discrimination will typically emerge when the market separation is given exogenously (e.g., through transportation or storage costs). Second-degree discrimination typically arises when self-selection devices are used.

To sum up, we have discovered that, for price discrimination to be possible, resale (i.e., transfers of commodities between submarkets) must be impossible or must be prevented. Transfers of demand, however, do not make price discrimination impossible: They make it less profitable. (As a consequence, sellers will try to reduce transfers of demand, possibly by discriminating more than otherwise.) A second condition has emerged naturally. It must of course be possible to sort customers according to the intensity of their demand. (As this sorting is a costly and delicate business, modern marketing methods have devised self-selecting techniques by which customers sort themselves.) This arrangement in turn plainly implies a third condition: There should in fact be differences in intensity in consumers' demand. Finally, the fourth and last condition that makes price discrimination possible is that the seller should have some monopoly power. For a long time, this condition was interpreted in the strong sense of an absolute monopoly (complete control over a market). Today economists[4] gradually begin to realize that duopolists, oligopolists, and small competitors in differentiated markets can price discriminate. The conditions under which a market equilibrium with price discrimination is possible are not yet fully understood. It is clear, however, that price discrimination is possible as soon as there is *some* monopoly power – as long as the firm's demand curve is not horizontal.

Price discrimination and business practices

The four conditions just discussed are listed very clearly in Telser (1965), who also emphasizes the link between trade practices and price discrimination.

First of all, many "abusive" practices become comprehensible as devices to accomplish price discrimination. At first sight, many trade practices appear as just "practices," irrational types of behavior about which economic theory has nothing to say that seem to be the result of habits. Very often, this is indeed how businessmen will describe them: "We've always had these sales conditions on the back of our invoices; sound commercial practice requires us to stipulate our sales conditions this way." Yet when analyzed in the framework of a model allowing for price discrimination, the very same practices can often be rationalized as devices that translate profit-maximizing conditions in practice and/or sort out customers or prevent resale. We have discovered how selling at delivered prices can be a form of third-degree price discrimination, with the implication that some customers may not be served, although they are ready to pay the delivered price posted in an adjacent market. In fact, resale of commodities to other markets is also made unprofitable through freight absorption.

On the other hand, few practices are abusive under all circumstances, as should be obvious, given that the same practice can be found in tightly monopolized or cartelized industries and in very competitive industries. When delivered prices appear in the framework of industrywide organized price schemes such as the basing-point system, an abusive practice is to be suspected. But when a firm grants a special price, transport costs included, to meet competition, one could hardly argue that there is an abuse of monopoly power.

Finally, even if a practice appears to be "abusive," in the sense that it reveals systematic price discrimination, it is not necessarily to be condemned per se. It may be better than having "simple" monopoly, that is, a simple monopoly price, if there is no way to restore competition. We shall thus have the difficult task of discussing the advantages and disadvantages of price discrimination in different circumstances: as a systematic device to restrict competition among oligopolists at the industry level; as a marketing device used by a monopolist (rather than a single price); and as a sporadic phenomenon reflecting the need for a seller to "meet competition."

Discriminating "against": A remark on semantics

Given that price discrimination is not good or bad per se, semantics are of some importance, the more so as the practice is illegal per se in the antitrust laws of a number of countries. Some authors suggest that we should speak of price "discrimination" only when it is "bad" or "illegal" and that we should substitute the words "price differentiation" when no abuse is involved. Economists cannot follow this suggestion, if only because they must keep economic and legal matters separate. Our positive analysis should not be influenced by normative considerations, and our normative analysis should not be influenced by legal stipulations. We shall try to keep to the definition just given and shall admit that there is price discrimination if and only if two varieties of a commodity are sold to two buyers at different net prices.

One implication may be worth mentioning right now. When can a customer be said to be discriminated against by a seller? Four different ways come to mind. The most brutal way of "discriminating" against customers is perhaps not to serve them at all, although they have a positive reservation price. A somewhat less brutal policy is to serve them an identical good or service at a higher price than that paid by some other customers. Much more subtle, though, is to sell some customers a different good or service but at a different *net* price. However, there is an even more subtle way in such such customers could be said to be "discriminated against": by giving them a lower price but taking more of their consumer surplus away. Imagine, indeed, that a buyer in a low-income group is asked to pay a low price for a small car but that this price is equal to that buyer's reservation price, whereas a rich buyer is asked to pay a high price for a luxury car, but in this case the price is lower than the reservation price. The entire consumer surplus is extracted from the poor, whereas the rich keep some of theirs. In a sense, the poor are "discriminated against."

Our definition implies that people are discriminated against only if they pay a higher *net* price, as in the second and third cases. In the first case, obviously, no price is being paid. The fourth case is worth discussing in its own right, as intuition suggests that price discrimination aims at taking the entire consumer surplus away from all customers, if possible. If in some situations some surplus is left to some people, we might expect the latter to be customers with *smaller* reservation prices: Why should the seller not try to extract the higher surplus? Yet we shall discover that the reverse is often true. It is often profitable to leave no surplus to the poor and to leave some to the rich!

A basic principle

If you can discriminate, it is profitable to do so. Given a number of separated markets[5] with different identifiable demands, a discriminating price policy is at least as profitable as a nondiscriminating one. This fundamental principle underlies my reasoning throughout the present book.

Perfect discrimination is clearly the most profitable discriminatory pricing policy one could imagine: The entire consumers' surplus is captured. But what about the different forms of imperfect discrimination? Are these also at least as profitable as uniform pricing? The answer is yes. (Proofs will be given or sketched as different types of imperfect discrimination appear.)

When larger profits are obtained, they are accompanied by a larger total output. Readers who are familiar with the abstract theory of "the discriminating monopolist" will find this a surprising and strong statement. Indeed, Robinson (1933, bk. 5) has shown geometrically – and Schmalensee (1981) has generalized this result using an algebraic approach – that if a single-price monopoly selling in two markets under constant costs is allowed to discriminate between them, total output is unchanged if both markets have linear demand curves. However, both Robinson and Schmalensee are careful to point out that this phenomenon depends critically on the assumption that both markets are served under *both* regimes. That this is a most unrealistic assumption will become clear in the course of my book: When some form of product differentiation (spatial, temporal, etc.) is introduced in the analysis, price discrimination typically serves to open *new* markets and thus to increase sales.[6]

Outline of the book

This book brings together four essays. The first essay discusses price discrimination in a spatial context. It is natural to start with spatial problems, first of all because the possibilities for (third-degree) price discrimination offered by the existence of costs of transportation are easy to visualize and simple to explain. As a result, many nonspatial forms of discrimination have been analyzed by analogy with – or have even been reduced to – spatial cases. These analogies will also be used to a large extent here. The spatial case will thus serve as a useful standard of reference and an introduction to more complicated situations. Essay II is devoted to price discrimination over time. Here the literature is very much in a state of flux, so that I shall have to draw rather heavily on my own research. The results I obtained using perfect information about future demand and cost conditions and uncertainty about future entry are based to a large extent on analogies with the spatial case. All I can hope for is that they will stimulate the reader's own thinking. Essay III tackles different forms of price discrimination based on income differences. In this area the literature has been expanding very rapidly during recent years, especially with reference to nonlinear pricing and commodity bundling. Strategies in the presence of imperfect information on prices also receive special attention. Essay IV links product selection and price discrimination. This is an entirely new area of research, on which scarcely any results are available, except possibly as far as quality uncertainty is concerned.

In all four parts, the analysis starts with a description of business practices used in different industries and trades as devices to accomplish price discrimination. These practices are then rationalized and are shown to be the result of profit-maximizing behavior at the firm level (and at the industry level, when possible). Each part discusses the extent to which they are socially optimal.

Space

CHAPTER 1

Business practices

Spatial pricing techniques typically use sales conditions such as "delivered" prices (the seller takes care of carriage) or fob prices (the seller sets a factory price and the buyer takes care of freight). In certain structural contexts, however, these techniques imply rather more than the choice of a particular type of sales condition: They can help to determine competitive behavior.

We shall concentrate on industrial structures such that the adoption of a given system is apt to have repercussions – favorable or unfavorable – on the competitive conduct of the relevant firms. These are industries that produce relatively homogeneous goods so that there is perfect substitutability at a given place between the goods of one manufacturer and those of another. Furthermore, freight is a significant factor in price formation, since the goods are of low unitary value and carriage is over fairly large distances. This last fact stems either from geographical concentration or from the small number of producers. In any case, bearing in mind the spatial differentiation, the number of competitors is low either because freight costs create a series of local oligopolies or because the number of producers in the whole of the relevant territory is low. Finally, the price elasticity of overall demand in the industry is low, so that sellers have a collective interest in avoiding industrywide price reductions.

This introduction, then, sets our reference framework. It is broad enough to take in a large number of industries, yet it is narrow enough to preclude abstract generalizations. After describing the price systems that are to be analyzed, we shall determine why firms find it worth adopting such techniques, both in a monopoly market (Chapter 2) and in an oligopoly market (Chapter 3). Chapter 4 considers the compatibility of the price systems with efficient spatial resource allocation and provides an opportunity to discuss perfect markets, quantitative interpretation of markets, and regional development.

Zone prices

A uniform delivered price is applied throughout a given territory.[1] When the unit transport cost is fairly high, and demand is concentrated at different places, a number of separate areas can be demarcated. Within each such area, a single delivered price applies to all points of delivery. An area might consist, for instance, of a member country of Benelux. Elsewhere it will consist of an economic region, a county or group of counties, and so forth, precise demarcation depending on the number and location of production and consumption centers, on political borders, and on the history of market-sharing agreements.

Between the areas, a rigid price difference is maintained, which implies that buyers (dealers or the final consumer) are prevented from buying or reselling in any area other than that in which they are located (or that which is allotted to them). There is thus a need for strict control of shipments. The simplest way of exercising this control is to ban buyers from handling their own carriage. Yet a ban is not essential; it may suffice to require payment of the delivered price applying in the buyer's area – even when the buyer obtains supplies in another area. In such cases, price gaps between areas must not exceed the cost of freight to each of the main centers of consumption, to exclude the possibility of arbitrage.

Within a given area, a ban on taking delivery at the factory itself ensures that the system will operate smoothly inside that area. Once again, however, more flexible arrangements may be possible. It is possible to go so far as to allow reimbursement (sometimes in part only) of freight charges where delivery is taken at the factory, but such a practice presupposes a highly disciplined trade and strict control of destination. To illustrate, consider three building materials: cement, plasterboard, and bricks.[2]

Cement is a nonstorable product with relatively high transport costs (10% to 15% of total costs, about 40% of the price at a distance slightly less than 250 km). In Belgium it is sold by the national cartel of cement producers at a uniform delivered price[3] – the same for the entire kingdom – when transport is by rail or water. (For transport by road, there is a uniform lower price within a radius of 10 km and a uniform upper price for distances above 110 km). *Fob-mill prices do not exist.*

Plasterboard is sold at similar conditions in the United Kingdom by British Plasterboard, Ltd. (BPB), which monopolizes the market for plasterboard and controls the entire supply of gypsum. Since 1968 there is one uniform delivered price for the entire United Kingdom. Yet transport costs represented on average 12.4% of total costs between 1967 and 1971. Transportation is by trucks. Delivery at the factory is not prohibited, but the rebate on the delivered price is only 2.5%, to discourage buyers from using their own trucks. BPB argues that fob prices would lead to a bad allocation of resources: The system of uniform delivered prices allows BPB to pass on any order to the plant that is capable of satisfying it at least cost. In other words, with a given delivered price, the

Table 1.1. *Phantom freight and freight absorption in the British brick industry*

Distance in miles	Transport cost incurred[a]	Transport cost charged[a]	Phantom freight or absorption[a]	Percentage of delivered price
5	1.55	2.01	+0.46	+4.07
30	2.49	2.62	+0.13	+1.09
40	2.90	2.85	-0.05	-0.41
60	3.69	3.32	-0.37	-2.94
90	4.62	3.97	-0.65	-4.91
120	5.70	4.66	-1.04	-7.46

[a] In pounds sterling per 1,000 bricks.
Source: The Price Commission, London.

problem reduces to the minimization of production costs and transport costs, for which a monopoly such as BPB is more efficient than a competitive market. Although BPB recognizes that uniform delivered prices involve discrimination against customers located farther away from the production plants, BPB argues that these prices are optimal and are preferred by the customers. It is also recognized, though, that uniform delivered prices deter new entry into the British plasterboard market.

Clay bricks are the monopoly of London Brick Company (LBC) since 1974. Transport costs are very important indeed, as they amount to about 30% of total costs. Delivered prices are uniform inside circular zones that are 5 miles wide (around the plant that executes a given order). From zone to zone the delivered price increases, but by less than the full transport cost. In addition, there is cross-subsidization, in the sense that customers located close to the plant pay more than the true cost of transportation ("phantom freight" is being charged), whereas customers farther away are being charged less. Table 1.1 indicates the phantom freight (+) and the freight absorption (−) obtaining in December 1973, in pounds sterling per 1,000 bricks.

The declared aim of this strategy is not only to enlarge LBC's geographic market penetration but also to increase the use of bricks as compared with other building materials. The resulting increase in production capacities is said to lead to cost savings and price reductions. In addition, selling at delivered prices does simplify life for sellers and buyers by improving the quality of the information on prices set by competitors and sellers and by reducing administrative costs.

Although LBC insists that fob prices increase cost, it allows buyers to take delivery at the factory, but only when demand conditions are normal. When demand is high, delivery at the factory is not allowed on the

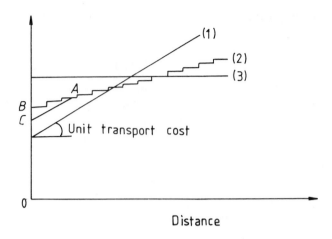

Figure 1.1. Delivered prices. The producing plant is supposed to be located at the origin of the axes. (1) Delivered price under fob-mill pricing. (2) Nonuniform zone prices (bricks). (3) Uniform zone price (cement, plasterboard).

grounds that this would disrupt the operations. When demand is low, LBC tries to maintain sales by granting local price reductions to outside areas (in which it would refuse to deliver when demand is high).

It is not clear whether those customers who take delivery at the factory are granted a rebate on the delivered price (charged for a distance of less than 5 miles). One thing is clear, though: Only those who receive a rebate larger than the transport cost (as incurred by them) have an incentive to take delivery at the factory. In Figure 1.1, these are the customers located to the left of point *A*, on the assumption that their unit transport cost is equal to the slope of the delivered price curve under fob pricing and that they get a unit rebate equal to *BC*. All customers located to the right of point *A* have an interest in letting LBC take care of the transport (whether by its own trucks or through hired transporters). Resale at a profit based on arbitrage is possible only in the area to the left of *A* and only for customers located between the factory and point *A* – on the assumption that rebate *BC is* granted. Without rebate, *no* customer is capable of taking delivery at the factory without actually suffering a *loss* (equal to the transport cost to and from the factory)!

The case of the British brick industry is particularly interesting because it shows how zone pricing (uniform delivered prices inside a zone) can be combined with nonuniform delivered prices (when comparing the delivered prices in adjacent zones). It also shows how price discrimination can be carried out in practice by charging phantom freight and absorbing freight between zones.

The basing-point system

Sale from a basing point (*point de parité* in French, *Frachtgrundlage* in German)[4] implies a delivered price equal to a base price plus the cost of carriage to the place of delivery calculated from a predetermined basing point, which need not necessarily be the place where the seller's factory is located. Consider a geographical area in which there are several centers of production. When all manufacturers calculate freight from a single basing point, we have what is called a *single-basing-point system*. When there are several basing points, we have a *multiple-basing-point system*. In the second case, the calculation of delivered prices can seem complex. What is the basing point for calculation of freight as regards a buyer at a specific place? In the system that we are to analyze, the formula is very simple: At every geographical location, the delivered price to be applied is equal to the lowest combination of a base price plus freight to that location (from the different basing points to which the base prices relate). This formula is applied by means of the "alignment" rule. Let us take a look at the formula in more detail.

The base price is the published price applicable at a given basing point. The industry decides on one or more basing points (e.g., a port such as Hamburg for foreign wheat imported by sea, or the city of Siegen for German-made fine sheet of ordinary steel, or perhaps even several cities, which may or may not correspond to actual centers of production). The freight to be added to the base price is worked out from a published tariff accepted by all concerned, such as a railway company's schedule of charges. For places not on railway lines or where the operation of official tariffs would be excessively complicated, the industry itself publishes (or asks the authorities to publish) a common tariff. All prices are delivered prices. The price to be charged at a given destination is the lowest possible delivered price calculated by comparing all the base prices and freight charges from corresponding basing points. Thus at a given place of destination only a single delivered price is possible, identical, and known with precision regardless of the seller and regardless of the distance covered in carriage to the place of destination.

It may thus happen that a seller applies a base price other than his (or her) own. In this case, there is alignment on a competitor's base price. By systematically setting an excessive base price, certain centers of production may find themselves aligning on the price of other centers for all their sales, including sales in their own immediate vicinity. On the other hand, the system has the inherent feature that the freight incorporated in the delivered price corresponds to actual cost of carriage only if the goods are actually dispatched from the basing point whose base price was used for calculation of the delivered price. If actual costs of carriage are higher than the freight thus calculated, the seller is absorbing part of the freight. If it is lower, the seller benefits from a phantom freight incorporated in the delivered price.

If the system is to work, buyers must be prohibited from taking responsibility for supplying their own means of transportation, or, alternatively, only such means of transportation as are controlled by the producers must be authorized, since this is the only way to ensure that at a given point of destination delivered prices are strictly uniform and arbitrage is impossible. Examples of single-basing-point systems are the "Pittsburgh plus," "Thionville," and "Oberhausen" systems enforced by American, French, and German steelmakers, respectively.[5]

A multiple-basing-point system is at present in operation in the European Common Market.[6] It was introduced in article 60 of the European Coal and Steel Community, at the urgent request of the steelmakers themselves – in particular the Benelux producers (see Fallon 1958 and Demaria 1958). The declared aims included (a) the creation of a perfectly competitive market (*sic*), there being only one single delivered price in any location; (b) the creation of a "perfect" market; (c) giving the centrally located producers (such as the Benelux steelmakers) the possibility of continuing to export to other European countries by meeting the local competition there (alignment), that is, without engaging in price wars. Figure 1.2 displays the basing points chosen for steel plate, together with the base prices (in Belgian francs) of the corresponding producers at some point in time.

Uniform fob prices

In the case of uniform fob prices,[7] the producers publish a mill price at which buyers may buy goods for carriage at their own expense; alternatively, if they prefer the producer to look after carriage, the actual cost can be added to the mill price. In any event, the net producer price (after deduction of freight) is the same whatever the destination, since at any point of delivery the delivered price is equal to the factory price plus actual carriage costs.

In a system such as this, the delivered price rises with the distance of the place of delivery from the factory or (if several firms are located at the same place) from the center of the production. Each center thus has a "natural" market where the delivered price of its goods is lower than that of competing centers of production.[8] The exent of the natural market changes with each change in factory prices and carriage costs. Assuming carriage costs are at a given level, the only way of penetrating the natural market of a competitor is to cut factory prices (the same for all buyers). Freight absorption and phantom freight are consequently impossible.

Figure 1.2. The multiple-basing-point system in Europe.

Fob prices with nonsystematic freight absorption

In the system that we have outlined,[9] the uniformity of the mill prices among the customers of the same firm means that each producer must reduce prices for all customers, either in order to obtain orders from places outside his natural market or in reaction to a price reduction announced by a neighboring center of production. Since we cannot expect a seller to react that way in real life situations, we are led to imagine a hybrid system such that buyers outside the seller's market could be quoted a special price.

A first possibility is to charge a special mill price for distant buyers. But this purely hypothetical possibility will not be considered here. It is unlikely to come about in practice, since the person buying at a special price could resell the goods at a profit within the seller's natural market, and the seller would thus have to reduce the factory price for all sales. The alternative is a system of uniform mill prices coupled with freight absorption outside the natural market to counter the delivered price that the buyer might have obtained from a closer center of production. The seller handles carriage and bears the cost of freight absorption where the sale is outside his or her natural market. The buyer always has the right to take delivery at the factory, but since factory prices are uniform, the risk of arbitrage is excluded. The means of transport is selected by the buyer in an fob sale. It will be seen that this system is no more than a basing-point system in which *each* factory is a basing point as far as the geographical structure of prices is concerned, except for one major difference: In this case, buyers can choose the mode of delivery and may find it is in their interests to take delivery at the factory. It is worth adding that this fourth system is really no system at all, since the freedom to choose mode of transport means that prices are unlikely to become petrified.

CHAPTER 2

The isolated firm

The aim of the foregoing chapter was to describe common spatial pricing techniques. There is much to be gained from extending the analysis and establishing the degree to which such techniques are profitable to individual firms. This chapter will first consider the equilibrium of an isolated firm that maximizes its own profit. The following chapter will consider the equilibrium of a group of competing firms.

The spatial theory of the firm proceeds from the fact that the location of buyers at different places permits a policy of *spatial price discrimination* where carriage costs are not negligible. By definition there is spatial discrimination when a firm sets net mill prices that vary from one buyer to another, according to the buyer's location. As this opportunity for discrimination is the specific result of geographical separation, the abstract theory of the discriminating monopoly will not suffice on its own: This theory must be adapted to the specific circumstances deriving from the existence of transport costs.[1]

Assumptions

Let us take a firm that has one factory and is the only firm to sell a homogeneous and heavy product in a given geographical area. To simplify matters, we assume that in that area demand is concentrated in three geographically separated places and can be represented by three identical linear demand curves. These "gross" demands depend on delivered prices and are to be distinguished from "net" demands, which depend on net factory prices.

It is worth noting from the outset that our assumptions imply no loss of generality. The results obtained for three demand locations can be extrapolated without difficulty to n locations. Furthermore, the conclusions of interest to us do not depend on the shape of the gross demand curves, so that the assumption of a linear curve, which considerably facilitates presentation, does not restrict the validity of our conclusions.[2] The same applies to the assumption of identical gross demand curves, since it will be seen that in fact they entail differing net curves and that only these net curves determine the equilibrium of the firm. The assumption of identical gross curves makes the impact of the existence of the spatial factor on the firm's policy all the more visible. Evidently the assumption becomes restrictive when the impact of phenomena other than transport costs comes up for analysis. Since any difference in the distance between the factory and places of demand entails differences in the net demand curves, it can also be assumed, without loss of generality, that these places are at equal distances from each other on a straight line. Let us therefore assume that demand D_0 is at the same location as the factory, demand D_1 at a certain linear distance, and demand D_2 at double that distance.

The situation facing the firm in these circumstances is represented in Figure 2.1a. Gross demand curve D_0 coincides with net demand curve d_0, since demand D_0 can be satisfied without any freight being payable. Curve D_0, which represents quantities demanded as a function of the delivered price, also represents gross demands D_1 and D_2. To sum up, $D_0 = D_1 = D_2$, since it is assumed that gross demand curves are identical. Net demand d_1 is obtained by drawing a straight line parallel with D_0, after deduction of one third of the intercept $0B$, the assumption being that the unit cost of carriage between the factory and the first distant center of consumption is $\frac{1}{3}0B$. Net demand d_2 is obtained similarly, the cost of carriage now being $\frac{2}{3}0B$. Horizontal line k represents the marginal cost of production, which is assumed to be constant.

Nonuniform discriminatory prices

What pricing policy will maximize profits in our firm in the circumstances described above? The theory of a discriminating monopolist immediately provides an answer: The firm will set its prices at such levels that marginal revenues corresponding to average revenues d_0, d_1, and d_2 will be equal to marginal cost k and therefore will be equal to each other. The demonstration of this discrimination rule is simple and well known, and there is no need to reiterate it here.

In Figure 2.1a, this rule leads to the net factory prices p_0, p_1 and p_2. As these net prices differ from each other, there is discrimination. By adding respective unit costs of carriage to net prices, I obtain delivered prices π_0 ($=p_0$), π_1, and π_2, which also differ. Two points must be made straightaway. First, the firm will be meeting demand from the three places. Second, it must be stressed that the difference between π_1 and π_0 is *less* than the cost of carriage (it is equal to half the cost of carriage because the demand curves are linear). The same applies to the difference between π_2 and π_0, so that the firm will find a systematic freight absorption policy on sales to the more distant buyers to be profitable.

The firm's total output may also be determined from Figure 2.1a. But I shall determine it rather in Figure 2.1b, which has the advantage of facilitating comparison with other pricing policies. Figure 2.1b is con-

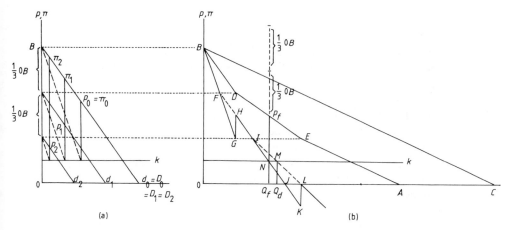

Figure 2.1. Equilibrium of the isolated firm. See text.

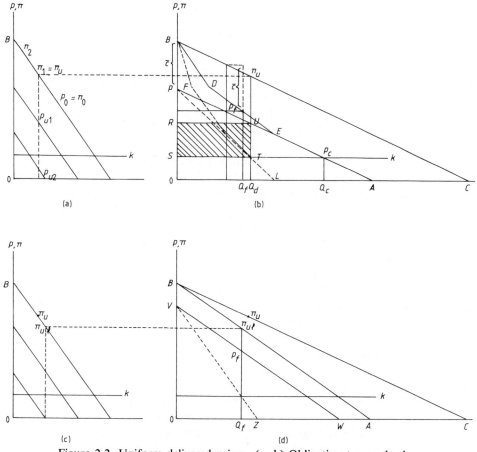

Figure 2.2. Uniform delivered prices. (a, b) Obligation to supply the entire territory. (c, d) Freedom to restrict the territory.

structed from the horizontal addition of demand curves (the usual method for the theory of discriminating monopoly). Straight line BC represents the horizontal sum of the three gross demand curves $(D_0 + D_1 + D_2)$ and does not interest us for the moment. Broken curve $BDEA$ represents the horizontal sum of d_0, d_1, and d_2. It is the aggregate *net* demand curve, constructed on the assumption that there is no price discrimination, that is, that the net mill price is the same in all three markets. I shall use it in the next section, to determine the uniform fob price.

Since there is discrimination, the aggregate marginal revenue that is of interest here is represented[3] by the regular broken curve $BFHIL$. It is the point of intersection between this curve and marginal cost k that determines total output Q_d.

Uniform fob prices

Where a firm has a monopoly in a given geographical area, the most profitable policy is, as we have seen, to apply different delivered prices with freight absorption. Nevertheless, the firm may use other tactics, for instance where it is obliged to do so by antitrust law or by the presence of competitors in control of neighboring geographical areas. Considerations relating to overall *market* equilibrium (taking in all the different geographical areas) may then come into play. We shall analyze these considerations in Chapter 3. For the moment, we shall assume that, for whatever reason, the relevant firm has adopted a less profitable policy than that of nonuniform discriminatory delivered prices.

The first possibility is setting a uniform fob price. This price is determined by the point of intersection between the marginal cost and the marginal revenue that corresponds to curve $BDEA$, since this curve implies equal net prices at the mill. In this case, the marginal revenue to be taken into consideration is represented by zigzag curve $BFGHIJKL$. Point of intersection N gives fob price p_f. It is easy enough to draw a graph establishing the loss of profit as against the operation of nonuniform discriminatory delivered prices. Since the profit of the firm is equal to the geometrical area between the marginal revenue and marginal-cost curves and the vertical axis, the loss of profit is equal to the sum of triangles FGH and IMN.

It will be seen that because it has set a fob price, the firm will no longer be able to supply the more distant customers. Simply drawing a horizontal line at level p_f, and transposing it from Figure 2.1b to Figure 2.1a, reveals that this price is higher than the net demand price on d_2. Alternatively, we can repeat the same exercise by adding to p_f, first, the cost of carriage $\frac{1}{3}OB$ and, second, $\frac{2}{3}OB$. These delivered prices correspond with a nonzero quantity on D_1 and a zero quantity on D_2.

It is thus not surprising to find that total output Q_f is less than total output Q_d yielded by discrimination. This is a general result: As compared with fob prices, freight absorption permits more distant markets to be supplied, output to be raised, and profits to be expanded. If we compare the discriminatory delivered prices π_0, π_1, and π_2 with p_f, and treating this uniform fob price as *the* net price, we find that π_0 implies phantom freight, whereas π_1 and π_2 imply freight absorption. In this sense, customers located near the mill subsidize customers located farther away.

Uniform delivered prices

By a uniform delivered price, I mean an identical price for a whole area – the geographical area controlled by the firm. Here the obligation to set a uniform delivered price is seen as a constraint imposed on the firm and implies a loss of profit as compared with the policy of nonuniform delivered prices just analyzed. The problem, then, is to determine the level of the single delivered price that will maximize profits under this constraint. For the sake of clarity we shall work from Figure 2.2, which reproduces the main data of Figure 2.1.

There are two possibilities. First, we shall assume that, apart from the obligation to set a uniform delivered price, the firm is obliged (e.g., by law) to supply the *entire* territory, in other words to set a uniform delivered price for the three places of demand (including the most distant). Second, we shall assume that the firm is free to restrict the geographical area in which the uniform delivered price is applicable and therefore is free to refuse to sell outside that area.

Obligation to supply the entire territory

As the firm has to set a uniform delivered price for all its three demands, gross total demand curve BC is used for the analysis and determines the firm's total output. Net total demand curve $BDEA$, just considered, is to be distinguished from straight line PA, which is obtained by deducting from BC a distance reflecting average cost of carriage (per unit sold) $\bar{c} = \frac{1}{3}OB$. This straight line PA measures average revenue yielded by the various possible total quantities and may here be interpreted as a net average revenue curve. Given the same delivered price, the same quantity is sold at the three centers of consumption (gross demands being identical), so that the average revenue is equal, for each unit sold, to the delivered price less the average cost of transport, that is, $\frac{1}{3}(0 + \frac{1}{3}OB + \frac{2}{3}OB)$, that is, $\frac{1}{3}OB$.

It is easy to show, once again, that the equality of marginal revenue and marginal cost determines constrained maximum profits and the uniform delivered price π_u. But this result, of course, is possible only at a reduced profit. We have already shown that a single fob price is less profitable than nonuniform delivered prices. The time has come to note that a uniform delivered price applying throughout the territory is in its turn less profitable than a uniform fob price. This can be shown in graph form with the average revenue curve PA. At a uniform delivered price π_u, the sale of quantity Q_d gives profits equal to shaded rectangle $RSTU$. This is smaller than the rectangle determined by the fob price (p_f).

The reader may wonder whether it would not be to the firm's advantage to set a uniform delivered price equal to the fob price plus the average cost of carriage. The answer is no. Let us add $\bar{c}$ to p_f and find the corresponding delivered price on gross total demand BC. This price yields a smaller output and smaller profits. The same applies to any uniform delivered price above π_u. Similarly, any uniform delivered price lower than π_u yields reduced profit despite increased output. Let us locate uniform price π_u on Figure 2.2a. We find that it gives three different net prices, π_1, p_{u1}, p_{u2}, and so there is discrimination. As all buyers are helping to cover total costs of carriage, there is both phantom freight and freight absorption. Buyers in the immediate vicinity of the factory are paying nonexistent freight charges that are lightening the burden on more distant buyers.

Freedom to restrict the territory

Nevertheless, close examination of Figure 2.2a will have made clear that, in the hypothesis under study above, the firm is selling at the third place of demand at a net price, p_{u2} that is lower than marginal cost k. Total profits are therefore also lower than those obtained on an fob price sale. Consequently, the firm can raise its profits by restricting its territory and refusing to supply the most distant demand.

If we take the two demand curves for the nearest places, the gross total demand curve moves from BC to BA. Let us deduct from BA a vertical distance reflecting the average cost of transport, being *half* of $(0 + \frac{1}{3}0B)$, in other words $\frac{1}{6}0B$. We then have straight line VW, which we reproduce in Figure 2.2d, incorporating the main data of Figure 2.2b. This straight line measures net average revenue, and a straight line VZ, measuring marginal revenue, corresponds to it. The point where marginal revenue equals marginal cost corresponds to output Q_f (obtained with the fob price) and to a net average revenue equal to p_f! From the firm's point of view, we are in the same situation as with sales at a fob price. Profits have risen through the restriction of the geographical territory. As for the uniform delivered price, it is at an intermediate level between p_f and π_u: It is obtained this time by adding the average cost of transport to the fob price and is equal to $\pi_{u\ell}$ ("free" uniform delivered price). Figure 2.2c shows that there is discrimination. This result is well known: It was obtained by Stevens and Rydell (1966) and by Beckmann (1968, pp. 33–4, and 1976).

Sale at marginal cost

The final item for discussion is sale at factory price equal to marginal cost, that is, to price $p_c = k$ in Figure 2.2b. At this price, we have zero profits (since marginal cost is constant and is therefore equal to average cost) and maximum output. This policy, which is frequently urged upon public enterprises, holds a central place in the theory of welfare economics and will be further discussed in Chapter 4.

Vertical integration into transportation

Two further remarks are in order at this stage. First, it should be clear that the unit transport cost is also the delivered price from the standpoint of firms offering transportation services, that is, carriers. This point is forcefully made by Greenhut, Hwang, and Ohta (1974). There should thus be a tendency among carriers to lower freight rates with greater distance. This tendency should, in turn, reduce delivered prices for distant customers. Second, it may be noted that a spatial price discriminator will find it profitable to integrate vertically into distribution, here into the transportation industry. This result is due to Schuler and Holahan (1978), who show that the maximization of the combined profits of a producer (who may or may not discriminate) and a hauler leads to a spatial price policy that is identical with the nonuniform discriminatory pricing policy that I just described.

Summary and conclusions

We have examined above the equilibrium of an isolated firm assuming a series of spatial price-setting techniques. We have been able to highlight the effect of spatial factors: The costs entailed by the geographical separation of buyers create possibilities of discrimination that firms find profitable. A policy of freight absorption appears eminently profitable, particularly when it gives rise to delivered prices that vary from one center of consumption to another. A uniform fob price yields less profit, although greater than those profits yielded by a uniform delivered price, unless firms are in a position to restrict their sales territory. In this case, restriction of the territory in which the uniform delivered price applies permits the seller to obtain the same net average revenue (and therefore the same profits) that a uniform fob price would make possible. Freight absorption also ensures the highest level of output (leaving aside sales at marginal cost) and permits buyers at the greatest distance from the place of production to be supplied.

We must now establish links between the pricing policies analyzed and the four pricing *systems* described in Chapter 1. Let us begin by stressing that the equilibrium of an isolated firm, which we have just analyzed, does not indicate why an industry adopts one given system rather than another. In business practice, different systems appear and are often applied side by side, in the same industry, although the foregoing theory suggests that it is always profitable for a firm to set nonuniform discriminatory delivered prices. This statement means that our analysis was incomplete and that the firm must be considered in relation to its competitors. The requirements of group equilibrium, it seems, may induce a firm to adopt other strategies, as we shall see in the next chapter.

Before we continue, however, we should consider some valuable lessons that can be learned from what I have already said. For instance, a policy of nonuniform discriminatory delivered prices that maximizes profits may take the form of a *system of zone prices* when the spatial configuration of demand indicates either concentration or a low degree of dispersion by area (as where there is one major town per area). For example, the situation in the British brick industry, as described in Chapter 2, is fully explained by Figure 2.1. The same policy may take the practical form of the adoption by a single firm (or a cartel) of *several basing points,* with base prices set at such levels that peripheral buyers benefit from freight absorption. On the other hand, systematic freight absorption, organized in the form of an obligation to *align,* seems to be fully outside the foregoing analysis. So does the phenomenon of *occasional freight absorption,* combined with a fob-mill price in relation to distant buyers. These phenomena are linked to the state of the market and in particular to competitive conditions.

CHAPTER 3

A group of firms

Let us therefore bring these competitive conditions, which involve the number of competitors, their location, and their production costs, into the analysis. In order to obtain results, we must unfortunately make a number of rather restrictive assumptions. In fact, I shall only· be able to study some particular cases, but my hope nevertheless is that they are fairly representative of spatial competition between oligopolists. The reader will notice that *discriminating* oligopolists are grouped together here. This grouping may cause some surprise, given that only monopolists are supposed to price discriminate, according to the standard literature.

Assumptions

Let us keep the assumption of linear demand curves and consider a given place of purchase.[1] At this place, the gross market demand curve is

$$\pi = \alpha + \beta q \tag{3.1}$$

where $q = \sum q_i$, q_i being the demand for firm i and $\alpha > 0$, $\beta < 0$. Suppose further that each firm has zero conjectural variations, that is, acts in a noncollusive way on the assumption that all $\partial q_j / \partial q_i = 0$. (This is the famous assumption made by Cournot.) Then $\partial \pi / \partial q_i = \partial \pi / \partial q (1 + \sum_{j \neq i} \partial q_j / \partial q_i) = \partial \pi / \partial q$ at this point in space. The firm's unit cost of carriage to that point is t_i. Equalization of net marginal revenue and marginal cost gives the equilibrium condition

$$\pi + \beta q_i = k_i + t_i \tag{3.2}$$

Let us suppose that there are m firms ($i = 1, \ldots, m$) in a position to sell the same homogeneous commodity at this buying point. The summation of these m firms gives the condition of market equilibrium (at one point)

$$m\pi + \beta \sum q_i = \sum k_i + \sum t_i \tag{3.3}$$

which, after division by m, can be rewritten as

$$\pi + \beta \frac{q}{m} = \bar{k} + \bar{t} \tag{3.4}$$

where $\bar{k} = \sum k_i / m$, $\bar{t} = \sum t_1 / m$.

39

To show that (3.4) determines the delivered price at any given point in space, rewrite (3.4) as

$$\pi\left(1 + \frac{\pi - \alpha}{m\pi}\right) = \bar{k} + \bar{t}$$

using the fact that $q = (\pi - \alpha)/\beta$, to find (after rearrangement) that

$$\pi = \frac{1}{m+1}(\alpha + m\bar{k}) + \frac{m}{m+1}\bar{t} \tag{3.5}$$

This equation[2] will enable us to determine the spatial configuration of π in different competitive conditions using the properties of $\bar{t}$.

Geographic concentration of production in a single location

The simplest case is the situation in which the competing firms are all located at a single center of production. The unit cost of transport is then the same for all firms, and $\bar{t} = t$, where t measures the unit transportation cost (or the distance measured in money terms) between the center of production and any given place of consumption. Equation (3.5) becomes

$$\pi = \frac{1}{m+1}(\alpha + m\bar{k}) + \frac{m}{m+1}t \tag{3.6}$$

whereas the price in the absence of transportation costs is

$$p = \frac{1}{m+1}(\alpha + m\bar{k}) \tag{3.7}$$

It will immediately be clear that the diagrammatic representation of π as a function of t gives a straight line[3] with a positive and less than unitary slope, since $m/(m+1) < 1$. In other words, a geographically concentrated group of competing firms benefits from freight absorption: Only part of t is incorporated in the delivered price (see Figure 3.1). Furthermore, as the number of firms rises, so price p falls and the slope becomes steeper, corresponding to freight absorption at a lesser degree. The sales area extends to the point where π is equal to the highest demand price that buyers are willing to pay, that is, intercept α (equal to OB in Figures 2.1 and 2.2).

Two centers of production in the same geographical area

Let us render the analysis a little more complicated by supposing that the firms are located at two separate centers of production and that there are m_1 firms at one center and m_2 firms at the other. Buyers are located on a line linking the two centers, which are separated by a distance d (see Figure 3.2).

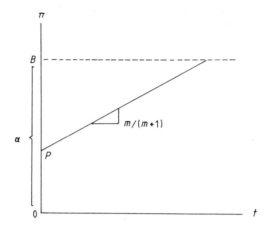

Figure 3.1. Geographical concentration of production.

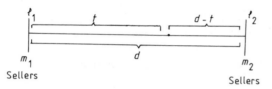

Figure 3.2. Two centers of production: Location.

For every purchase on that line, the transportation cost is t from center l_1, and $(d-t)$ from center l_2. The average transportation cost $\bar{t}$ is

$$\bar{t} = \frac{1}{m_1 + m_2} [m_1 t + m_2 (d - t)] \tag{3.8}$$

Let $m = m_1 + m_2$. From Equation (3.5) we see that the delivered prices will obey

$$\pi = \frac{1}{m+1} (\alpha + m\bar{k}) + \frac{1}{m+1} [m_1 t + m_2 (d - t)] \tag{3.9}$$

From center l_1, these delivered prices rise at the constant rate

$$\frac{1}{m+1} (m_1 - m_2) \tag{3.10}$$

with distance. That is to say that, if most of the firms are located at l_1, and only a few at l_2, so that $m_1 > m_2$, delivery prices will rise in linear fashion from l_1 as in Figure 3.3a. This trend may explain sales on a *single basing point* (e.g., the Pittsburgh plus, Oberhausen, and Thionville

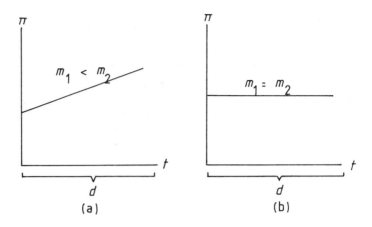

Figure 3.3. Two centers of production: Prices. See text.

systems) by an entire industry, even by firms that are geographically distant from the principal center of production taken as the basing point.

Figure 3.3b illustrates the situation where different centers of production are equal in size ($m_1 = m_2$). Here it is in the industry's interest to adopt a *uniform delivered price*, the curve representing π being horizontal.

Spatial variations in competitive conditions

From the foregoing results the reader may imagine a variety of more complicated practical situations and may in particular determine the spatial configuration of delivered prices in situations where the geographical areas that can be supplied by the centers of production overlap only partly. For instance, two centers of production may be in competition only in a central area on each side of which one of the centers of production has a sales monopoly. The delivered price schedule will then turn out to be a combination of three straight lines with different slopes that vary with the number of competitors in each of the areas.

Figure 3.4 illustrates the spatial configuration of π that maximizes profits for two centers of production that set their prices on the terms described. Center l_1 has two firms and is therefore more important than l_2, where there is only one firm. If center l_2 did not exist, the first center would control the geographical area that extends right up to point D. If center l_1 did not exist, the second center would control the area from l_2 to A. The fact that they both exist narrows the area down to Y for l_1 and to Z for l_2. The natural market of center l_1 extends only up to Y, where its delivered price is equal to the marginal cost at l_2 plus transportation

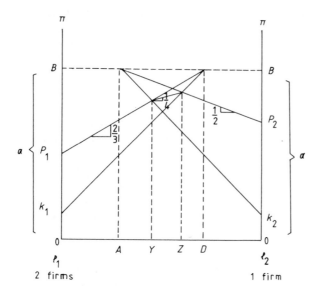

Figure 3.4. Spatial variations in competitive conditions.

cost. The natural market of l_2 extends up to Z, where its delivered price is equal to k_1 plus the transportation cost from l_1.

Between Y and Z, the larger center sets delivered prices, following a straight line with a smaller slope $(2-1)/(3+1) = \frac{1}{4}$. In this area, center l_2 must accept decreasing delivered prices as the distance to the point of sale rises. This constraint may explain *alignment* on a competitor's delivered price ("meeting competition"). Such alignments may take place only occasionally. However, to avoid a collapse of the geographical structure of prices described in Figure 3.4, particularly where there are geographical shifts in demand or recessions, the industry as a whole stands to gain by institutionalizing alignment, that is, by adopting the rule of systematic alignment, which is the most important feature of sales from *multiple basing points*. (In Figure 3.4, l_1 and l_2 are then basing points.)

Competitive pressures and entry

With several centers of production in the same geographical area, an increase in the total number of firms (m) will *increase* the degree of freight absorption – and therefore of price discrimination – according to Equations (3.9) and (3.10). In this sense,[4] an increase in competitive forces will lead to *more,* not less, price discrimination!

However, this conclusion is reached under the rather restrictive assumptions of homogeneous commodity and zero conjectural variations. Furthermore, the way in which the entry of new firms affects the prices has not been studied in detail: Greenhut and Greenhut (1975) simply refer to an increase in m, without further analysis. In two recent papers, Norman (1981a and 1981b) dropped these assumptions and considered more closely the entry of new firms, to find that within his richer theoretical framework there is still nothing inconsistent in postulating the coexistence of competition and spatial price competition through freight absorption. In certain circumstances, stronger degrees of competition are indeed associated with higher degrees of spatial price discrimination.

In his 1981b paper, Norman is able to show that freight absorption is greater, not only when noncollusive firms adopt noncoincident locations, but also when, in addition, products are more differentiated (when cross-price elasticities of demand are smaller). When he departs from the simple Cournot assumption of zero conjectural variations, Norman finds that, if coincidentally located oligopolists *collude* to reduce competitive pressures between themselves, an *increase* in spatial price discrimination will follow. On the other hand, collusion between noncoincidentally located oligopolists has an ambiguous effect. However, an increase in discrimination on a particular product is more likely, the more "competitive" that product is, that is, the greater the extent to which consumers perceive it as being a substitute for other products in the market.

What happens in the case of nonzero conjectural variations (without explicit collusion)? Here an increase in conjectural variations can be expected to lead to an increase in spatial price discrimination in the case of coincident location but will have ambiguous effects when producers are located separately.

Norman (1981b) concludes:

> The existence of spatial price discrimination in particular markets is not *a priori* evidence of lack of competitive pressures. But neither can a simple connection be drawn between the degree of competition and the degree of spatial price discrimination. Discrimination between spatially separated consumers by means of freight absorption may indeed reflect and be the result of intense competitive pressures in particular markets, but this is more likely if the competitors in such markets are not themselves spatially concentrated. On the other hand, discrimination may be the consequence of collusive agreements between coincidentally located producers, or of attempts by such producers to anticipate the actions of their competitors.
>
> Certainly, the simple (spaceless) foundations upon which current policies are based need to be re-examined. It would appear, however, that such re-examination must be based upon empirical analysis which takes rather fuller account of inter-connections between producers, of the

extent to which they produce differentiated or substitute commodities, and of the locational choices they have made. [1981b, p. 25]

In his 1981 paper "Spatial Competition and Spatial Price Discrimination," Norman (1981a) takes a closer look at the effects of potential entry of new firms. This entry is supposed to act through a limit price. The lower this limit price (with respect to the maximum price – intercept α – that the consumers are ready to pay and with respect to marginal costs of production), the more *uniform pricing* is likely to occur, and the higher the degree of price discrimination is likely to be. Again, it cannot be concluded that freight absorption is prima facie evidence of the lack of competition in a particular market.

"Tacit collusion" and imperfect information

To what extent does the adoption of one or other of the spatial pricing systems described in Chapter 1 promote price competition or help to eliminate it? I should add that this question concerns market conduct in a given market structure. The structure is that described in Chapter 1: I am considering industries producing a relatively homogeneous product of low value per unit of weight requiring carriage over fairly large distances. Demand is inelastic, and supply is oligopolistic, if only because space as such creates oligopolistic relationships.

The emphasis on oligopolistic structure makes it mandatory to discuss price competition with reference to "tacit collusion." In a legal environment where explicit price agreements are not enforceable, so that joint profit maximization is not a realistic assumption,[5] oligopolists are supposed to replace explicit agreements by "tacit collusion" in the standard antitrust literature. These tacit agreements are supposedly reached through an exchange of information[6] on prices, sales conditions, and possibly other relevant data such as production data and investment projects. Creating perfect information is somehow thought to be a sufficient condition for oligopolists to collude on prices. That is why direct exchange of information among competitors is considered illegal or at least prima facie evidence of collusion in countries with a vigorous antitrust legislation. Sellers are allowed to gather information on their competitors only through indirect means, for example, through their customers.

If oligopolists are recognized as being in a game-theoretic situation, and if agreements are not enforceable and are therefore not binding, then "tacit collusion" appears to me to include the so-called noncooperative Cournot–Nash equilibria. These equilibria are such that "no player could increase his own payoff by deviating from his equilibrium strategy, given that the other players use their equilibrium strategies" (J. W. Friedman 1977, p. 149). When firms are in a Cournot–Nash equilibrium, there is no reason to make agreement. To find Cournot–Nash equilibria, firms *have* to gather information, not only on general business conditions (such as aggregate supply and demand conditions), but especially on their competitors' shipments, prices, inventories, investment projects, and so forth. The fact that oligopolists engage in information-gathering activities – and spend much time and effort in it – is thus no evidence, per se, of collusive behavior.

However, in a world without uncertainty, the improvement of information on the competitors' strategic variables may also help to reach "tacit agreements" or "quasi-agreements,"[7] that is, equilibria in which the profits of some firms are above the levels attained in a Cournot–Nash equilibrium (without leading to full joint profit maximization). What happens in real life situations, in which uncertainty is always present and signals may be misunderstood?

Spence (1978) has shown that under these conditions the set of attainable equilibria shrinks to a subset. Indeed, when firms react to signals rather than to competitors' strategies observed without error, then it may become profitable to "cheat," that is, to deviate individually from one's equilibrium strategy (to expand one's market share secretly). The set of possible equilibria is reduced to those – in the neighborhood of a Cournot–Nash equilibrium – where the probability of not being detected[8] is small enough.

The adoption of a particular pricing technique may, in a spatial framework, have direct implications for the probability of detecting deviating behavior and thus for the ease with which equilibria are found and maintained. Spatial price discrimination may thus be linked with the competitor's efforts to find and maintain a Cournot–Nash equilibrium or a quasi-agreement in its neighborhood. Let us consider this matter in more detail.

A system of zone pricing may, first of all, be the result of explicit market-sharing agreements that break up a geographical market into submarkets. The logic where "price competition" is concerned is then obvious: There can be no competition either at the production stage or at the distribution stage inside a zone, and buyers have no incentive to obtain their supplies from manufacturers nearer by. The system is typical of the major international cartels that segregated national territories (reserved for national cartels) and subdivided these national markets into regional markets (reserved for regional cartels or a local manufacturer). A uniform delivered price also drastically reduces the probability that a firm trying to deviate from it will not be detected. Tacit agreement is made easier to the same extent. However, the results obtained by Norman (1981a and 1981b) suggest that one should be careful: The existence of uniform delivered prices is not prima facie evidence of the existence of tacit collusion, since uniform pricing may also result from competitive pressures due to the threat of entry (or to product differentiation).

There has been considerably more discussion of the basing-point system. Outlawed in a number of individual cases in the United States since the 1940s, it was officially adopted by Article 60 of the European Coal and Steel Community (ECSC) Treaty and still applies in the coal and steel industries in Europe, as we saw in Chapter 1. This system is all the more worthy of discussion as it developed historically, in the United States, in a legal context where price agreements, particularly on a regional basis, were prohibited. This is not to suggest that the system cannot work under a price-fixing arrangement; it is known to have been applied by well-organized cartels such as the German steel cartel,[9] and it preceded their formation.[10] But the system is of particular interest here in that it could be the sequel to a geographical market-sharing agreement. If such an agreement were prohibited, would the adoption of a basing-point system be apt to promote tacit collusion? The answer is yes. The introduction of a basing-point system as described in Chapter 1 creates conditions that favor tacit collusion where the structural situation is that which we have assumed.

First, it leads to perfect information on prices: The definition of the delivered price is such that any seller and any buyer can establish it with the highest degree of precision and a minimum amount of research. As has been stressed on a number of occasions, tacit agreement between members of an oligopoly is possible only where all the members know exactly what prices the others are charging. Where the unit value per unit of weight is low, carriage costs constitute a significant price factor, and the *delivered* price is the subject of attention. As soon as there is any uncertainty as to the exact delivered price, buyers may exploit this fact to obtain secret price reductions and then may carry out arbitrage through resale, so that general price levels may fall through the weakening of the geographical structure of delivered prices.[11]

Second, the rule of systematic alignment implies that the effect of any price reduction by a competitor is automatically neutralized. Although certain appearances may be to the contrary, alignment thus has no competitive virtues. Although it may, at first sight, indicate aggressive conduct, in reality it makes undercutting competitors' prices impossible. Alignment is a defensive tactic: Assuming equal prices, the sellers can tie traditional customers to them wherever such customers may be located.

However, alignment also implies cross-hauls, that is, an inefficient use of resources, with the result that profits are reduced. Collusion in the framework of a multiple-basing-point system must therefore be short of joint profit maximization. The following quotation from Smithies is in order:

In the Cement case before the [Federal Trade] Commission in the fall of 1942, counsel for the Commission states: "If a single corporation owned all the mills and attempted to operate them, that is just what it would do to prevent them from competing with each other. Such a monopoly would act just as respondent manufacturers under separate ownership are acting when they use the [multiple] basing point system." This statement is incorrect. A monopolist would never adopt the basing-point system, since he could always increase his profits by leaving the price pattern unchanged and eliminating cross-hauling. It follows that if, as is contended by its opponents, the existence of the system implies collusion, it is collusion short of complete agreement. [1942, p. 706]

It may be worth adding that tacit collusion can be reinforced by various aspects of the way in which this system operates and particularly through the selection of basing points. The choice of a single basing point where there are several centers of production enables the dominant center to impose its price leadership. The point chosen might be the place where the price leader has the main factory. It can also correspond to the location of small, marginal, and distant competitors whose natural markets are thought to deserve protection (while reserving the benefit of phantom freight for the main center). But price leadership is not incompatible with the existence of several basing points, for base prices can be set at such levels that numerous competitors are obliged to align systematically on the base price of a single basing point (so that other base prices never count).

The vast majority of writers on this subject agree with the foregoing diagnosis. Whereas the view that a basing-point system tends to sharpen competitive conduct is rarely held, we more frequently meet the argument[12] that this system develops spontaneously and inevitably in industries with high fixed costs, unstable demand, and an oligopolistic structure. This argument is not convincing when we bear in mind that the system arises from explicit agreements (frequently reached laboriously) and that it is not easy to keep in operation. There are numerous opportunities for breakdowns. At times of serious depression, the temptation to grant clandestine rebates (on the delivered prices resulting from the system) is likely to wear down adhesion to the agreement; at times of economic boom, shortage of supply may permit sales at individual prices higher than those of the system; finally, and most important of all, imports from nonmember countries can destroy the whole system. When it does work, this fact in itself is evidence of intentional adhesion to a tacit price agreement.

Uniform fob prices are sometimes used by organized cartels and arise under tacit collusion. Although price information is less perfect as regards delivered prices, since buyers may use their own means of transport, it is perfect as regards mill prices. The exclusion of alignment confines each center of production to its own natural market, and tacit price fixing is fostered.[13]

The following quotation from Smithies is revealing. Smithies assumes two identical firms for ease of exposition, to show that uniform fob prices allow joint profit maximization:

> If the two competitors sold on a uniform mill-net basis and acted as quasi-coöperators, they would charge the same prices and would jointly realize the same (equal) profits as would a monopolistic owner of the two plants who restricted himself to selling on an f.o.b. mill basis. The reason for this is that each competitor assumes that he can gain no new territory through price cutting, but must be content with maximizing his revenue in half the market. Therefore, he will charge the ideal monopoly price in his half of the market. It is obvious in this case that f.o.b. mill selling is more profitable than basing-point selling, since [...] the mere existence of cross-haul assumes that the total basing-point profits of the two producers must be less than the two-plant monopolist's profits. Also on our present assumptions that the competitors are identical, we can conclude that in equilibrium their profits will be equal. Hence we can conclude that, in quasi-coöperation, they will have neither a joint nor a several interest in preferring the basing-point system to f.o.b. mill selling. [1942, p. 710]

In practice, the choice between uniform fob and basing-point pricing will depend on the relative sizes of the competitors[14] and on the geographical stability of demand.[15] Competitors of comparable size will, ceteris paribus, adopt fob-mill prices,[16] since this allows them to eliminate cross-hauls and thus to raise joint profits. The fob-mill system is also the simplest to operate. If, in such a system, demand develops along parallel lines, each natural market develops at the same rate, and market shares (or production quotas) can be safeguarded simply by maintaining each operator's natural market. If undesirable shifts in natural demarcation lines were to arise, for instance, through the development of new means of transport, corrections could still be made by adjusting differences between factory prices. On the other hand, if regional demand shifts are frequent and on a large scale, alignment becomes necessary and basing points with it. A center for which demand is falling can then maintain its market share by supplying growth regions without endangering the structure of prices.

Our fourth system of fob prices with nonsystematic freight absorption was clearly devised in order to offset the disadvantages of the other systems and to provide useful reference criteria. It provides the best prospects for promoting competitive behavior. First, freedom to choose terms of delivery and means of transport means that there is no certainty as to the delivered price applying at various places of destination. Second, interpenetration of natural markets remains possible, but alignment on the local price leader is no longer compulsory nor even systematic: Undercutting is possible. Furthermore, intermediaries could carry out arbitrage operations by reselling in other natural markets where it is profitable to do so. The result would thus be a network of natural markets with flexible and rather blurred boundaries. Last but not least, I am ready to argue that a combination of fob prices and discriminatory delivered prices – as long as the latter are not systematic in the sense of a mandatory alignment – is better than any of the other delivered price systems. But this point raises questions of welfare and Pareto optimality, which deserve a more systematic treatment.

CHAPTER 4

Welfare implications

The preceding chapters add to our understanding of the logic of the chief spatial pricing techniques. The time has come to evaluate these techniques in the light of welfare economics. We have seen that spatial discrimination ensures maximum output, since it enables distant customers to be prospected. One is tempted to deduce – as Greenhut and Ohta (1972) and Greenhut and Greenhut (1975) have done – that this is therefore the best pricing policy from the standpoint of social welfare. This chapter aims to demonstrate that the deduction is not entirely correct. I shall argue that a combination of fob pricing and discriminatory delivered prices (that is, buyers may choose between the two) is the best solution that can be obtained in an imperfect world. (This combination was described in Chapter 1 as a system of fob prices with nonsystematic freight absorption.)

The unconstrained spatial Pareto optimum

The theorems of welfare economics usually relate to a nonspatial economy. Such an economy is Pareto-optimal when, at the same time and for the same pricing system, the marginal rates of substitution between any given pair of goods are equal for all consumers, the marginal rates of substitution between any pair of factors and products are equal for all firms, and marginal rates of transformation between any factor and any commodity are equal for all firms using that factor and manufacturing that commodity. Such an optimum is defined for a given income distribution, and no value judgment on that income distribution is therefore possible from it. As long as consumers and producers make their choices independently of each other, and assuming the market is not saturated, any competitive equilibrium is a Pareto optimum, and vice versa. Competitive equilibrium arises where, each market being in equilibrium, all consumers maximize their utility and all producers maximize their profits.[1]

These theorems can be applied to a spatial economy only to the extent that the spatial element is correctly integrated. From the outset the definition of goods must be enlarged, and we must stress, with Debreu, that "a good in one place and the same good in another place are *different*

51

economic objects and it is vital to specify the place where the good is available" (1959, p. 29). A ton of steel manufactured in Oberhausen and delivered in Frankfurt and the same ton of steel delivered in Munich are to be regarded as distinct products for economic purposes. The equilibrium price of these various "goods" being given, firms will choose to manufacture the good or goods whose price is highest (and will thereby maximize profits).[2] Firms produce "distant" goods (goods for sale at a distance from the place of manufacture) only if they can be sold at a net price that is at least as high as the price of the "nearest" good (in other words, the net price obtained on a sale at the place of manufacture). Freight absorption is thus incompatible with a competitive equilibrium and therefore with a Pareto optimum. All sales are thus at fob prices: Firms supply distant customers only if the customers bear all costs of carriage. And if, by way of hypothesis, it were necessary to sell at discriminatory delivered prices (whether uniform or not), firms would sell at only one place, namely the place where their plant is located.

The foregoing reasoning considers the properties of competitive equilibrium and deduces that optimal allocation is incompatible with sales at discriminatory delivered prices. The same result can be obtained by direct analysis of the optimum, as is shown by Mougeot[3] (1975, chap. 2) in a recent work in which he generalizes a model by Negishi (1960). In addition to the constraint of a given income distribution, Mougeot adds a number of constraints reflecting the spatial nature of the economy. Features of the economy then include fixed location of economic agents and regional availabilities of given factors. Transportable resources, whose utilization involves the services of a transport firm and therefore payment of transport costs, are distinguished from fixed resources that can be used only locally. There are n markets, with a variable number of consumers, located in n regions (defined as points in space to simplify analysis), and m transportable goods. These goods can be produced in each of the regions by a variable number of multiproduct firms and are taken to the user by a carrier.

The properties of the optimum are worked out by maximization of the vector of individual utilities:

$$(U_{1_1} \ldots U_{G_1}, U_{1_2} \ldots U_{G_2}, \ldots, U_{G_n}) \tag{4.1}$$

where

$$U_{g_j} = U_{g_j}(q_{g_j}^i \ldots q_{g_j}^m) \qquad g_j = 1, \ldots, G_j; \quad j = 1, \ldots, n \tag{4.2}$$

is the ordinal index of utility for consumer g_j residing at place j, and q^i for g_j represents the quantity of good i consumed by individual g_j residing at j.

The vector of (4.1) is to be maximized subject to a series of constraints expressing the equilibrium of the market at each place and for each good (including transport services), the technological constraints on production and transportation, and the regional endowments of transportable and nontransportable factors of production. This maximization, incidentally, in no way implies interpersonal comparisons.

To solve this problem, we use the Kuhn–Tucker theorem, which considers it equivalent to a new problem where the maximization of vector (4.1) is replaced by maximization of a linear combination of its components,

$$\sum_{g_j} \sum_j \alpha_{g_j} \cdot U_{g_j} \tag{4.3}$$

where the α_{g_j} are interpreted as the inverse of the marginal utility of income of consumer g_j. Expression (4.3) can be interpreted as a social welfare function. The value of weights α_{g_j} reflects the income distribution.

The maximization of the Lagrangian, composed of the sum of (4.3) and of these constraints, a multiplier (dual variable) being associated with each constraint, gives a set of conditions that redefine the Pareto optimum in a spatial context. This set is really a redefinition and not just a second-best optimum (describing the least undesirable situation possible, the true optimum being out of reach). In other words, it is recognized that the conditions of the nonspatial optimum, outlined at the beginning of this section, are generally inapplicable in a spatial context, and the problem is redefined through the explicit introduction of spatial differentiation.

Of the conditions that are valid in a spatial context, let us consider only those of direct interest to our problem. The first relates to the consumer optimum and is written

$$\alpha_{g_j} \frac{\partial U_{g_j}}{\partial q_{g_j}^i} - \pi_j^i < 0; \qquad \left(\alpha_{g_j} \frac{\partial U_{g_j}}{\partial q_{g_j}^i} - \pi_j^i \right) q_{g_j}^i = 0 \tag{4.4}$$

where π_j^i is the dual variable associated with the market equilibrium constraint and can be interpreted as the price of good i at place j.

The inequality and equation in (4.4) express this alternative: Either good i is bought by individual g, in which case the product of its marginal utility by coefficient α for g_j is equal to the price, or this product is less than that price and the good is not bought. Consequently, the price system no longer has that property of unity which is a feature of the nonspatial model: "Prices vary with location, but at each place there is a single system. In practice there are as many systems as markets, so there are n price systems. The unity of the price system therefore depends exclusively on the unity of the market. As soon as distance is taken into consideration, a single market is inconceivable and prices therefore vary from place to place" (Mougeot 1975, p. 114). Although, at each place, all the properties of the nonspatial optimum are found (equality for all individuals of the marginal rates of substitution), it is not possible to define an overall optimum (which would imply a single price system). The optimum defined here can therefore only be relative; in other words it depends on a given income distribution and on the geographical distribution of natural resources and productive equipment.

As for the production optimum, all the classical conditions of the optimum are evidently found when the place of production and place of consumption are the same: The sale is at marginal cost, so that marginal rates are equal between firms. Where the place of production and place of consumption are not the same, so that a firm located in region h may sell good i in any region j: "The price of that good at j is equal to the sum of the marginal cost of transport from h to j and the marginal cost of production. Where the price on the outside market is lower than the sum of these marginal costs, the good is not sold" (Mougeot 1975, p. 118). We may conclude that economic efficiency demands that spatial differentiation of products caused by transport costs be fully reflected in delivered prices.

Constrained welfare maximization

In the preceding analysis, welfare was maximized without profit constraint. I now want to maximize ($W = \mu S + \Pi$) with μ between zero and one.

Consider a linear region with N_i buyers per location ($i = 1, \ldots, n$). To simplify, I shall suppose each consumer to have an identical linear gross demand curve

$$q_i = a - b\pi_i \tag{4.5}$$

where π_i is the *delivered* price. By definition, the *net* price (at the mill) is equal to ($p_i = \pi_i - t_i$), where t_i is the unit transportation cost between the mill and the point of delivery (the point where the N_i customers are located).

The linearity of the gross demand curve makes it possible to compute the consumer surplus as the sum of the N "Harberger" triangles, or as

$$S = \frac{1}{2} \sum_{i=1}^{n} N_i \left(\frac{a}{b} - \pi_i \right) q_i \tag{4.6}$$

and the profit equation is

$$\Pi = \sum_{i=1}^{n} N_i (p_i - k)(a - b\pi_i) \tag{4.7}$$

k being the constant marginal cost of production. It should be stressed that discrimination is implied in the way Π is defined (there is only one marginal cost, common to all points of delivery).

Maximization[4] of ($W = \mu S + \Pi$) with respect to the *net* prices p_i leads to

$$p_i = \frac{a(1-\mu)}{b(2-\mu)} + \frac{k}{2-\mu} - \frac{1-\mu}{2-\mu} t_i \tag{4.8}$$

When $\mu = 1$, we get the unconstrained optimum, implying that $p_i = k$ or that $\pi_i = k + t_i$ for all locations. There can be no freight absorption or phantom freight. When $\mu = 0$, we obtain the .well-known profit-maximizing absorption of one-half the freight:

$$p_i = \left[\frac{a}{2b} + \frac{k}{2} \right] - \frac{1}{2} t_i \tag{4.9a}$$

or

$$\pi_i = \left[\frac{a}{2b} + \frac{k}{2} \right] + \frac{1}{2} t_i \tag{4.9b}$$

The constrained optimum lies somewhere between the two, depending upon the choice of μ. Admittedly this is not an earth-shaking result. Yet it confirms good common sense, which says that there is no point in trying to prohibit freight absorption entirely but that one should aim at reducing it to some extent. This point is elaborated and illustrated in the next section and is further discussed with reference to individual welfare.

Nonlinear net prices and welfare

In an ideal world, in which there is competition, economic efficiency demands that all goods be sold at fob prices. By competition, I mean not pure competition but rather what Beckmann (1968, 1971, 1972) called "spatial monopolistic competition," each industry comprising many small firms selling spatially differentiated products. In such a world, uniform fob prices indeed ensure greater output (per firm) and greater consumer welfare (per geographical area) than discriminatory prices – see Holahan (1975) and Norman (1981a).

However, perfect competition is an ideal that cannot be realized in practice, and even "spatial monopolistic competition" is rarely encountered in practice. It is doubtful, therefore, whether the spatial Pareto optimum should be used as a criterion on which to base policy measures (such as antitrust policy). One should at least reconsider the problem of the optimal pricing technique on the assumption that a single firm or cartel serves a particular market or operates under spatial oligopolistic competition. It is not obvious, to say the least, that the best thing to do is to impose fob pricing by law in these situations, knowing that (a) firms are profit maximizers and have therefore an incentive to charge discriminatory delivered prices and (b) competitive forces may lead to uniform – and therefore again discriminatory – prices.

Suppose that there is sufficiently strong and lasting monopoly power – for whatever reason – for the spatial unconstrained Pareto optimum to be an unattainable goal, at least in the short run. Then it is of considerable interest to ask whether it would not be better not to impose fob pricing blindly but to look for the best among the pricing techniques that monopolists and oligopolists are likely to use in fact. This best can only be a second best by comparison with "the" spatial Pareto optimum. But it can provide a reasonably operational policy goal worth pursuing in practice as long as monopoly power cannot be curbed.

Consider the case of a firm with a monopoly in a given geographical area, with no outside competitors. This was the situation analyzed in Chapter 2. Holahan (1975) shows that, in this case, spatial discrimination provides a greater consumer surplus than a uniform fob price. The mathematical demonstration of this point is rather laborious and would overburden the present book. But an intuitive demonstration can be given from Figure 4.1, which represents the spatial evolution of delivered prices (as a function of t), under the various pricing techniques analyzed in Figures 2.1 and 2.2.

First, compare nonuniform discriminatory delivered prices (π_d) with delivered prices derived from a uniform fob price (π_f). The former are lower than the latter from distance OV. Consumers located in the immediate vicinity of the factory pay a higher price if there is discrimination ($\pi_0 > p_f$). Those located at distance $\frac{1}{3}OB$ benefit from a discriminatory delivered price ($\pi_1 < \pi_f$) that is lower than the fob price plus cost of carriage ($\pi_f = p_f + t$), so that some compensation is possible. But customers located at distance $\frac{2}{3}OB$ gain in welfare from discriminatory price π_2, whereas, at that distance, price π_f, derived from adding the cost of carriage to the fob price, would be prohibitive ($\pi_f > \alpha$). In sum, then, there is a net gain.

Now compare nonuniform discriminatory delivered price (π_d) with uniform delivered prices, assuming the latter to be applied throughout the geographical area (π_u). In the immediate vicinity of the factory, the former is lower than the latter; at the most distant place of demand, the opposite situation obtains; halfway between the two places, $\pi_d = \pi_u$. As the positive and negative gaps compensate each other, the two policies appear to have equivalent effect, except that the uniform price is

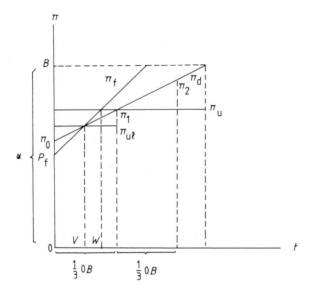

Figure 4.1. Delivered prices and welfare.

even more favorable to distant customers and less favorable to those nearer by.

The uniform price (π_u), applied throughout the geographical area, consequently entails a net gain as compared with delivered prices derived from a uniform fob price (π_f). As for the uniform price ($\pi_{u\ell}$), obtained where firms are in a position to refuse to supply the most distant buyers, it is equal to π_f at distance OV. The upward difference at the factory is equal to the downward difference at distance $\frac{1}{3}OB$, which is the boundary of the sales territory: This policy is equivalent to selling at a uniform fob price under the approach taken.

To sum up – and this is an argument frequently advanced in industrial circles[5] – geographical discrimination (through the setting of prices π_d or π_u) is beneficial to the community at large because freight absorption benefits distant buyers.

At this point, we might improve our understanding of the argument just developed by referring to nonlinear pricing (which is discussed at some length at the end of Chapter 10). Prices are said to be "nonlinear" when they are quantity dependent. And a nonlinear price schedule can be said to be Pareto-superior to a linear price (i.e., one that is uniform with respect to quantity) that is different from marginal cost, because it is always possible to find a nonlinear schedule such that those customers who gain from it gain more than those who are discriminated against (see the discussion of Figure 10.6). What we have discovered in our discussion of Figure 4.1 is not only that the discriminatory delivered prices π_d can be Pareto-superior to uniform fob prices, because the position and the slope of π_d with respect to π_f can be chosen such that customers east of point V gain more than those west of V lose. We have also discovered that π_d is *necessarily* Pareto-superior, because it is profitable for monopolists to choose π_d such that this condition is satisfied. When the delivered price is uniform, then the monopolist will spontaneously restrict the market area and will charge $\pi_{u\ell}$, which is equivalent to selling at a uniform fob price. To get the Pareto-superior price π_u, the obligation to satisfy the entire market area must be imposed.

Having gone this far, I might as well try to push the argument even further, asking whether π_d (and therefore π_u) could be Pareto-superior not only from the point of view of aggregate welfare but also with respect to the preference of *each individual* agent (customers and producers). Willig (1978) shows that nonlinear prices Pareto-dominate uniform prices at that individual level when individuals are given the possibility to choose between the two (see Figures 10.7 and 10.8 and the discussion of them). The same is true for π_d as compared with π_f.

To see this point, let us introduce the concept of *"nonlinear net prices,"* defined as net prices that are distance dependent. Any list of delivered prices, according to which buyers located at various distances are charged prices such that *net* prices (at the mill) vary, is thus "nonlinear" in distance. Discriminatory delivered prices are therefore nonlinear by definition[6] and have this property in common with two-part tariffs, block tariffs, and quantity discounts (see Chapter 10).

Now put the origin in Figure 4.1 at p_f, the fob-mill price. Then π_f is a straight line through the origin with a slope equal to the unit transport cost (so that the new price is independent of the distance) and corresponds to a ray representing "linear" pricing, whereas π_d corresponds to a two-part tariff. Suppose that the customers located east of V are poor farmers in the mountains, whereas those west of V have rich farmland in the valley. Then π_d might be Pareto-superior with respect to π_f, even from the individual point of view. But suppose the reverse happens to be true: The distant buyers are the large rich farms, whereas west of V the land is poor. In assessing the benefit to the community at large, we simply counted the losses and gains per customer, giving each of them an equal weight. We might now decide to give people with poor land a better chance and oblige the monopolist to sell fob until distance V and to sell at π_d prices farther away. In other words, we impose the solid lower envelope[7] of π_f and π_d in Figure 4.2. It is clear that it Pareto-dominates the straight line through the origin π_f (uniform fob pricing) from the individual point of view. The seller could hardly object, since he or she

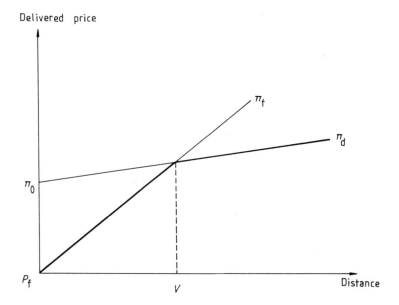

Figure 4.2. Nonlinear net prices and welfare. π_f implies a uniform net price; π_d implies a nonlinear net price.

will make more profits than under fob-mill pricing (although not as much as under π_d pricing). Customers west of V get the lowest delivered price they could hope for, given the mill price p_f, and are unaffected by the price reductions given to distant buyers. Customers east of V also get the lowest delivered price they could hope for and are unaffected by the gain obtained by those, west of V, who use their own trucks to take delivery at the mill.[8]

The preceding discussion is valid for an isolated monopolist (or for a regional or national cartel). What if we have a small number of spatially separated sellers? To the extent that they do have the monopoly of their natural markets, the conclusion just reached remains valid: The possibility of taking delivery at the mill at the fob price is an improvement compared with a case in which all prices are delivered prices.

As far as the competitive behavior of oligopolists is concerned, imposing the condition that customers should always have the opportunity to take delivery at the mill (and to do their own transportation) has the additional property of creating an area, around the factory, in which delivered prices are not known with certainty, since costs of transportation differ from buyer to buyer. As a result, competitive pressures may be higher, at least if the neighboring competitors penetrate far enough into each other's natural markets. In any case, lower delivered prices around a factory would make entry by competitors into local markets more difficult (as they would have to absorb more freight).

Perfect markets

The implications of welfare economics, reformulated to take account of spatial features, can usefully be highlighted in a discussion of the concept of a "perfect market." They help to reveal the fallacious nature of the argument put forward by certain writers, most of them apparently European,[9] to the effect that the unity of the price is an element of market perfection,[10] even in a spatial context.

The argument is that discriminatory delivered price systems (uniform zone delivered prices, multiple basing points with alignment) guarantee price unity, either throughout an entire geographical area or at every possible geographical location, so that the form of market imperfection that results from the incorporation of actual transport costs into delivered prices can be eliminated. The systems further guarantee perfect market information. This argument is highly speculative and is purely conceptual. Originally, the elements of perfection (perfect information, price unity, standardization, etc.) described the conditions for the smooth operations of a stock exchange or an organized commodities market. Once elevated to the level of a model, and associated with atomistic perfect competition, the concept of a perfect market then becomes a normative criterion, and reality must at all costs be adjusted to it.

In the industrial structures that we are considering, this concept is highly irrelevant, since it ceases to be a condition of smooth operation. In Chapter 3 we saw that perfect information must be removed from the list of criteria of perfection where the market is oligopolistic, the product is of low unit value, and the price elasticity of demand is low. Welfare economics shows that the same applies to price unity where delivered prices are concerned. The entire discussion turns on the uniformity ("linearity") of the *net* prices: Uniformity of delivered prices is irrelevant.

The implications are clear. Consider the zone price system. A uniform delivered price covering a whole area does not reflect spatial differentiation at all: The most distant buyers are given better treatment than those nearer to the center of production because of the systematic freight absorption. There is systematic discrimination against well-located buyers. This is at most a second-best optimum, and for reasons related to the extent of the market served, *not* to the uniformity of delivered prices.

Consider the basing-point system. In a market with several centers of production, it would be absurd to call for introduction of a single basing point by referring to the model of a single-price perfect market. Not only would this give maximum encouragement to a price leadership policy, as we have already seen, but also peripheral centers of production (with regards to the basing point) would artificially benefit from phantom freight to the detriment of buyers located in their vicinity. Having several basing points would probably be Pareto-superior. And systematic alignment would add a nonlinearity aspect that would again be Pareto-superior with respect to the single-basing-point system.

Finally, it is evident that spatial differentiation is best reflected in prices set on a uniform fob basis. Even then, it should not be deduced that the fob system would create a perfect market in the structural context that is being considered, for the total exclusion of isolated reductions (of delivered prices) would be damaging to active price competition. All in all, it seems more prudent and more realistic to abandon the concept of a perfect market, which leads to dogmatism or to misunderstandings.

Regional developments

In all that has been said so far, it has been assumed that sellers and buyers were located at determined places. The time has now come to drop this restrictive assumption and to consider the potential impact of spatial pricing techniques on location changes and thence on regional development. As regards the adaptation of the sellers' location to the regional development of demand, it is clear that the uniform fob system ensures the quickest adaptation through the establishment of new plant in regions where demand is expanding. The geographic dispersion of centers of production is thus promoted.[11] Any formula that allows for freight absorption favors traditional locations and thus makes for geographical concentration.

Next consider the potential effect of geographical pricing systems on the location of buyers. The problem arises particularly where buyers are themselves manufacturers and process a basic product. Here a distinction must be drawn. It would seem that *uniform delivered prices* should deprive the buyer of any interest in locating a factory near that of the manufacturer of the basic product. Geographical dispersion of demand is therefore encouraged. Under a system of *uniform fob prices,* buyers, ceteris paribus, will find it worthwhile to establish themselves near the center of production of the basic product. However, since the system guarantees rapid geographical adaptation of the production of the basic product, the dispersion of production ultimately entails dispersion of demand.

In contrast, the establishment of a *basing-point* system is apt to spark a cumulative process of geographic concentration of buyers around the basing point of the dominant center of production (which is usually the oldest center as well).[12]

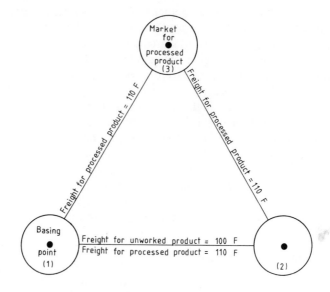

Figure 4.3. Basing point and geographical concentration. Delivered prices for basing point (1) are 500F for unworked product and 600F for processed product. Delivered prices for point (2) are 600F for unworked product and 700F for processed product. Thus at the market (3), delivered prices are 710F for processed product from point (1) and 810F for processed product from point (2).

The process is particularly clear in the case of a *single basing point*. Suppose that a basic product is manufactured at two centers of production l_1 and l_2, and that processing industries are located at the same centers (half at each). For some reason l_1 is taken as basing point (see Figure 4.3). Delivered prices consequently rise from l_1 to l_2. The cost of production is the same at the two centers (let us assume 500F per ton) and equal to the base price 500F at l_1. The cost of carriage between the two centers is 100F per ton for the basic product. The delivered price at $l_2(\pi_2)$ is 600F.

Suppose that processing industries place half their orders for the basic product with each center, so that each of the centers is on an equal footing. The result is an average net price of 500F both at l_2 and l_1. Center l_2 receives 600F per ton on local sales and 400F on sales at l_1. (This statement, of course, assumes that demand is higher at l_2, which is unrealistic but essential if the two centers are to produce identical amounts.) Further suppose that the cost of processing the basic product is the same at both centers (100F per ton). The unit cost of carriage of the processed product from one center to the other is 110F. The cost of the processed product is $500F + 100F = 600F$ at l_1, and $600F + 100F = 700F$ at l_2. Processors at l_1 cannot sell at l_2, for the cost of carriage is prohibitive. A fortiori, processors at l_2 cannot sell at l_1. Each center thus has a monopoly on its local market.

At first sight, because demand is assumed to be higher at l_2, the choice of basing point does not affect the location of processors. But in fact opportunities are not equal. To illustrate this statement, let us introduce a third market for the processed product at l_3. The cost of carriage of the processed product from the first two centers to l_3 is the same, say 110F per ton. Nevertheless, only processors located at the basing point for the basic product will be able to sell at l_3, since their delivered prices at l_3 are $600F + 110F = 710F$, as against $700F + 110F = 810F$ for processors located at l_2. Processors therefore have a clear interest in location near the basing point for the basic product. This interest, in its turn, promotes expansion of basic product production capacity at the basing point and destroys the equality of opportunities that was assumed at the outset. For as long as a single basing point is maintained at l_1, the process is irreversible and cumulative.

What, then, is the situation in a *multiple-basing-point system?* If each center of production has its own basing point, and if there are no price-fixing agreements, the system creates no distortion. But these ifs are highly unrealistic. In practice, the system is designed to reinforce a price-fixing agreement and to safeguard the interests of the dominant centers. These centers will impose a geographical price structure of such a nature that delivered prices will rise with distance from the dominant center. Peripheral centers will be forced to operate base prices that are at least as high as those of the basing point, even if their production costs are lower. The typical spatial configuration of prices is then as described in Figure 3.4. The same cumulative concentration process works in favor of the geographical area where the dominant basing point is located. This area tends to be intensely and traditionally industrialized.

Time

CHAPTER 5

Business practices

In a spatial context, at least one of the conditions that make price discrimination possible is automatically satisfied: Space separates selling points, and to overcome distance a cost (time lost plus possibly the pecuniary expense of transport) is involved. Consequently, as we have seen, net demand curves are automatically different even if gross demand curves are identical in different locations. At first sight, there seems to be no reason why the same should not be true in an intertemporal framework. Time separates yesterday from tomorrow, and to overcome it a cost (the psychological cost of waiting plus possibly the actual cost of storing) is incurred. This statement is certainly true for storable goods. What about nonstorable goods? When inventories cannot be carried, a larger reserve capacity may be the only way to satisfy future demands, so that capacity costs may play the same role as inventory costs. Whatever the case, the pricing of storable goods over time seems to raise problems other than the pricing of nonstorable goods, and it may be important to distinguish carefully between the two types of goods.

I shall also consider two special cases of storable goods. In one case, there is a given stock, and production consists in extracting units from it: This is the problem of exhaustible resources, such as petroleum and natural gas. One expects prices to rise as one approaches exhaustion (as the resource is growing scarcer), and one wonders how simultaneously to determine the time shape of the price and of the rate of production. In the other case, the product is a durable, so that it can be used more than once. Here, the price probably declines the more the durable is used. I shall discuss this problem of *used* durables in Essay IV, where attention will be given to quality uncertainty. In the present essay, I shall consider the pricing of *new* durables as time elapses (as of the moment of their introduction in the market).

Storable goods and normal-cost pricing

Inventories exist at the retail and wholesale levels but also at the manufacturer's level, which will interest us most. It is of some importance to realize that the behavior of these manufacturers' stocks in the aggregate is the composite of the rather disparate fluctuations of various parts, because both the motives that control inventory policy and the ability of manufacturers to implement their policies promptly and completely differ. In his classic study of the role of inventories in business cycles, Abramovitz (1948) argues that manufacturers' stocks must be divided into at least three major categories: (a) raw materials, (b) goods in process, and (c) finished goods.

Any materials or supplies purchased by a manufacturer and not yet employed in the process of fabrication at the plant constitute raw materials, however much they may have been fabricated at earlier stages. They normally constitute about 40% of manufacturers' stocks and would follow fluctuations in output if manufacturers had perfect control over their stocks. In fact, they follow cycles in output with a lag. Goods in process consist of commodities that the manufacturer has begun to manipulate but that are not yet in the condition in which they are usually sold. They compose about 20% of all manufacturers' stocks and should be directly proportional to output. Finished goods are commodities a manufacturer is ready to sell either to distributors or consumers or to other manufacturers for further fabrication. These (inevitably) make up about 40% of all manufacturers' stocks and can be partitioned into goods made to order and goods made to stock. The former are simply in the pipeline between production at one end and delivery at the other, account for perhaps 15% to 20% of stocks of finished goods, and rise and fall with shipments. Goods made to stock vary inversely with shipments.

In this essay, the term "inventories" will always designate finished goods made to stock and stored at the manufacturer's level or at the (wholesale and retail) distributor's level, as the case may be.[1] A completely different theoretical analysis may be necessary for inventories of raw materials or of goods in process.

The best evidence available on how manufacturers of storable goods price their products over time (e.g., over the business cycle) is perhaps still that gathered by the Oxford Economists' Research Group during the late 1930s, published in the *Oxford Studies in the Price Mechanism* by Wilson and Andrews (1951) and rationalized in Andrews's *Manufacturing Business* (1949). The answers given to the questionnaires and at interviews by about thirty-eight entrepreneurs are summarized as follows by Hall and Hitch:

> The most striking feature of the answers was the number of firms which apparently do not aim, in their pricing policy, at what appeared to us to be the maximization of profits by the equation of marginal revenue and marginal cost....
>
> An overwhelming majority of the entrepreneurs thought that a price based on full average cost (including a conventional allowance for profit) was the "right" price, the one which "ought" to be charged. In some cases this meant computing the full cost of a "given" commodity,

and charging a price equal to cost. In others it meant working from some traditional or convenient price, which had been proved acceptable to consumers, and adjusting the quality of the article until its full cost equalled the "given" price. A large majority of the entrepreneurs explained that they did actually charge the "full cost" price, a few admitting that they might charge more in periods of exceptionally high demand, and a greater number that they might charge less in periods of exceptionally depressed demand. What, then, was the effect of "competition"? In the main it seemed to be to induce firms to modify the margin for profits which could be added to direct costs and overheads so that approximately the same prices for similar products would rule within the "group" of competing producers. One common procedure was the setting of a price by a strong firm at its own full cost level, and the acceptance of this price by other firms in the "group"; another was the reaching of a price by what was in effect an agreement, though an unconscious one, in which all the firms in the group, acting on the same principle of "full cost," sought independently to reach a similar result. [1951, pp. 112–13]

To compute "full cost," prime (or direct) cost per unit is taken as the base, a percentage addition is made to cover overheads (or indirect cost), and a further conventional addition (frequently 10%) is made for profit. Interest on capital is mostly included in the addition for profit rather than in overheads.

As for the possible effect of interest rates on the holding of inventories, the answers were on the whole negative, as reported in Meade and Andrews (1951) and in Andrews (1951). Sayers, however, explained these negative answers by the historical circumstances of the 1930s: "It is true that when in the thirties interest rates were low, business men were inclined to pooh-pooh their significance; but when in the twenties they were high, the business men were loud in emphasizing (e.g. in the Federation of British Industries) the depressive effects of dear money: indeed, it was partly because such an agitation was going on that the Macmillan Committee was appointed in 1929. I cannot help wondering what answers an 'Oxford inquiry' would have evoked in the twenties" (1951, p. 14).

The full-cost principle was rebaptized "normal cost" principle by Andrews (1949, pp. 157–61), to insist on the fact that it leads to a price that the businessman considers normal. To estimate the normal cost – this estimate always refers to the future, as the computation is done in order to determine a price – a "normal" level of output must be chosen. This budgeted output "will frequently be a notional one which can be described as covering that proportion of capacity, or a little less, which the business man can hope to achieve on the average, taking the good years with the bad" (Andrews 1949, p. 165). Ex post realized profits will fall in recession years and will rise in good years because of the difference between the overheads actually realized and the estimates of average overheads used to determine the price.

More recent empirical work tends to confirm the normal-cost principle. Using data for a number of British industries, Godley and Nordhaus (1972) were able to show that observed prices behaved in a way that is surprisingly similar to the behavior of prices computed on the basis of costs normalized for the business cycle. These prices follow the evolution of normal costs, *not* the evolution of demand or current costs. Nordhaus summarizes the available evidence as follows: "Prices are set on the basis of costs normalized for the cycle. We found, rather surprisingly, that prices were almost completely determined by normal costs. More precisely, once costs have been converted to normal average costs (costs are read off a cost schedule at the normal value of output) there was at most a whisper of an effect of the *actual* level of demand and costs on actual prices" (1976, p. 60).

As for the role of interest rates, Sayers's conjecture is probably correct. Changes in interest rates probably have an impact on prices and inventories when the level of interest rates is high and no impact when that level is low. Although systematic empirical studies relating to this statement seem to be missing, it is at least not contradicted by some econometric findings by Eckstein and Wyss (1972).

Macroeconomists today seem to be great believers in the normal-cost principle. Most price equations appearing in macroeconomic models – to explain the prices of particular industries – are indeed based on it. And theoreticians with the most diverse approaches openly state their adherence to it: See Kaldor (1976, p. 705) or Malinvaud (1976, pp. 9–10), for example. A microeconomist would like to do more and to understand why firms are using the normal-cost principle. How can demand change without affecting the price? How can costs change without affecting the price? If setting marginal cost equal to marginal revenue is not the rule that is followed in practice, as Hall and Hitch and Andrews suggest, what other principle is to be invoked? The most satisfactory answer – at least to my taste – would be that normal costing is a rule of thumb that somehow allows firms to maximize profits without using calculus and without being myopic to the point of maximizing profits instantaneously, year by year (or day by day? or minute by minute?). The following chapter will suggest that the theory of price discrimination, when applied intertemporally, suggests precisely this type of answer because it implies that profits are maximized over several periods – with the implication that prices are sticky, whereas inventories fluctuate greatly.

Storable goods and seasonal price schedules

The fluctuations of demand and costs to which I have referred occurred over the trade cycle and covered therefore several years. I now want to draw attention to the corresponding seasonal variations within one year and to notice that these might lead to a completely different type of pricing, such as a monthly price schedule with sharp movements according to the seasons. These movements are not the result of the "interplay of demand and supply" on the market, since they are announced twelve months in advance (and therefore are completely controlled by the businessmen) and often happen during months in which demand, for example, is zero (so that demand can hardly be said to be the driving force behind the price change). A real life example will help make my point clear.

Consider the Belgian nitrogen fertilizer market. The final demand for fertilizers originates at the farm and is characterized by a rather extreme seasonal shift. Nitrogen fertilizers are used, each year, during a period of three months, on average from March till May. This period varies somewhat according to the climate and the type of fertilizer. Final demand is almost instantaneous: As farmers have only limited storage facilities, intertemporal demand transfers occur only over a limited number of months and typically extend forward only until December or January.

Vertical integration into distribution is almost totally absent. Producers have limited storage capacities, and these are minimal compared with nine months' production, which suggests that the intermediate market (the distributors) can supply storage more efficiently than the producers could. For analytical purposes, the situation can be described as one in which all storage is supplied by the distributors. These distributors are very numerous, very small, and competitive. There admittedly is one strong farmers' cooperative, but it happens not to be strong in nitrogen fertilizers.

On the production side, one cartel has controlled production (and imports, if any) entirely since 1932. Before that crucial year, prices fluctuated according to an irregular seasonal pattern. Since then, *fixed seasonal price schedules, announced each year in the spring for the coming twelve months,* appear. In 1932 precisely the Belgian market was closed to foreign competition by a series of agreements among the Belgian and other European cartels and by government intervention. The announced price is the price at the retail level. Its time shape is the same as that of the intermediate price, because the latter is equal to the retail price minus a wholesalers' rebate. This rebate is a constant (12 BF per 100 kg in 1977–8). The declared aim of the seasonal price schedule is to encourage purchases in the fall and early winter (from October until February, to be precise). For technical reasons, production has to be continuous and smooth during the year, and producers could not build up stocks efficiently in sufficient quantities to supply the required quantities in the spring.

Table 5.1. *Seasonal price schedules for nitrogen fertilizers (Belgian francs per 100 kg)*

Month of delivery	Ammonium nitrate[a]		Ammonium nitrate[b]		Urea[c]	
	p_t	Δp_t	p_t	Δp_t	p_t	Δp_t
1976						
July	386	0	352	0	709	0
August	386	0	352	0	709	0
September	386	6	352	6	709	6
October	392	6	358	8	715	6
November	398	7	364	7	721	7
December	405	6	371	6	728	6
1977						
January	411	4	377	4	734	4
February	415	3	381	3	738	3
March	418	0	384	0	741	0
April	418	0	384	0	741	0
May	418	0	384	0	741	0
June	418	0	384	0	741	0

Note: p_t = wholesale price per 100 kg.
[a] 26% nitrogen.   [b] 21% nitrogen.   [c] 46% nitrogen.
Source: Société Carbochimique.

As can be seen in Phlips (1962a, chap. 10, figs. 5, 7, 8, and 11), the typical time shape is as follows: The price increases stepwise during the months when final demand is negligible, that is, until February or March (according to weather conditions); then the price is constant for two or three months; finally there is a sharp drop, the lowest level being reached in June or July. This low level is, in fact, the starting point of a new seasonal price schedule.

Table 5.1 presents the price lists announced on July 1, 1976, for the coming twelve months for three basic types of fertilizer. It is of interest to notice the following stipulations in the producers' sales conditions. Orders (from wholesalers) must be sent in before the first day of the month in which they have to be carried out; however, the producers always have the right to postpone delivery until some later month; when there is a postponement, the price announced for the month of actual delivery (*not* the price for the month for which the order was placed) will be applicable. Although these stipulations are rather drastic, wholesalers do not object, because complete certainty about future final prices, coupled with known margins, implies almost complete certainty about yearly profits. (Profits would be entirely certain if final demand were certain and if storage costs during the coming twelve months were known with certainty.)

All in all, intuition suggests that, although nitrogen fertilizer producers do produce for storage, they must find ways of shifting the supply of storage from their own premises to the distributors'. If they had been able to carry the stocks themselves, they would have set prices that did not reflect – or did not totally reflect – storage costs. Here they seem to be obliged to announce prices that fully cover storage costs, to induce distributors to supply storage well in advance. One wonders to what extent this obligation is related to the atomistic structure of the final market for fertilizer. In other words, would not the seasonal price schedule have been flatter if the number of distributors had been small?

Exhaustible resources

At this point, it seems natural to extend the discussion somewhat by considering commodities that are storable without being reproducible, so that their stock is given. These are the so-called exhaustible resources, such as oil, coal, gold, and the basic metals. When the Organization of Petroleum Exporting Countries (OPEC) cartel discusses a new oil price, it might be facing a problem analogous to the one the Belgian nitrogen fertilizer cartel must solve each summer – except that the time horizon might be much longer than an agricultural season and that not only the price but the rate of extraction from the soil must be determined.

One thing is clear: Since the creation of the OPEC cartel, the price of oil is higher than before. OPEC has abruptly raised the *level* of oil prices, as can be seen[2] from Figure 5.1e (see the abrupt raises in 1973 and 1979–80). But what about the time shape of oil prices? They could be said to have been sticky during the 1950s and 1960s. Since 1973 they have been seen to rise at varying rates. To say that these prices reflect "the law of supply and demand" is an easy way out and, to my taste, a most unsatisfactory answer, especially since a large part of the oil reserves are controlled by a few producers who are capable of controlling the price of oil. We shall have to find out what kind of economic reasoning is followed by those who actually fix prices.

The discussion in Chapter 7 will mainly refer to the price of oil. The other prices in Figure 5.1 are given for purposes of comparison. It is surprising to see how similar the time shapes are, particularly since the early 1970s. Could it be that a same third force is acting on these prices? In particular, one wonders to what extent higher and higher interest rates might be responsible for – or at least linked to – the spectacular rise during the past eight years.[3]

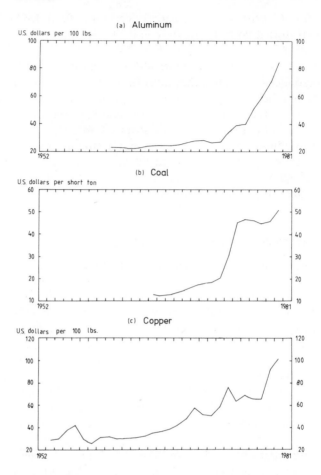

Figure 5.1. Prices of exhaustible resources. (*Source:* © 1982, Institut de Recherches Economiques et Sociales, Louvain-la-Neuve. Reprinted by permission.)

New durable goods and skimming

"Sticky" prices were seen to be irresponsive to changing demand conditions. We have seen that seasonal prices rise more while demand is nonexistent than when demand is high. We have also seen that oil prices are manipulated upward in a spectacular way by a cartel. To leave the reader in a state of complete bewilderment, it remains to pinpoint other cases, in which a monopolist manipulates prices downward in the face of increasing demand. (Let readers be reassured that the theory of intertemporal

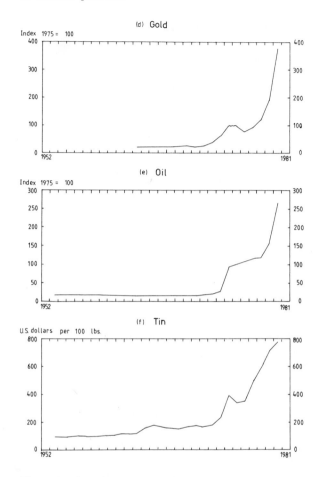

Figure 5.1 (*cont.*)

price discrimination will provide the unifying principle that rationalizes these apparently different types of behavior.)

New goods, such as television sets, hand calculators, video cassettes, a new movie,[4] a new book, and so forth are typically reduced in price gradually over the product life cycle. A book publisher issues a hardcover edition first. After a few months, the leftovers go to specialized bookshops that sell the same hardcovers – though absolutely new – at much reduced prices, and the publisher puts an even cheaper paperback edition on the market. Dean (1949, pp. 419–21) called this phenomenon "skimming pricing."

Let us from a historical perspective view the prices of radio receivers when they were sold for the first time in the 1920s. Table 5.2 shows the

Table 5.2. *Catalog price of*
"Ducretet-Thomson" radio
receiver, France, 1926-1939

Year	Price[a]	Model[b]
1926	3,755	RM6 (6)
1928	3,755	RM6 (6)
1931	3,960	CD5 (5)
1932	3,746	R4 (4)
1934	1,990	C55 (5)
1935	2,180	C636 (6)
1936	2,950	C736 (6)
1937	1,700	C850 (5)
1938	1,850	C930 (5)
1939	1,950	D30 (5)

[a] In francs.
[b] Numbers in parentheses are numbers of lamps.
Source: Fourastié (1959), p. 565.

catalog price for Ducretet-Thomson radio receivers in France during the period 1926-39, as reported in Fourastié (1959). (The first radios were sold, in France, in 1924.) The prices refer to different though comparable models, as indicated. The quality of these models improved considerably over the period. The first model (RM6) was difficult to assemble and to handle. By 1934, the C55 could be used without batteries, and frequencies could be changed without problem (Fourastié 1959, pp. 228-9). Yet eleven years after its introduction on the market, a radio cost less than half its initial price!

In his books, Fourastié argues that technical progress makes such price decreases possible. He is no doubt correct, especially during a longer period. I doubt, though, whether technical progress explains everything. Especially in the very first years of a product's existence, when quality improvements must imply higher costs of production, high prices seem to result from a desire to make certain that buyers with inelastic demand buy the product first. Since a buyer typically needs only one unit of the good, lowering the price will allow the producer to reach different, more price-conscious consumers. It seems worth checking whether this alternative rationalization is compatible with profit maximization.

Table 5.3 – taken from Fourastié (1959) – provides another, rather spectacular, example of a price decrease for a new durable: the bicycle! In five years' time (from 1892 to 1897) prices were reduced by 50%.

Table 5.3. *Catalog price of "Hirondelle" bicycle, France, 1892–1908 (in francs)*

Year	Most expensive model	Cheapest model	Tire
1892	500	360	—
1893	420	275	—
1894	380	250	—
1895	365	209	22
1896	318	180	20
1897	256	214	20
1898	275	214	19
1899	300	237	19
1902	300	190	16
1903	300	190	15
1904	300	190	16
1905	300	190	16
1907	350	130	16
1908	350	130	14

Note: Tire prices for 1892–1894 are not available.
Source: Fourastié (1959), pp. 500, 501, 503.

By 1899 they had become sticky and seemed to behave according to the normal-cost principle.

It is striking that many of the durables considered belong to the category of leisure goods. I suspect that these are the goods for which the sensitivity to price differs greatly among a population, notably as a function of wealth, income, or age. Wealthy people – especially their children – want to be the first to buy new gadgets such as a bicycle (in the nineteenth century), a radio (in the 1920s), or a video cassette (in the 1980s). It is only after a producer has satisfied their demands at the highest possible price – irrespective of the cost of production – that the producer starts wondering what a normal cost of production could look like and what a normal price could be.

My final example is even more spectacular and concerns the price of electronic computers in the United States during the period 1955–65. Chow (1967) constructed a price index for computers corrected for differences in quality. This index (Table 5.4) is an average of the ratios of observed rentals to the rentals that would have been charged if the models had been introduced in the year 1960. Given quality, a computer was ten times cheaper in 1965 than in 1954, whereas the stock of computers grew from an estimated 1960 rental of about $370 thousand (per month) at the end of 1954 to about $194 million at the end of 1965.

Table 5.4. *Price index for computers*

Year	Stock ($ thousands)[a]	Price index[b]
1954	370.3	3.2554
1955	991.7	2.9610
1956	2,389.9	2.5336
1957	5,087.6	2.3168
1958	8,362.0	2.0342
1959	12,549.0	1.5884
1960	19,072.0	1.0716
1961	38,264.0	0.9042
1962	64,349.0	0.6873
1963	95,815.0	0.5712
1964	136,845.0	0.4186
1965	194,136.0	0.3416

[a] Estimated 1960 rental.
[b] Base year = 1960. Prices have been corrected for differences in quality.
Source: Chow (1967), p. 1124.

"An average annual rate of growth of 78 percent would have accomplished this" (Chow 1967, p. 1117).

Nonstorable commodities and the Green Tariff

After emphasizing the pervasiveness of sticky prices for storable manufactured goods, I have illustrated cases in which prices were systematically moving upward or downward. The time has come to illustrate a last case of prices that oscillate in a systematic or random way. The cases that come to mind refer to nonstorable goods, particularly services.

In service industries, variations in demand cannot be met by variations in inventories, because the product is technologically not storable. In other industries, storage costs may be prohibitive because of the bulk or other properties of the products, as in the case of pipeline transportation. In such cases, prices do tend to follow oscillations in demand. Telephone calls are cheaper at night than during the day. Hotels advertise weekend specials, to fill rooms that would otherwise stay empty. Heating oil is more expensive in the winter than in the summer. But the most typical fluctuation, perhaps, is the daily oscillation of the price of electricity, due to the fact that customers tend to consume electricity mostly in the morning (between 7:00 and 9:00 a.m.) and in the late afternoon (between 5:00 and 7:00 p.m.), whereas generating capacity is limited and storage costs prohibitive.

One of the most elaborate electricity tariffs that tries to cope with demand variations is the Green Tariff of Electricité de France (EDF) – so called because of the color of the cover of the brochure in which it first appeared.[5] In 1958 the Green Tariff was first offered on an optional basis to high-voltage consumers. Ten years later it was made standard for all high-voltage consumers and became available to residential customers in a simplified version.

Mitchell describes how the Green Tariff adapts prices to the main typical variations in demand:

> The different tariff periods are defined in terms of the effect of increased demand on the requirement for additional generating capacity. *Peak hours* are those time periods when an additional megawatt of demand substantially increases the risk of an outage due to a shortage of capacity and thus, in the long run, requires that generating capacity be increased to maintain a given level of system reliability. The *shoulder hours* are considered to be the time period when additions to system demand only somewhat increase the risk of capacity shortage. *Off-peak hours* are the time periods when increased demand on the system causes no increase in the probability of shortage...
>
> During the four coldest winter months, November through February, Electricité de France experiences its greatest demand and consequently has its highest operating costs and greatest risk of shortage (partly because some hydroelectric resources are unavailable). For these months there are three distinct periods:
>
> *Peak hours:* 7 a.m. to 9 a.m. and 5 p.m. to 7 p.m., Monday through
> Saturday.
> *Shoulder hours:* 6 a.m. to 10 p.m., except Sunday and peak hours.
> *Off-peak hours:* 10 p.m. to 6 a.m. and all day Sunday.
>
> Since running costs and risk of shortage are lower in the other eight months of the year, the Green Tariff introduces seasonal pricing in the months of October and March by eliminating the peak hours and charging at the winter shoulder rate for electricity consumed during the entire 6 a.m. to 10 p.m. period (except on Sunday), so that only shoulder and off-peak rates apply. And in the summer months (April through September), when running costs are even lower because of reduced demand and the availability of water from the spring runoff for hydroelectric facilities, only shoulder and off-peak hours of the day are differentiated: moreover, the summer shoulder and off-peak rates are less than winter rates. In all, the Green Tariff has five tariff periods: peak, shoulder, and off-peak in the winter; and shoulder and off-peak in the summer. [1978, pp. 67–9]

The resulting time shape of the kilowatt-hour (kWh) charges, as effective in 1975 for service at medium voltages, is displayed in Figure 5.2, taken from Mitchell (1978, p. 68).

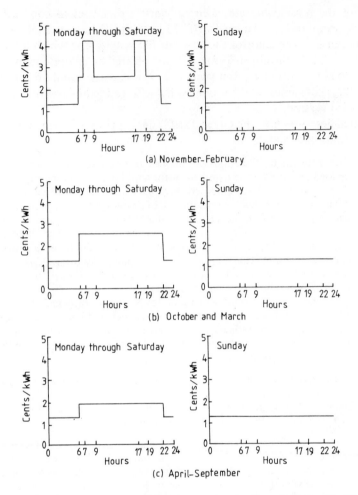

Figure 5.2. Kilowatt-hour charges under the French Green Tariff for service at medium voltages, 1975. (*Source:* Mitchell 1978, p. 68.)

CHAPTER 6

Storable commodities

In Essay I, great care was taken to make clear at which point in space (at the mill or at the customer's location) a price is applicable and over which geographical distance a delivered price may be valid and therefore constant (or "uniform"). We must now recognize that similar questions must be solved by the seller (often simultaneously with the spatial problems) with respect to intertemporal pricing: At what moment in time is a price applicable and over what time period can it possibly remain valid and therefore unchanged (or "rigid," or "sticky")? We are thus led into the problem of price stickiness over time. Why do certain prices change every so often, whereas other prices remain constant for months, if not for years?

From the start I want to make a distinction between prices determined in well-organized competitive markets, such as auctions for raw materials, and the so-called administered prices, fixed by manufacturing businesses. The former are determined as the result of a tatonnement process involving the instantaneous demands and supplies of traders, speculators, or intermediaries, and this often happens simultaneously in a spot market and in a futures market.[1] The latter are the only prices that interest us in this book, so that a firm is always considered to be in a monopolistic or oligopolistic situation and has therefore the possibility of fixing its prices itself. In general these prices are sticky, in the sense that they do not change with every variation of demand and costs, as we saw in Chapter 5. Furthermore, when there is a change in price, the increase (or decrease) is often said to be smaller than with competitive prices.[2] What could be the reason?

Analogies between space and time

The concepts and methods used in spatial economics can be used to analyze pricing over time. We shall see that some conclusions reached in Essay I simply carry over to intertemporal problems. It will suffice to redefine the variables (and indexes) in an appropriate way.

Indeed, although not perfect, certain analogies between space and time are far-reaching and provide a better understanding of the problems involved. In his book on capital theory, Bliss (1975, chap. 3) emphasizes

81

Table 6.1. *Analogy between space and time*

Space	Time
Geographical distance	future date (t)
Point of delivery	date of delivery
Point of production	present moment ($t=0$)
Frontiers of market area	planning horizon (T)
Transport cost	storage cost
Delivered price	future price (π_t)
Net mill price	discounted price $[\pi_t/(1+r)^t]$
Uniform delivered price	constant future price

that time differentiates economic commodities in the same way that space does. We know that a physically identical commodity delivered in two different points in space is to be treated as two different commodities from an economic point of view. Why? Because spatial location is taken into account in the buyers' preference ordering and in the sellers' production set. On the market, the result is that, on the one hand, households are ready to pay more for a bottle of milk delivered on the doorstep than for the same bottle to be picked up at the supermarket, and that, on the other hand, producers do take account of costs of transportation when determining their prices. The same is true for a physically identical product delivered at two different points in time.

To make the analogy more explicit, it is useful to list a number of concepts used in a spatial context, as in Table 6.1, and to define the corresponding temporal concepts. (The reader is urged to write down the concepts corresponding to the left column before looking at my right column.) Whereas a spatial analysis refers to a firm with a given location, an intertemporal analysis is set up with reference to the present moment ($t=0$) or "today." This moment is the beginning of a time period – the planning period – over which the plan to be determined extends. This period lasts until a terminal date (T) – given or to be determined – that defines the planning horizon. To the concept of distance (from the production point) therefore corresponds the concept of the future date, defined with respect to the present ($t=0$). One unit of distance becomes one unit of time, that is, one time period.

Time can be continuous or discrete. In continuous time, t is a point in time. When time is treated as discrete, the period (a week, a month, a year) is defined as the smallest unit of time inside which there are no subperiods. When the period is a week, you might imagine that decisions are made on Monday morning and that whatever is decided for ($t=0$) is carried out during the week without question (as if the business manager came into the office only on Monday morning to give orders and then vanished until the following Monday). This method of treating discrete time is very widespread and was given good standing in chapter 9 of Hicks's *Value and Capital* (1936). (Hicks imagines that markets are open only on Mondays, so that only on Mondays can contracts be made and new prices fixed.)

Transport costs are costs associated with moving a commodity through space. The cost of storage is the corresponding concept over time. Indeed, to store a commodity is to move it (its selling date) from today till later. This notion suggests that the analogy with the spatial theory discussed in Essay I is valid for goods produced for storage, not for commodities that are to be transformed (raw materials and goods in process). Plainly the storable goods considered here, which are "finished" from the seller's point of view, may be considered by the buyer as goods to be transformed during the production process. What matters is that there be a production in t of a commodity to be sold not in t but in a later period.

To the concept of a delivered price corresponds the concept of a future price (π_t) announced today (in $t = 0$) as being valid in the future period t or at the future date t. What, then, is the equivalent in an intertemporal context of the net mill price (defined as the delivered price minus transportation cost)? It must be the value, today, of future price π_t, namely, its discounted value ($a^t \pi_t = p_t$), where a^t is the discount function $[1/(1 + r)]^t$ in discrete time. In continuous time, the corresponding discount function is e^{-rt}. It indicates that a price realized later is worth *less* today. (Please check! Today, $a^t = a^0 = 1 = e^0$.) If interest charges are the only costs of storage to be taken into account, then r is simply today's rate of interest, and discounting[3] is seen to be the correct way to "deduce" storage costs from future receipts. Otherwise, storage charges and allowances for risk have to be deducted from π_t before it is discounted.

Now that we have carried the analogy between time and space this far, the time has come to recognize that there are limitations. There is, in fact, an essential difference: *Time differs from space in that it runs in one direction only.* Tomorrow necessarily comes after today. For our problem, this means that transportation over space is possible in any direction (including reverse transportation to the point of departure), whereas displacement of production is possible into the future only. The decision to produce for stock means that stocks are piled up today and available for sale tomorrow: Tomorrow the firm cannot reverse policies and decide to reduce yesterday's production. In other words, to use Samuelson's (1957) expression, storage allows us to move goods from the present to the future at a finite cost, but we cannot move these goods back from the future to the past at a finite cost. This creates an asymmetry that is typical for intertemporal analyses. Without it, we could apply spatial theory to intertemporal problems without further thought by simply redefining the variables. In fact we must be careful to take into account the fact that decisions in ($t=0$) determine the situation at the beginning of ($t=1$): If one has piled up stocks in ($t=0$), these are on hand in ($t=1$) and any new production plan elaborated in ($t=1$) must take this circumstance into account. (We are prisoners of the past.)

One additional remark: As time passes, firms must check at the beginning of each period (each "Monday") to see whether they are on a path that is intertemporally optimal (from their point of view). Each Monday, a new plan, valid from ($t=0$) until ($t=T$), could be elaborated – given that each new Monday corresponds to ($t=0$) with a concomitant displacement of the horizon T. This option creates a consistency problem, as the new plan could be different from the one put in operation a week ago. At the limit, plans could be revised each Monday, so that actual decisions taken in successive t's could be interpreted as belonging to initial segments (or points) of optimal paths that are never followed to their ends.[4]

Intertemporal price discrimination

In Essay I, the theory of the discriminating monopoly was shown to be a most useful tool to explain some observed spatial configuration of prices. Given the analogies between space and time just discussed, one cannot but wonder whether this theory could also help us to understand some temporal features of industrial prices. The answer is yes, at least for goods produced for storage. The next section will try to show how normal-cost pricing can be interpreted as a form of intertemporal price discrimination. In this section, I want to explain the mechanics. To do this, I shall follow Shaw's pioneering 1940 paper on the theory of inventory.

I start with a quotation from Shaw which I find worth reading and rereading:

> The guiding principle of the firm's operating plan, is, of course, the *ex-ante* maximization of the difference for the expectation interval[5] between discounted sales proceeds and discounted prime costs. It is the task of management to select from alternative income–outgo streams the one which promises the highest capital value. A characteristic of this stream which is particularly instructive for present purposes is that the discounted marginal revenue and the discounted marginal cost for one date are equalized as closely as possible with one another *and* with the marginal revenues and marginal costs discounted from the remaining dates in the operational period. Any plan which fails to substitute a higher for a lower discounted marginal revenue or a lesser for a greater discounted marginal cost, where substitution is possible, falls short of the optimum.

Inventory is the product of the desynchronization of output and sales that intertemporal substitutions of discounted marginal revenues and discounted marginal costs require. Profitable opportunities for substitution are opportunities to obtain a positive net yield upon investment in inventory. The capital value of inventory is the sum of the discounted gains to be won by substitution, and it is maximized when the capital value of the enterprise is maximized.

There is an evident parallelism between the theories of inventory accumulation and discriminating monopoly. The former defines optimum distribution of a total supply between markets that are separated in time. The latter defines optimum distribution of a total supply between markets that are separated in space. Assuming appropriate discounting of future quantities, the definitions of optima are identical: "... profits will be at a maximum when the marginal revenue in each market is equal to the marginal cost of the whole output."[6] In the analysis that follows, the parallelism has been exploited rather intensively. [1940, pp. 468-9]

It is remarkable that the parallelism[7] between inventory accumulation and price discrimination was perceived so clearly only a few years after the publication of Jean Robinson's *The Economics of Imperfect Competition*. Implicit in the passage just quoted is the discovery that the maximization of discounted present and future profits leads to new insights into the intertemporal pricing problem only if the firm is given the opportunity to accumulate inventories of finished goods. If the quantity produced is always equal to the quantity sold – an assumption made in all the microeconomic textbooks that I know – then intertemporal and instantaneous profit maximization lead to the same conclusion: To maximize profits, a firm must equalize marginal revenue and marginal cost in each period, instantaneously. If, however, the quantity produced can be different from the quantity sold, so that inventories can accumulate (when that difference is positive) or can decumulate (when the rate of production is smaller than the rate of sales), then intertemporal profit maximization leads to new insights. One discovers (a) what I shall call an intertemporal discrimination rule, *different* from the standard marginal-cost-equals-marginal-revenue rule, and (b) as a consequence, that the simultaneous determination of prices, output, and sales – and therefore inventories – over time is a special case of the theory of the discriminating monopoly.

The textbook marginal-cost-equals-marginal-revenue rule says that price and output (or sales) are determined by the *intersection* of marginal revenue and marginal cost. The intertemporal discrimination rule says something different: In Shaw's words, it says that (discounted) marginal costs and revenue are equalized *throughout the planning period.* With shifting revenue and cost curves, this equality could imply intersection only by a miracle (if the effects of discounting were exactly compensated by shifts in the opposite direction). In general, intertemporal profit maximization must imply equilibrium values of production and sales at which marginal costs and marginal revenue, though equal, do not intersect.

To clarify this point, I shall follow Shaw in his analysis of three cases: (a) the case of a perfectly competitive firm facing an infinitely elastic marginal revenue curve; (b) the case of an imperfectly competitive firm that sells at a rigid conventional price, determined, for example, by a state authority or by a cartel; (c) the case (which interest us) of an imperfectly competitive firm that sells at a variable price and determines this price (and therefore sales) simultaneously with its output, so that its price policy cannot be separated from its inventory policy (which results from the difference between output and sales). The first two are special cases of the third. Once we understand why inventories are accumulated with given competitive or conventional prices, we shall be able to understand better how intertemporal price discrimination (case c) creates additional opportunities for inventory holding through expansion of immediate output and deferred sales.

Consider a single firm, assumed to be producing a final good in an established plant. To simplify the presentation, suppose that its processes of manufacture are completed within a week and that the output is available for sale in the same week. Decisions are made by the management on Monday of each week and are not subject to change until the succeeding Monday. The planning horizon extends over two weeks, so that total output for weeks 1 and 2 must be equal to total sales for weeks 1 and 2. If production in week 1, x_1, exceeds sales in week 1, q_1, then x_2 must fall short of q_2 by equal amounts: Part of q_1 is then retained in inventory (s_1) for subsequent sale.

One additional assumption is necessary to make inventory accumulation possible in cases where prices are determined by a competive market. I shall have to assume that the demand function of the second week is not precisely known. (As a result, it will be necessary to discount it not only for interest but also for risk.) If this function were known with certainty (in the first week), then a competitive firm would not find it profitable to abandon the myopic instantaneous rule of equalizing price and marginal cost to fix the rate of production in each week. (Remember that such a firm can sell as much as it wants at the prevailing price in any week. Why then would it incur storage costs?) In the case of a conventional price or of an imperfectly competitive firm capable of fixing its own (variable) price, it will not, to the contrary, be necessary to assume uncertain demand (or cost) functions for the second week: Even with demands and costs known with certainty, the possibility of intertemporal price discrimination will make inventory accumulation profitable.

Figure 6.1 is a geometric summary of the calculations of a *perfect com-*

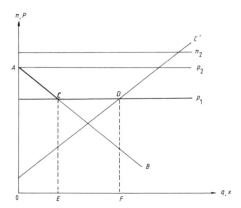

Figure 6.1. A perfectly competitive firm on Monday of week 1.

petitor for Monday of week 1. This firm faces a given competitive price p_1 and forecasts that the price will rise next week to π_2. The present value of π_2 is p_2. After deduction of an allowance for risk (which is supposed to increase with the proposed volume of inventory), the horizontal line p_2 becomes the downward-sloping line AB, representing net discounted marginal revenue of week 2, as seen on Monday of week 1. Summing AB and p_1 horizontally gives the aggregate marginal revenue ACp_1 for supplies that are salable in either week 1 or week 2. C' is the marginal cost of production in week 1.

Anticipated changes in the cost function have no direct bearing on this firm's inventory policy. There is no incentive to escape rising factor prices by storing in week 1 or to delay production if factor prices are expected to fall in week 2. The cost function for week 2 therefore does not enter the picture, and production in week 1 is determined simply by the equality of current price p_1 and current marginal cost C'.

However, the anticipated increase in selling price does create an incentive to substitute deferred sales for immediate sales of current output, that is, not to sell the entire output of week 1. The profit-maximizing plan for Monday of week 1 is to produce $0F$ and to keep $0E$ of it in stock. Indeed, at point C the curve AB intersects p_1, so that marginal revenues are the same on both markets (in both weeks). They are also equal to marginal cost FD, but that fact has nothing to do with the inventory policy: It is the automatic result of the fact that p_1 is horizontal. In other words, equality of discounted marginal *revenues* alone is the principle that governs investment in inventory by perfectly competitive firms. As long as AC is above p_1, the firm has an interest in deferring sales until

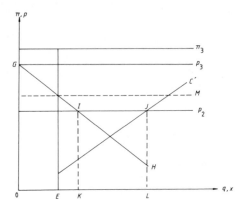

Figure 6.2. A perfectly competitive firm on Monday of week 2.

next week, so that $0E$ *(not EF)* measures inventories. Indeed, to the left of C, present returns forgone (p_1) are less than discounted marginal returns in the future.

Shaw's conclusions are that, for a perfectly competitive firm, (a) production for stock is contingent upon an expected rise in selling price (unless π_2 lies above p_1, all of $0E$ is sold at once) and (b) total output is likely to be unaffected by inventory policy.[8]

It is of some interest to consider the situation this competitive firm faces on Monday of week 2. It is depicted in Figure 6.2. Whether the firm likes it or not, $0E$ stocks are on hand. The current price p_2 is now precisely known (and is probably different from the expected π_2) as is C'. The horizon includes week 3, so that expected π_3 and the corresponding p_3 and GH enter the picture. It is essential to notice that the position of GIp_2 relative to C' is dependent upon the volume of carry-over, $0E$, as the marginal cost curve for the current week is shifted to the right of the vertical axis by this amount. Although production in week 2 is the same as it would have been if no inventories had been carried over from week 1, the proportion that is accumulated in week 2 is smaller, because of the carry-over. (Any current price, in week 2, above M would lead to a decision to decrease the inventory existing on Monday of that week.) "This is confirmed by reflection upon the fact that, since inventory and new output are eligible for the same markets, they are logically indistinguishable elements of a total supply" (Shaw 1940, p. 475).

Next we consider an imperfectly competitive firm that sells at a conventional price. Whereas in the previous case the yield to inventory arose from the substitution of deferred for immediate sales, inventories can be profitable for this firm only to the extent that immediate output is

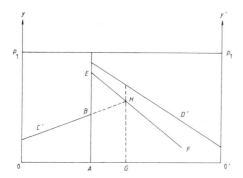

Figure 6.3. An imperfectly competitive firm selling at a conventional price on Monday of week 1.

substituted for deferred output. This interoutput substitution is profitable because it leads to savings in costs. Whereas substitutions between sales are outlawed by the nature of a conventional price, the stimulus for investment in inventory may be either adverse cost prospects or forecast of increases in total sales at the conventional price or both.

Figure 6.3 represents the situation such a firm faces on Monday of week 1. The conventional price, known to be valid for this week and for week 2, is p_1. The sales quota for week 1 is $0A$, and the sales quota anticipated for week 2 is $0'A$, measured from the $0'y'$ axis. Changes in costs are uncertain: C' is the known marginal cost curve in week 1, whereas D' is the marginal cost curve anticipated for week 2. The latter has to be corrected for interest, for risk, and for storage allowances. These corrections give curve EF, which may be described as representing discounted marginal net savings from interoutput substitution.

Indeed, suppose production $0A$ were chosen, in accordance with the sales quota. Then savings could be realized by increasing production in week 1, since at A the marginal cost in week 1 (AB) is less than the discounted value of marginal cost in week 2 (AE). An increase in production in week 1, that is, interoutput substitution, reduces the present worth of total costs for the output aggregate ($00'$) until point G is reached, with a total saving of BEH. At H, marginal cost of week 1 is equal to discounted marginal cost of week 2. Here equality of marginal *costs* alone is the rule that guides inventory policy.

On Monday of week 2, the C' curve will again have shifted to the right as the result of the carry-over AG. The point H moves downward along the redated EF curve, which implies a *reduction* of the output of week 2 (which is indeed measured from $0'y'$) and therefore a reduction in total output for both weeks. Shaw concludes that "stock on hand displaces new output for both weeks, in the proportions that are required to equalize discounted marginal costs. The displacement effect is attributable to the limited opportunity for substitution, for which the rigid sales volume and the slopes of the cost curves are responsible, as well as to the dampening influence of rising marginal allowances for carrying charges and risk'' (1940, p. 477).

We are now ready to tackle the more general case of a monopolistic firm that is capable of fixing its own price together with its rate of production. (The price in turn determines the rate of sales, and the difference between production and sales gives the change in stocks, we should remember.) The rule that governs investment in inventories is now a combination of the ones that were valid in the preceding cases. Not only must discounted marginal revenues be equal from one week to the next, and similarly for discounted marginal costs: Discounted marginal revenues must be equal, *in addition,* to discounted marginal costs. This is the "intertemporal discrimination rule" formulated in the quotation given in the beginning of this section and discovered independently by Smithies (1939). The remainder of this chapter is devoted to discovering some of its implications. For the time being,[9] I want to show how it works in the framework of our two-week planning horizon.

In the case of the competitive firm, the presence of an allowance for risk, resulting from the uncertainty about next week's price, made it profitable to hold inventories in the face of an expected rise in price. In case b, the marginal-cost curves could cross (see Figure 6.3) even without a correction for risk of the D' curve. In the present case, I shall suppose that future cost and demand functions are known with certainty, to stress the fact that intertemporal price discrimination makes inventory holding profitable, even in the absence of uncertainty. Not only will inventories be voluntary – as they were already in cases a and b. They will also be totally unrelated to the presence or absence of uncertainty about future demand and cost conditions.

In Figure 6.4a, two different demand curves are represented, the highest one representing the demand for week 2. For the sake of legibility, no provision is made for discounting the demand for week 2. The same is true for the marginal-cost curves C_1' and C_2'. If this firm were to maximize profits instantaneously, in each week, with no attempt at price discrimination, it would choose points A and B to determine its prices and output (equal to sales). The advantages of intertemporal price discrimination and investment inventory are evident, however. Add the demand curves horizontally, to find aggregate marginal revenue as explained in Chapter 2. Find the aggregate marginal-cost curve corresponding to the sum of the marginal-cost curves. The intersection of these two aggregate

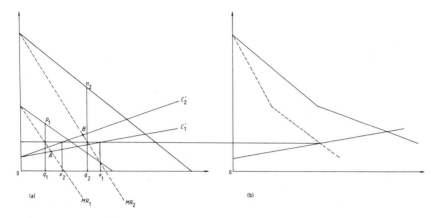

Figure 6.4. An intertemporally discriminating firm on Monday of week 1.

curves, in Figure 6.4b, determines the level at which marginal costs and marginal revenues must be equal from week to week. Following the horizontal line back to Figure 6.4a, the firm finds the plan q_1, x_1, q_2, x_2, which gives a higher profit.

Sales in week 1, q_1, are smaller than they would have been if point A had been chosen (and q_2 is larger than the sales determined by point B): There is intersales substitution, as in case a. Output x_1 is larger than with myopic profit maximization, and x_2 is smaller, so that immediate production is substituted for deferred production, as in case b. In addition, total production is larger than it would have been without discrimination. Adding $0x_1$ and $0x_2$ gives a larger total, since the points x_2 and x_1 are both on the right side of points A and B, respectively.

A further implication of intertemporal price discrimination should be noticed: Price is higher in week 1 and lower in week 2 than if intertemporal discrimination were not practiced. (Compare p_1 with the myopic price determined by point A, and π_2 with the price determined by point B.) "Upward pressures upon prices [or costs] of final goods cast their shadow before them" (Shaw 1940, p. 479).

Plainly $(x_1 - q_1)$ is the increase in stocks during week 1, and $(x_2 - q_2)$ is the decrease planned for week 2. On Monday of week 2, there will be a carry-over of $(x_1 - q_1)$, and this will in turn affect the firm's policy during week 2. It will not, in fact, produce x_2 and sell q_2. The carry-over shifts the cost curves to the right, with the result that the intersection point in Figure 6.4b moves downward:[10] Output is reduced in week 2 (compared with x_2), sales are larger than q_2, and stocks will be lower at the end of week 2 than was planned in week 1.

Normal-cost pricing

Reverting to Monday of week 1, and to Figure 6.4, it is a remarkable feature of the intertemporal discrimination rule that it makes the firm choose a level of marginal cost, to determine production in any week, that is higher than point A (on the lower cost curve C_1'), and lower than point B (on the higher cost curve C_2'). This suggests that the intertemporal discrimination rule may provide a theoretical underpinning for the practice of normal cost pricing.

To see this point more clearly – but also to do justice to Smithies (1939), who developed the theory of price discrimination independently from Shaw, using calculus of variation techniques – I want to consider a planning horizon that includes several time periods and to handle the problem in continuous time.[11] Smithies's contribution may be summarized and illustrated as follows. Suppose the firm has a time horizon that extends from $(t=0)$ to $(t=T)$. At each t, there is a known instantaneous demand function with the announced future price $\pi(t)$ as its argument. (It corresponds, in spatial economics, to what Greenhut and Ohta 1975 call the "gross" demand function, defined in terms of delivered prices.) Suppose also, for convenience, that the only costs of holding inventories are interest costs, so that the process of discounting automatically deals with them. Then $e^{-rt}\pi(t)$ $[r=r(0)]$ corresponds to the "net" price at the mill. Even with identical "gross" demands, "net" demands are different *and* are separated over space. The same is true over time, because time runs automatically and in one direction only. On the cost side, the present value of marginal costs is supposed to be an increasing function of the rate of production.

If $q=q(t)$ measures the rate of sales and $x=x(t)$ the rate of production, whereas $\pi=f(q,t)$ is the demand function at time t and $[c=\phi(x,t)]$ is unit cost, then the problem is to maximize

$$\int_0^T e^{-rt}(\pi q - cx)\, dt \tag{6.1}$$

with respect to q and x, subject to the constraint that the total quantity sold is equal to the total quantity produced during the whole period, that is,

$$\int_0^T (x - q)\, dt = 0 \tag{6.2}$$

As the difference between x and q defines the rate of change of inventories $[ds/dt=s'(t)]$, (6.2) can be rewritten as

$$\int_0^T s'(t)\, dt = 0 \tag{6.2a}$$

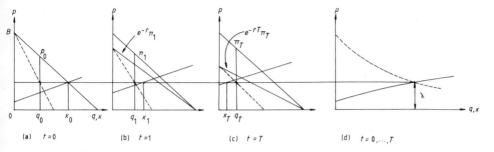

Figure 6.5. Normal-cost pricing. See text.

The problem is thus a classical variational problem with isoperimetric constraint. Its solution, which determines the optimal path of x, q (and therefore s), *and* π, gives the intertemporal discrimination rule

$$e^{-rt}\left(\pi + \alpha\,\frac{\partial \pi}{\partial q}\right) = e^{-rt}\left(c + x\,\frac{\partial c}{\partial x}\right) = \lambda \qquad (6.3)$$

where λ, the multiplier associated with Equation (6.2a), is a constant. The rule says that *the discounted marginal revenue from sales and the discounted marginal cost of goods produced at all points of time must be equal and constant.*

Notice, however, that the nonnegativity constraint $s(t) \geqslant 0$ for $(0 \leqslant t \leqslant T)$ is ignored in the exposition given above. If we had $\pi = f(q)$ and $c = \phi(x)$, that is, if the demand and cost functions did not shift over time, then (6.3) would imply that x was growing while q was decreasing: The firm should sell as much as possible right from the start – more in fact than it produces – so that the optimal path starts with a negative inventory! To circumvent this difficulty, and to make voluntary inventories possible, Smithies assumes that the demand and cost schedules are shifting upward according to exponential trends with constant growth rates larger than r and such that $g_1 < g_2$, where g_1 is the growth rate of the demand schedule and g_2 is the growth rate of the cost schedule. Then the optimal solution implies that x decreases over time while q is increasing with p: The expectation of increasing costs and prices makes it profitable to build up inventories to be sold later on.

Figure 6.5 depicts a situation in which, for simplicity, only the cost schedules are shifting upward over time. The equilibrium value of λ is determined after horizontal summation of the discounted marginal revenue and marginal cost curves and gives the horizontal line that helps find the equilibrium values of x, q, and π.

Inspection of Figure 6.5 reveals two features that are interesting in connection with the problem at hand. First, with constant demand schedules over time, the change in price from one period to the next (sometimes referred to as the "temporal price spread") is smaller than the marginal cost of storage. We thus have a nice analogy with price discrimination across space: Freight absorption here takes the form of an "absorption" of storage costs and occurs whenever the demand curves are not too convex. Second, the level of the (constant and discounted) marginal cost at which discounted marginal revenues are equated cannot be the same, in general, as the one at which instantaneous profits are maximized. In fact, its optimal level is computed over periods 0 to T, so that we might call it a "total" or "normalized" marginal cost. I dare to suggest that "normal" costing, with the implied normalization over the business cycle, may be a rule of thumb for the computation of this "total" marginal cost in practice. In Figure 6.5, λ is indeed at a "normal" level,[12] in the sense that it is above the point of intersection of the marginal cost and revenue curves at $(t=0)$ and below it at $(t=T)$.

The rate of interest

As a result of the Oxford Inquiry in the 1930s, normal-cost theoreticians suggested that changes in the rate of interest do not affect prices. This was the general feeling of businessmen in the 1930s, when interest rates were low, but not in the 1920s, when interest rates were high. Could it be that interest rates have a perceptible influence only when they are high? The intertemporal discrimination rule says yes, adding that this influence will be the more visible the worse the business conditions.

To see this, it is necessary to solve[13] Equation (6.3) for $\pi(t)$ as a function of sales $q(t)$. The solution differs according to market structure and can be written as

$$\pi(t) = \left\{ \lambda + [p(0) - \lambda]\, \frac{q(0)}{q(t)} \right\} e^{rt} \tag{6.3a}$$

In perfect competition, we would have $\lambda = p(0)$, according to Equation (6.3), since $\partial\pi/\partial q = 0$. In perfect competition, prices would thus fully reflect storage costs in the sense that $\pi(t) = p(0)e^{rt}$, or $\dot{\pi}/\pi = r$. (I make this statement with some reservations, since a competitive firm will produce for storage only if there is some uncertainty, as just noted.)

In monopolistic competition (when there are many competitors), prices do reflect the rate of interest. Indeed, the solution implies a price change $\dot{\pi} = r\pi - \epsilon e^{rt}\dot{q}q^{-2}$, where π and q are measured in index form and ϵ is a very small number. When $\dot{q} > 0$, $\dot{\pi}/\pi$ is smaller than r, so that we could say that there is "absorption" of storage costs by analogy with freight absorption in spatial economics. Yet the influence of r should be perceptible, especially when r is large compared to q and the change in $q, \dot{q}$.

When monopoly power becomes really big, the picture changes entirely. Now the solution of Equation (6.3) can be written as

$$\pi(t) = \left\{ \frac{1}{q(t)} + \delta\left[\frac{q(t) - 1}{q(t)} \right] \right\} e^{rt} \tag{6.3b}$$

which, in turn, implies $\dot{\pi}/\pi \simeq r - \dot{q}/q$. Prices are approximately inversely proportional to q, as δ is a very small number. It is not surprising, then, that monopolists are seen to increase prices dramatically when demand goes down and to stabilize prices when demand goes up and rates of interest are low. But when r is high, even monopolists will have to raise prices, whether demand goes down or not (when selling storable goods). In fact, they appear to tend to make sure that total revenue $\pi(t)q(t)$ grows along the path traced by e^{rt}. The expression for $\dot{\pi}/\pi$ implies that prices are (approximately) rigid when $r \simeq \dot{q}/q$. When r is large and $\dot{q}/q < 0$, stagflation occurs, whereas the condition $\dot{q}/q > r$ leads to decreasing prices.

The relationship between price dynamics and the rate of interest under different market structures, as just discussed, should not be too difficult to implement empirically. (These findings actually do not seem to be contradicted by the available empirical evidence. See, e.g., Eckstein and Wyss 1972.) And two things are clear: (a) A negative correlation between administered prices and demand over time should not be discarded offhand as implausible, and (b) stagflation coupled with high interest rates fits perfectly well into this model.

The policy implications are interesting. In a world such as the one I have described, it is hard to see how a reduction of demand could reduce inflation: In monopolistically competitive markets, demand has no perceptible influence on prices, whereas under monopoly a reduction in demand can only increase prices. It is even harder to see how high interest rates could help control inflation – except through a suicidal policy of bankruptcy or of ending the production of storable goods.

Oligopoly and sticky prices

The "pervasiveness of price stickiness across time and space" is not only a recognized fact; it is also[14] a "phenomenon in search of a theory" (Nordhaus 1976). We saw in Essay I that some progress has been made recently in the theoretical explanation of the spatial configuration of industrial prices. The preceding section has derived some results that help explain stickiness over time when competitors are numerous or when the firm has no competitors at all. But what if competitors are few?

In the field of industrial organization, a long controversy originating in a presentation before the Kefauver Committee by G. Means culminated in the more sophisticated discussion of the so-called administrative inflation hypothesis linking rigid prices with market concentration. A huge amount of empirical evidence was put forward, but it was often conflicting or inconclusive. That it was so should cause no surprise, as formalized theoretical results, necessary for the construction of meaningful empirical tests, were essentially lacking. The theoretical assumptions from which the empirical work originated boil down to two conflicting approaches. On the one hand, there is Stigler's presumption, which he formulates as follows:

> The traditional economic theory argues that oligopoly and monopoly prices have no special relevance to inflation. A monopolist (to take the simpler case) sets a profit-maximizing price for given demand and cost conditions. If inflation leads to a rise in either demand or costs, a new and usualy higher price will be set. The price will usually be above the competitive level at any given time, but its pattern over time will not be other than passively responsive to monetary conditions. [1962, p. 8]

On the other hand, the adherents of normal-cost pricing argue that prices are insensitive to demand fluctuations (and even to actual costs), since they are set by applying a markup to direct costs normalized for the business cycle (i.e., direct costs read off a cost schedule at the normal value of output). The markup is the same for all firms within an industry but varies from industry to industry: it is thus industry determined.

If it is true that the intertemporal discrimination rule is a rationalization of normal-cost pricing, one cannot but wonder whether an industry whose members behave according to this rule would behave in the way described by normal-cost theory. In particular, one wonders whether prices would be sticky in the sense that they do not react to shifts in demand but follow direct costs according to a markup linked to some industry characteristics.

Suppose, then, that m firms in a given industry pursue the policy of intertemporal price discrimination. Because they produce a homogeneous product, they must sell at an identical price. For each firm $(i=1,\ldots,m)$ we have, from (6.3), at $t=0$

$$p + q_i \frac{\partial p}{\partial q_i} = k_i \tag{6.4}$$

where k_i represents its normalized marginal cost (taking the optimal value λ_i), $p=f(q,0)$ is the industry's demand function at $t=0$ with $q=\sum_i q_i$, and $\partial p/\partial q_i$ is the slope of the demand function for firm i.

First, let

$$\frac{\partial p}{\partial q_i} = \frac{\partial p}{\partial q} \tag{6.5}$$

Each firm influences the market price, by its sales, in the same way that a change in total sales does. An alternative and perhaps more illuminating interpretation is to notice that, as

$$\frac{\partial p}{\partial q_i} = \frac{\partial p}{\partial q} \cdot \frac{\partial q}{\partial q_i} = \frac{\partial p}{\partial q} \cdot \left(1 + \sum_{j \neq i} \frac{\partial q_j}{\partial q_i}\right)$$

where $\partial q_j / \partial q_i$ is a "conjectural variation," (6.5) amounts to assuming that firm i believes that the other firms will hold output constant when it changes its own output. It does not imply that the firms have equal shares of the market, since (6.4) can be written, using (6.5), as

$$p\left(1 + \frac{q_i}{q} \cdot \frac{1}{\eta}\right) = k_i \tag{6.4a}$$

where q_i / q is the market share and η is the elasticity of demand for the industry. Equation (6.4a) can be a noncooperative Nash equilibrium,[15] in the sense that no firm has an incentive to change when condition (6.4a) is realized for all firms.

Aggregating over the m firms, we see that

$$mp + q \frac{\partial p}{\partial q} = \sum_i k_i$$

or, after dividing through by m,

$$p\left(1 + \frac{1}{\eta m}\right) = \bar{k} \tag{6.6}$$

where $\bar{k} = \sum_i k_i / m$.

It would suffice that all firms agree to fix prices according to the average $\bar{k}$ of their normalized marginal costs for (6.6) to determine a cooperative solution (in which all firms have equal market shares). This type of collusion does not contradict our historical knowledge of pricing practices.

Whether there is collusion or not, if the industry's demand curve can be approximated by

$$p = \alpha + \beta q \tag{6.7}$$

so that $\eta = p/\beta q = p/(p-\alpha)$, then (6.6) can be written as[16]

$$p = \left(\frac{1}{m+1}\right)\alpha + \left(\frac{m}{m+1}\right)\bar{k} \tag{6.8}$$

so that p appears as a linear function of the intercept (α) of the industry's demand curve and the average normalized marginal cost.

Two comments are in order. First, for given m, that is, for a given market structure, an increase in global demand has a smaller impact on the price than an increase in the average marginal cost. This conclusion is compatible with normal-cost theory and with the findings by Godley and

Nordhaus (1972) reported in Chapter 5. Second, compare two industries with a different concentration ratio. In the more concentrated industry (small m), cost increases are less fully transmitted into prices than in the less concentrated industry (large m). But the price is more sensitive to changes in demand in the former. These results can easily be tested and are far apart from what is sometimes suggested on intuitive grounds (see Ross 1973, p. 189). At any rate, (6.8) casts doubt upon regression analyses[17] in which the concentration ratio appears as an independent variable in addition to demand and cost variables and suggests partitioning cross-section industry data according to the level of the concentration ratio.

The conclusions derived from (6.8) remain valid when assumption (6.5) is weakened to become

$$\frac{\partial p}{\partial q_i} = \gamma \frac{\partial p}{\partial q} \tag{6.9}$$

where

$$\gamma = \left(1 + \sum_{j \neq i} \frac{\partial q_j}{\partial q_i}\right)$$

so that the impact of changes in a firm's sales is a multiple ($\gamma > 1$ and is identical for all firms) of the impact of changes in total sales. Now (6.8) reads

$$p = \left(\frac{\gamma}{m + \gamma}\right)\alpha + \left(\frac{m}{m + \gamma}\right)\bar{k} \tag{6.10}$$

The larger is γ, the larger is the sum of the conjectural variations $\partial q_j / \partial q_i$ and the smaller is the transmission of cost changes. A larger γ reflects a better cooperation among firms. If it is true that cooperation is easier the smaller m is, so that γ increases when m decreases, then cost increases should have an even smaller impact on prices in more concentrated industries, compared with less concentrated industries, whereas the difference in the impact of demand between the two groups of industries should be more pronounced. However, for given m, the difference between the influence of global demand $\gamma / (m + \gamma)$ and the influence of marginal cost $m / (m + \gamma)$ tends to be less pronounced when cooperation is stronger.

Uncertain entry

We now return to the case of a single supplier in the market and introduce the circumstance that potential entrants exist. Although the firm (or cartel) is still allowed to discriminate intertemporally, its optimal policy will be influenced by the necessity of balancing high profits associated with discrimination against the loss of profits due to entry of additional suppliers.

It is natural to discuss the firm's policy in the framework of the model set up by Kamien and Schwarz (1971), which has the advantage of offering a probabilistic approach while permitting industry demand to grow over time. However, the Kamien–Schwarz model will have to be adapted. Indeed, although it allows time t to vary inside a preentry period (and a postentry period) and demand to grow with t, it does not allow for intertemporal price discrimination. In what follows, profits in the preentry period will be made to depend upon the rate of sales and the rate of production, to make the holding of inventories – and therefore intertemporal price discrimination as just defined[18] – possible.

> *Assumption 1.* Profit at time t is $\Pi_1(q,x,t)$ for all t in the preentry period; Π_1 is a strictly concave function of its arguments and is specified as $\Pi_1 = \pi q - cx$; $\pi = e^{g_1 t}[f(q)]$ and $c = e^{g_2 t}[\phi(x)]$.

Notice that $g = (g_1 - g_2) < 0$. As before, q and x are the decision variables: q determines π for given g and t. Remember also that $s'(t) = x - q$.

Post-entry profits vary inversely with g according to Assumption 2. Indeed, the more demand grows, the bigger the entrant will be, and the smaller the incumbent's profit will be.

> *Assumption 2.* Profit at time t is $\Pi_2(g)$ with t in the postentry period; $0 \leqslant \Pi_2(g) < \max_{q,x} \Pi_1(q,x,t)$; and $\Pi_2'(g) \leqslant 0$.

There is no need to modify the Kamien–Schwarz model with respect to the forces that govern entry. Let $F(t)$ denote the probability that entry has occurred by time t, with $F(0) = 0$. The conditional probability of entry at time t is $F'(t)/[1 - F(t)]$. Given that entry has not yet occurred, the entry probability is an increasing, convex function of product price at time t.

> *Assumption 3.* $F'(t)/[1 - F(t)] = h[\pi(t);g] \geqslant 0$; $h(0,g) = 0$, $dh/d\pi \geqslant 0$, $d^2h/d\pi^2 \geqslant 0$.

The hazard rate, $h(\pi)$, reflects the ease of entry into the market.

The problem is to maximize the present value of expected future profits, under these assumptions, with respect to q and x. As q determines π, our task amounts to finding simultaneously the optimal path for π, q, and x, as in Mills (1962) and Hay (1970), but with uncertainty about entry rather than about the quantity demanded.

Formally, the firm maximizes

$$\int_0^\infty e^{-rt}[(\pi q - cx)(1 - F) + \Pi_2 F]\,dt \qquad (6.11)$$

where $F = F(t)$, and $g_2 > r$, subject to

$$F'(t) = h[\pi(t)][1 - F(t)]$$
$$F(0) = 0$$

and the constraints on inventories, already discussed,

$$\int_0^\infty s'(t)\, dt = \int_0^\infty (x - q)\, dt = 0 \tag{6.12}$$

and

$$s'(t) \geqslant 0 \qquad \text{whenever } s = 0 \tag{6.13}$$

Before discussing the solution to this problem, it is of some interest first to take up the special case considered by Kamien and Schwarz in which $x = q$ for all t, that is, the case where the firm never produces for inventory, to emphasize the impact of uncertain entry. Then the constraints on inventories are automatically satisfied, and the Hamiltonian reduces to

$$H = e^{-rt}[(\pi - c)q(1 - F) + \Pi_2 F] + \psi(t)h(\pi)(1 - F) \tag{6.14}$$

The necessary conditions are, if q is optimal,

$$\partial H/\partial q = \left[e^{-rt}\left(\pi - c + q\,\frac{dp}{dq} - q\,\frac{dc}{dq} \right) + \psi(t)\,\frac{dh}{d\pi}\,\frac{d\pi}{dq} \right](1 - F) = 0 \tag{6.15}$$

$$\psi'(t) = -\partial H/\partial F = e^{-rt}(\pi q - cq - \Pi_2) + \psi(t)h(\pi) \tag{6.16}$$

with transversality condition

$$\lim_{t \to \infty} \psi(t)F(t) = 0 \tag{6.17}$$

$F(t)$ is a nondecreasing function bounded above by unity as $h \geqslant 0$. So long as entry has not occurred, (6.15) therefore implies that it is no longer optimal to equate current marginal revenue and current marginal cost: The current marginal cost of entry $[e^{rt}\psi(dh/d\pi)(d\pi/dq)]$ must be added to current marginal revenue before we equate it to current marginal cost. The auxiliary variable $\psi(t)$ indeed measures the rate of decrease of the objective function (6.14) due to an increase in the probability of entry, and $dh/d\pi > 0$ and $d\pi/dq < 0$, so that $[e^{rt}\psi(dh/d\pi)(d\pi/dq)]$ is positive and can be interpreted as the current marginal cost of entry (for the existing firm), given that entry has not occurred. (This result is another example of the fact that discounted profit maximization leads to an optimal price policy implying marginal revenue below marginal cost, whenever state variables appear in the problem, as shown by Jacquemin and Thisse 1972. Here the state variable is F, the probability that entry has occurred.)

It is to be expected that the intertemporal price discrimination rule (equality and constancy of discounted marginal revenues and costs) will, in turn, have to be amended in the full problem (with production for inventory) defined in (6.11) to (6.13), which we now consider. The solution of the necessary conditions gives the decision rule (for the preentry period, when $s(t) > 0$):

$$e^{-rt}\left(\pi + q\,\frac{d\pi}{dq}\right) + \psi\,\frac{dh}{d\pi}\,\frac{d\pi}{dq} = e^{-rt}\left(c + x\,\frac{dc}{dx}\right) = \lambda \quad (6.18)$$

which is very different indeed from (6.15). Although (6.15) refers to current values, (6.18) requires that, as in the intertemporal discrimination rule (6.3), the equilibrium values be constant over time, so that $\left(c + x\,\frac{dc}{dx}\right)$ is again *normalized* marginal cost.

Consider an industry in which m firms apply the rule laid down in Equation (6.18), so that for each firm i

$$p + q_i\,\frac{dp}{dq_i} + \psi_i\,\frac{dh}{dp}\,\frac{dp}{dq} = k_i \qquad (6.19)$$

when $t = 0$. The marginal hazard rate obeys the formula

$$\frac{dh}{dp}\,\frac{dp}{dq_i} = \frac{dh}{dp}\,\frac{dp}{dq}\left(1 + \sum_{j \neq i}\frac{\partial q_j}{\partial q_i}\right) \qquad (6.20)$$

Suppose that $\sum_{j \neq i}\partial q_j/\partial q_i = 0$. Then the equation

$$p\left(1 + \frac{q_i}{q}\cdot\frac{1}{\eta}\right) + \psi_i\,\frac{dh}{dp}\,\frac{dp}{dq} = k_i \qquad (6.21)$$

shows that, with given production costs, demand, and market shares, the price must go down as the marginal cost of entry goes up for any firm. Alternatively, with given price, costs of production, and demand, the firm will reduce its market share, and so on.

Aggregating over the m firms and dividing through by m, we find

$$p = \left(\frac{1}{m+1}\right)\alpha + \left(\frac{m}{m+1}\right)\bar{k} - \left(\frac{m}{m+1}\right)\bar{\psi}\,\frac{dh}{dp}\,\frac{dp}{dq} \qquad (6.22)$$

using the linear specification (6.7) to represent the industry's demand curve. The average cost (or loss of profit) due to entry $\bar{\psi}(dh/dq)(dp/dq)$ appears as a separate variable, affecting the price, and has the same impact as a change in cost, but with the sign reversed. This fact suggests the necessity of introducing a barrier-to-entry variable in empirical work on administrative inflation (with which, of course, a positive regression coefficient should be associated).

One implication is that the price will be constant when the increase in average demand ($\Delta\alpha/m$) plus the increase in average normalized marginal cost $(\Delta \bar{k})$ happens to be compensated by an increase in the average cost of entry $[\Delta \bar{\psi}(dh/dp)(dp/dq)]$.

Finally, consider the case where

$$\sum_{j \neq i} \partial q_j / \partial q_i \neq 0 \qquad \text{and} \qquad \gamma = 1 + \sum_{j \neq i} \partial q_j / \partial q_i$$

Then (6.22) becomes

$$p = \left(\frac{\gamma}{m + \gamma}\right)\alpha + \left(\frac{m}{m + \gamma}\right)\bar{k} - \left(\frac{\gamma m}{m + \gamma}\right)\bar{\psi} \frac{dh}{dp} \frac{dp}{dq} \tag{6.23}$$

The better the cooperation among firms, the larger γ and the stronger the negative impact of the threat of entry on price.

A first empirical test

The theory outlined above leads to a number of propositions about industry behavior that can be falsified empirically and are therefore of interest. They can be collected as follows:

1. For a given market structure, an increase in global demand (for the industry) has a smaller impact on the price than an increase in the average marginal cost of production evaluated at the normal level of output.
2. In more concentrated industries, cost increases are less fully transmitted into prices than in less concentrated industries.
3. In more concentrated industries, changes in demand are more fully transmitted into prices than in less concentrated industries.
4. Proposition 1 is weakened when the firms in the industry cooperate.
5. Propositions 2 and 3 are reinforced when the firms in the more concentrated industries cooperate.
6. Barriers to entry have a positive impact on prices.
7. The introduction of a barrier-to-entry variable should lead to better results in a regression based on cross-section data, as far as propositions 2 and 5 are concerned.
8. The better the cooperation among firms, the stronger the positive impact of the barrier-to-entry variable on price.

Propositions 1 and 7 have been abundantly verified in the administrative inflation literature and can be regarded as well established. Verification of Propositions 4, 5, and 8 requires data on collusion per industry that are very hard to collect and is postponed for later work. The tests presented here will therefore concentrate on Propositions 2, 3, and 7.

Suitable data are at hand: These are the cross-section data on Belgian, Dutch, and French industries I used on other occasions.[19] For each industry, the price level is measured by the wholesale price index in the year

1964 (1958 = 100) for Belgium and the Netherlands and in 1965 (1959 = 100) for France. Direct unit production costs are taken to approximate normalized marginal cost (k) and are the simple average of unit materials costs and unit salary and wage costs, which are measured respectively as

$$\frac{MC_{t'}/MC_t}{Q_{t'}/Q_t} \quad \text{and} \quad \frac{SW_{t'}/SW_t}{Q_{t'}/Q_t}$$

$t'=1964$ or 1965 and $t=1958$ or 1959. Both t' and t are (mild) recession years and are supposed to be years for which the rate of output was normal. MC_t is the total cost of purchased fuel and materials less the net increase in inventories in year t, whereas SW_t represents total salaries and wages for the industry in year t. It is implicitly assumed that m, the number of firms, remained constant between t and t'.

$Q_{t'}/Q_t$ is used as a proxy for α, the level (intercept) of industry demand, and is defined as

$$\frac{S_{t'}/S_t}{P_{t'}/P_t}$$

where S_t is the value of industry shipments in year t and $P_{t'}/P_t$ is the wholesale price index used as the dependent variable. This approximation is defensible on the grounds that the period covered was a period of rising prices and rising sales in real terms. (More refined estimates of α could of course be constructed, especially in a time series approach.)

All industries included in the sample produce storable products (with a variable durability, inevitably). For Belgium, only seventeen matching observations could be collected. For the Netherlands and France, the corresponding numbers are forty-three and forty, respectively. However, this already small sample had to be subdivided into two subsets, one with a "small" and one with a "large" concentration ratio (C), as the theory suggests that the regression coefficients differ according to the number of firms in the industry and therefore according to the concentration ratio.

The proposed test is to compare the regression coefficients associated with the demand and the cost variables, respectively, in the two subsamples. (It may be emphasized, again, that the regression equations have no intercept and also that the concentration ratio should *not* be included as an additional variable.)

In earlier work, this set of (admittedly rather poor) data never led to clear-cut results, probably because the underlying regression models were based not on firm theoretical grounds but rather on the usual ad hoc assumptions. It is a happy surprise to be able to present the following results, which appear to confirm Propositions 2, 3, and 7,

Table 6.2. *Regression results ignoring the threat of entry*

	Demand	Cost	N
Unconcentrated group			
Belgium ($C<50$)	0.097	0.918	9
	(0.125)	(0.152)	
Netherlands ($C<50$)	0.025	0.928	27
	(0.033)	(0.046)	
France ($C<40$)	0.007	0.992	25
	(0.017)	(0.029)	
Pooled	0.012	0.973	61
	(0.015)	(0.024)	
Concentrated group			
Belgium ($C \geqslant 50$)	0.058	0.915	8
	(0.082)	(0.104)	
Netherlands ($C \geqslant 50$)	0.024	0.898	16
	(0.039)	(0.058)	
France ($C \geqslant 40$)	0.057	0.972	15
	(0.027)	(0.044)	
Pooled	0.050	0.916	39
	(0.025)	(0.037)	

Note: Parenthetical numbers in cells are standard deviations.

at least when one looks at the results obtained after pooling the data for the three countries. (The national samples are too small for us to expect much from the results per country, which are reported for the sake of completeness.)

Table 6.2 reports results (by ordinary least squares, or OLS) relevant to Equation (6.10), which ignores the possible threat of entry. Table 6.3 gives OLS results on the same data after adding a barrier-to-entry dummy[20] and relates the Equation (6.23). Standard deviations appear in parentheses. N is the number of observations per subsample. There is no point in reporting R^2, as the regressions are run without intercept.

The pooled results in Table 6.2 provide an indication that the regression coefficient for the cost variable is larger in the unconcentrated group of industries and that the coefficient for the demand variable is larger in the concentrated group.[21] However, the standard deviations are sufficiently large to cast doubt on the significance of these differences. Now compare the pooled results in Table 6.3 and notice that the differences are more pronounced, whereas standard deviations are comparable to those of Table 6.2 or smaller. Although far from conclusive, the evidence

Table 6.3. *Regression results with a barrier-to-entry dummy*

	Demand	Cost	Barrier to entry	N
Unconcentrated group				
Belgium ($C<50$)	0.022	0.956	13.677	9
	(0.116)	(0.133)	(7.536)	
Netherlands ($C<50$)	0.032	0.901	10.939	27
	(0.030)	(0.043)	(4.156)	
France ($C<40$)	−0.002	0.985	7.087	25
	(0.017)	(0.028)	(3.960)	
Pooled	0.001	0.962	10.298	61
	(0.014)	(0.021)	(2.548)	
Concentrated group				
Belgium ($C\geqslant50$)	0.050	0.889	3.630	8
	(0.140)	(0.383)	(52.324)	
Netherlands ($C\geqslant50$)	0.020	0.942	−6.317	16
	(0.039)	(0.068)	(13.752)	
France ($C\geqslant40$)	0.073	0.845	12.702	15
	(0.025)	(0.066)	(5.371)	
Pooled	0.054	0.873	4.982	39
	(0.025)	(0.052)	(4.220)	

Note: Parenthetical numbers in cells are standard deviations.

suggests that Propositions 2 and 3 are not rejected by the data,[22] whereas Proposition 7 is clearly verified.

The cost of storage and the number of sellers

At this stage the reader no doubt wonders what happens to the prices when the number of sellers becomes large. Intuition suggests that the price will tend toward the competitive price, which is known to have a time path defined by $\pi(t) = p(0)e^{rt}$ and therefore to have a relative rate of change ($\dot{\pi}/\pi$) equal to the rate of interest. On the other hand, the reader might recall that the rate of interest was used until now as a measure of storage costs, to simplify the presentation. If there are storage costs other than the rate of interest, intuition again suggests that a competitive price will have to reflect these, as seems to be the case with the seasonal price schedules for nitrogen fertilizers discussed in Chapter 5. That these intuitions are correct can be shown as follows.[23]

Seasonal price schedules are based on discrete (typically monthly) price changes. An approach in discrete time is therefore indicated. Consider seller i, whose profit function is defined as

$$\Pi_i = \sum_{t=1}^{T} [\pi_t(q_t) \cdot q_{it} - c_t x_{it} - C_i(s_{it})] \tag{6.24}$$

$\pi_t(q_t)$ is the reciprocal market demand function, since $q_t = \sum_i q_{it}$, $i = 1, \ldots, m$, where q_{it} is the quantity sold by this seller in period t, there being m sellers in this industry. Marginal costs of production c_t is supposed to be given and identical for all sellers, to simplify. Indeed, I want to concentrate on $C_i(s_{it})$, the cost of storage per unit of time. The quantity produced is x_{it}.

The cost of storage behaves as the sum of a number of components. In his authoritative 1958 paper on "The Supply of Storage," Brennan defines three such components: the outlay on physical storage, the risk-aversion factor, and the convenience yield on existing stocks.

The total outlay on physical storage is the sum of rent for storage space, handling (or in-and-out charges), interest, insurance, and so forth. This outlay increases as the quantity of stocks held by a firm increases. Brennan thinks it increases at a constant rate (the marginal outlay is constant) until total warehouse capacity is almost fully utilized. Beyond this level, marginal outlay rises at an increasing rate. The convenience yield is a concept well known to specialists of futures markets[24] but is rather ignored by general economists. It plays a crucial role in determining the general shape of the cost-of-storage function $C_i(s_{it})$. Brennan defines it as follows:

> Suppliers of storage are mostly engaged in production, processing or merchandising with storage as an adjunct. The costs of storage must be considered as charged against the business operation as a whole. Given day-to-day fluctuations in the market, a producing firm can meet a sudden and "unexpected" increase in demand by filling orders out of finished inventories or by adjusting its production schedule or by some combination of these. The convenience yield is attributed to the advantage (in terms of less delay and lower costs) of being able to keep regular customers satisfied or of being able to take advantage of a rise in demand and price without resorting to a revision of the production schedule. Similarly, for a processing firm the availability of stocks as raw materials permits variations in production without incurring the trouble, cost and perhaps delays of frequent spot purchases and deliveries. A wholesaler can vary his sales in response to an increased flow of orders only if he has sufficient stocks on hand.
>
> The smaller the level of stocks on hand the greater will be the convenience yield of an additional unit. It is assumed that there is some quantity of stocks so large that the marginal convenience yield is zero. [1958, pp. 53-4]

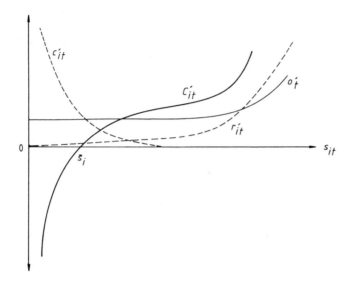

Figure 6.6. The marginal cost of storage for firm i.

The risk-aversion factor is also an increasing function of the level of stocks. The greater the quantity of stocks held, the greater will be the loss to the firm from an unexpected fall in the future price. At some critical level of stocks, this loss would endanger the firm's credit position, and the risk of loss would rise sharply.

Total storage costs $C_i(s_{it})$ are equal to the outlay on physical storage *plus* the risk of loss *minus* the convenience yield. The marginal storage cost (C_{it}') is then equal to the marginal outlay (o_{it}') *plus* the marginal risk factor (r_{it}') *minus* the marginal convenience yield (c_{it}'), as depicted in Figure 6.6. The determination of the shape of the total cost of storage $C_i(s_{it})$ is left to the reader as an exercise.

The level of inventories evolves over time according to

$$s_{it} - s_{it-1} = x_{it} - q_{it} \tag{6.25}$$

for $i = 1, \ldots, m$. We assume that initial stocks take the value $\bar{s}_i$, at which the cost of storage is minimal:

$$s_{i0} = \bar{s}_i \tag{6.26}$$

Indeed, it would be unrealistic to assume zero initial stocks, as that would imply a very high cost of storage. As for the terminal stocks, they must also be equal to $\bar{s}_i$,

$$s_{iT} = \bar{s}_i \tag{6.27}$$

In other words, all the firms must, over the planning period, sell as much as they produce, and $C'_{iT}=0$.

The first-order conditions are derived backward, as is usual in dynamic programming. At the final period T one finds

$$\pi_T + q_{iT} \frac{d\pi_T}{dq_T} + C'_{iT} - \lambda_i = 0 \qquad (6.28a)$$

$$-c_T - C'_{iT} + \lambda_i = 0 \qquad (6.28b)$$

where λ_i is the multiplier associated with (6.25). By introducing (6.28b) into (6.28a) we get

$$c_T = \pi_T + q_{iT} \frac{d\pi_T}{dq_T}$$

or marginal production cost is equal to marginal revenue. For a period $(t<T)$ we find

$$\pi_t + q_{it} \frac{d\pi_t}{dq_t} - \pi_{t+1} - q_{it+1} \frac{d\pi_{t+1}}{dq_{t+1}} + C'_{it} = 0 \qquad (6.29a)$$

$$c_{t+1} - c_t - C'_{it} = 0 \qquad (6.29b)$$

These conditions can be interpreted as follows: each firm's sales policy is such that the change in marginal revenue equals the marginal cost of storage (Equation [6.29a]); each firm adjusts its inventories so as to equalize its marginal cost of storage with the (given) change in production costs (Equation [6.29b]). Using the equilibrium conditions for periods $(t+1),\ldots,T$, we may rewrite (6.29a) and (6.29b) as

$$R'_{it} + \sum_{\tau=t}^{T} C'_{i\tau} = c_t + \sum_{\tau=t}^{T} C'_{i\tau} = \lambda_i \qquad (6.30)$$

where λ_i is a positive constant[25] and $R'_{it}=\pi_t+q_{it}d\pi_t/dq_t$. This is a generalized intertemporal discrimination rule. It says that *marginal revenue corrected for present and future marginal inventory costs must be equal to marginal cost of production corrected in the same way and constant over time.* Notice that marginal revenue is equal to marginal cost at all t, although not at the levels where marginal revenue and marginal cost intersect nor at a constant level!

Equations (6.29a) and (6.29b) can also be written as

$$C'_{it} = \Delta\pi_t + \Delta(\pi_t\eta_{it}) = \Delta c_t \qquad (6.31)$$

where η_{it} is the elasticity of firm i's reciprocal demand, that is,

$$\eta_{it} = \frac{q_{it}}{\pi_t} \cdot \frac{d\pi_t}{dq_t}$$

and the operator Δ designates the first differences between period $(t+1)$ and period t. According to Equation (6.31), $[\Delta(\pi_t \eta_{it}) > 0]$ implies that $\Delta \pi_t < C'_{it}$. By analogy with the spatial concept of "freight absorption," one could say that firms are absorbing inventory costs when $\Delta(\pi_t \eta_{it}) > 0$, which will be the case when η_{it} is rising in absolute value, for example, when π_t is rising.

When the number of firms becomes large, η_{it} tends to zero. To see this point more formally, suppose all firms are equally small, so that $q_{it} = q_t/m$. Then $\eta_{it} \to 0$ as $m \to \infty$, and

$$\Delta \pi_t = C'_{it} = \Delta c_t \tag{6.32}$$

Competitive prices fully reflect storage costs.

Equation (6.32) could explain the time shape of seasonal price schedules, such as those (for nitrogen fertilizers) depicted in Table 5.1, in the following way. Until August, the distributors make only negligible purchases and try to keep their cost of storage at its minimum, so that $s_{it} = \bar{s}_i$ and $C'_{it} = 0$. As a result, $\Delta p_t = 0$. From September till November, we have $\Delta p_t = C'_{it}$, where C'_{it} is positive and increasing. Indeed, the distributors begin to increase their stocks in September. As of December, farmers begin to order: Δp_t decreases until March because C'_{it} decreases. From March until June, final demand is very high, so that stocks are at their minimum level (to the extent that the scheme works well, so that no shortages or excess stocks appear). Then $C'_{it} = 0$ and $\Delta p_t = 0$.

Vertical integration into distribution

Suppose now that the m firms just discussed are in fact distributors who sell a commodity (e.g., nitrogen fertilizers) on a final market. Then c_t is nothing but the (given) intermediate price at which they purchase the commodity from its producers.

Having a competitive final market can then be seen to have dramatic consequences. First of all, when m, the number of distributors, becomes large, intertemporal price discrimination becomes impossible, as we just saw. Second, final and intermediate prices tend to be equal at each period, because of the same equation (6.32). If producers want their distributors to carry stocks, they must offer them an intermediate price that changes over time at a rate that fully reflects storage costs.[26] A further implication is that producers may find it worthwhile to integrate forward into the distribution sector and to set up their own distribution system in order to be able to practice intertemporal price discrimination.

In a static framework, vertical integration is said to be motivated – among other reasons – by the desire of a monopolist to internalize the downstream marginal revenue curve. This motivation has a long tradition in economic theory (see Machlup and Taber 1960) and was recently reemphasized by Greenhut and Ohta (1976). I am ready to argue that this traditional literature on vertical integration misses an important dynamic aspect because it neglects the storage problem. If the product has to be stored before it can be sold to the final consumer, producers forgo profits if they must let prices increase at a rate equal to the rate of interest (because of competitive pressures in the distribution sector). By setting up their own distribution system, producers may hope to gain sufficient control over the industry's supply of storage to make intertemporal price discrimination possible, that is, to absorb storage costs to some extent. The analogy with the case of a firm facing several carriers in a spatial framework, analyzed by Schuler and Holahan (1978), is clear.

When distribution is under control, the producer will follow the policy derived in the preceding section. Instead of letting both the final price and the (now internalized) intermediate price rise at a rate equal to the rate of interest, he or she will set prices in such a way that the change in final marginal revenue equals the marginal cost of storage (Equation [6.29a]). And he or she will adjust inventories so as to equalize the marginal cost of storage with the change in the marginal cost of production (Equation [6.29b]). This action amounts to equalizing marginal revenue and marginal production cost – both corrected for present and future marginal inventory costs – over time, according to Equation (6.30).

CHAPTER 7

New commodities, exhaustible resources, and intertemporal welfare

The "storable" goods discussed in Chapter 6 were not only storable but also producible: In each time period considered, inventories could be increased through new production. What would become of our theory of intertemporal price discrimination if the commodity under analysis were storable without being producible? Remember (from Chapter 5) that we would be considering a so-called exhaustible resource, such as coal, oil, iron, and so forth. The answer is that the (third-degree) intertemporal price discrimination rule remains formally valid, although with a completely different economic interpretation. The difference is due to the fact that (new) production is impossible, so that – if the rate of sales and the rate of extraction from a coal mine or an oil field are taken to be equal for the sake of simplicity – the change in stocks is equal to the rate of extraction, that is, the rate of sales. Intertemporal output substitution is impossible, as the good is not "produced": All the owner of a coal mine can do is to postpone extraction, substituting deferred sales for immediate sales, or to accelerate extraction, substituting immediate sales for deferred sales.

To explore the implications of this rather fundamental point, I shall discuss again here the different cases that were considered in Chapter 6 and show to what extent the results obtained there are identical with those obtained in the literature on exhaustible resources. Implications about price stickiness over time or about the influence of the rate of interest will be seen to carry over to exhaustible resources, if some variables are correctly redefined. The theory of exhaustible resources thus appears as a special case of the theory of intertemporal price discrimination.

The storable goods discussed in Chapter 6 are also well established commodities, in the sense that they are of general use and have been produced for some time, so that it makes sense to talk about "normal" rates of production over a business cycle, say, and about normal costing. For new storable goods (such as minicomputers or video cassettes) that have never been sold or produced before, normal costing may be impossible, given the absence of information on changes in demand and costs, so that forecasts would be at most uninformed guesses and therefore worthless. In the case of new goods for which the given stock is the result of past production, such as a new movie or a new book that is available for sale, future costs – and therefore normal costs – are irrelevant. I shall argue that here it is the theory of first-degree intertemporal price discrimination (or a second-degree approximation of it) that is relevant. My discussion of the pricing of new durables will thus naturally introduce us to Essays III and IV, which are entirely devoted to methods of approximating first-degree price discrimination with the help of second-degree discrimination.

I shall also present a short discussion of intertemporal welfare economics. The available results mainly stem from the exhaustible resources literature and are therefore directly applicable to all storable goods. However, just like the spatial Pareto optimum, the intertemporal Pareto optimum might not be the best criterion to use in real world applications, so that we might have to look again for second-best results.

Intertemporal substitution with given prices

As far as I could determine, Gray's 1914 "Rent under the Assumption of Exhaustibility" was the first paper to discuss the economics of exhaustible resources. Unfortunately, it considered only the case where prices of the resource are given: Not until publication of Hotelling's 1931 paper "The Economics of Exhaustible Resources" was the problem of the joint determination of price and the rate of extraction solved.

Gray considers the owner of a coal mine who sells his coal at a given price and establishes the following principle:

> The owner of a valuable coal deposit ... desires to derive the maximum benefit from the limited supply which he owns. If for any reason less benefit can be derived by immediate removal and sale of the coal than by waiting until some future time, it may be profitable to postpone utilization.
>
> The simplest condition that might produce this result is an expected alteration in the price of coal. If the price is rising and the prospect is that the rise will continue, the owner of the mine will find it to his interest to take out but little coal in the present. This is true because the resources at his disposal are limited. Obviously this motive would not exist if the basis of income were perpetual. Likewise a lowering of the prices of those factors which enter into the expenses of production will make profitable a postponement of removal. On the other hand, a decrease of prices of the product or an increase of the prices of the factors of expense, in so far as such changes are continuous or anticipated, will create motives for rapid utilization. [1914, pp. 470–1]

The reader should have no difficulty in establishing the parallel between this reasoning and Shaw's analysis of the case of a perfectly competitive firm producing for storage, as illustrated in Figures 6.1 and 6.2. "To take out but little coal in the present" is just another way of substituting deferred sales for immediate sales, when the price of the product is expected to rise.

The fact that "the resources at his disposal are limited" introduces a new element, though, that strengthens the result. In the case of a producible good, a perfectly competitive firm can sell as much as it wants at the prevailing price and therefore postpones sales only if price changes are uncertain. For a perfectly competitive coal mine, uncertainty is not a necessary condition for intertemporal substitution, because the available stock is given: This constraint on the total available implies that postponement of extraction is always worth considering when prices are rising. For the same reason, changes in factor prices – which do not affect a perfectly competitive firm's inventory policy – always make it worthwhile to consider postponement or rapid utilization.

Subject to the same qualifications, a parallel can be drawn between Shaw's second case – the case of an imperfectly competitive firm which sells at a conventional price, illustrated in Figure 6.3 – and Gray's reasoning on the influence of costs of extraction. First of all, says Gray, it is not true that extraction will be pushed to the point where price is equal to marginal cost. The exhaustibility of the natural resource dictates a different course: The owner of the mine may well hesitate to proceed beyond the point of maximum average returns per unit of expense, that is, beyond the point of minimum average cost, as we would say today. The argument may be illustrated by Table 7.1, taken from Gray (1914, p. 472), which shows the results of removing various quantities of coal from a mine during a definite period of time. Each ton of coal is worth $1.00, so that marginal revenue is 100 throughout the table.

The mine owner in the situation represented by Table 7.1 will take out only 400 tons of coal during a year, not 900 (at which marginal cost equals marginal revenue). Why? Because, if more than 400 are removed, each ton will yield a smaller net return than if its removal were postponed until it could be effected at the minimum expense. Obviously, the static theory of the firm does not apply. (Actually, it would apply only if coal were (a) inexhaustible *and* (b) not storable. As soon as a commodity is storable, static theory does not apply, as we saw in Chapter 6. Exhaustibility simply reinforces the argument.) To be correct, though, our discussion should have been conducted in terms of the present value of expenses and returns. Indeed, the tendency to postpone for future removal all coal that makes average cost rise is counteracted by the fact that postponement

Table 7.1. *Variations in the net return in the removal of coal in a given period of time*

Quantity of coal removed (tons)	Value of coal removed ($)	Expense of removal per 100 tons ($)	Total net return ($)	Average net returns per 100 tons ($)	Increase in expense due to the removal of each additional 100 tons	Net return of each additional 100 tons after the point of maximum net returns per 100 tons
100	100	120	−20	−20	—	—
200	200	100	00	00	—	—
300	300	80	60	20	—	—
400	400	50	200	50	—	—
500	500	52	240	—	60	40
600	600	55	270	—	70	30
700	700	59	287	—	83	17
800	800	64	288	—	99	1
900	900	68	288	—	100	0
1000	1000	73	270	—	—	—
1100	1100	79	231	—	—	—

Source: Gray (1914), p. 472.

of a return decreases its value today. The present value of a ton removed at minimum expense in the future may be smaller than the net return of the same coal removed today at a higher cost.

Table 7.2 reproduces the last column of the preceding table, that is, the net returns of each additional 100 tons as of a total of 400 tons, together with the present value of these returns if postponed for one or more years, when the rate of interest is 10%. The optimal rate of extraction will now depend on the total quantity of coal available. If only 1,200 tons were to be extracted, then there would be no reason to extract more than 400 tons a year. The total would be exhausted after three years, and in the third year the last 400 tons removed would still have a net return with a present value of $41.66, which is more than the net return of adding 100 tons (for a total of 500 tons) in the first year. However, when the total to be extracted is higher, it becomes optimal to extract more than 400 the first year and then progressively less in successive years. For example, when the total available is 3,700 tons, the owner finds it profitable to extract 600 tons the first year, 500 the second, third, and fourth years, and 400 the fifth, sixth, seventh, and eighth years. Indeed, if extraction were pushed to 600 tons in the second year, it would give a present value for the marginal net return of $27.27, less than the $29.41 of 400 tons in the eighth year. A similar reasoning shows that 500 is not optimal after the fourth year.

The upshot is that profit maximization with a given price leads to equalization of the present value of net returns over time, about $30 in this numerical example. As the selling price is constant, the process amounts to equalizing the present value of marginal costs – exactly as in the case of a firm selling a storable good at a conventional price (illustrated in Figure 6.3).

Hotelling's rule and the intertemporal price discrimination rule

The simultaneous determination of prices and rates of extraction leads to an even more fascinating discussion. Hotelling introduces it by drawing a parallel between the conservationist movement and the influence of monopoly power. Fifty years later[1] these remarks seem still highly relevant, especially with respect to the oil market, where the OPEC cartel has monopolized a large part of the known reserves:

> Contemplation of the world's disappearing supplies of minerals, forests, and other exhaustible assets has led to demands for regulation of their exploitation. The feeling that these products are now too cheap for the good of future generations, that they are being selfishly exploited at too rapid a rate, and that in consequence of their excessive cheapness they

Table 7.2. *Present values of the net returns derived from the removal of coal at different future periods with interest at 10% (in dollars)*

	Tons	Present value							
		Year 1	Year 2	Year 3	Year 4	Year 5	Year 6	Year 7	Year 8
Maximum average net return per 100 tons	400	50	45.45	41.66	38.46	35.71	33.33	31.25	29.41
Net return of each additional 100 tons	500	40	36.36	33.33	30.76	28.57	26.66	25.00	23.52
	600	30	27.27	25.00	23.07	21.42	20.00	18.75	17.64
	700	17	15.45	14.16	13.07	12.14	11.33	10.62	10.00
	800	1	0.90	0.83	0.76	0.71	0.66	0.62	0.58
	900	0	0	0	0	0	0	0	0

Source: Gray (1914), p. 475.

are being produced and consumed wastefully has given rise to the conservation movement...

In contrast to the conservationist belief that a too rapid exploitation of natural resources is taking place, we have the retarding influence of monopolies and combinations, whose growth in industries directly concerned with the exploitation of irreplaceable resources has been striking. If "combinations in restraint of trade" extort high prices from consumers and restrict production, can it be said that their products are too cheap and being sold too rapidly?

It may seem that the exploitation of an exhaustible natural resource can never be too slow for the public good. For every proposed rate of production there will doubtless be some to point to the ultimate exhaustion which that rate will entail, and to urge more delay. But if it is agreed that the total supply is not to be reserved for our remote descendants and that there is an optimum rate of present production, then the tendency of monopoly and partial monopoly is to keep production below the optimum rate and to exact excessive prices from consumers. The conservation movement, in so far as it aims at absolute prohibitions rather than taxation or regulation in the interest of efficiency, may be accused of playing into the hands of those who are interested in maintaining high prices for the sake of their own pockets rather than of posterity. [1931, pp. 137–8]

Hotelling starts by assuming that the owners of a natural resource will want to maximize the present value of all their future profits, just as any other entrepreneur might, and establishes the following basic principle: Under perfect competition, owners of operating mines will be indifferent as to whether they receive now a price p_0 for a unit of their product or a price $p_0 e^{rt}$ after time t. It is not unreasonable, therefore, to expect that the price will be a function of time and of the form

$$\pi(t) = p_0 e^{rt} \tag{7.1}$$

When this is in fact the case, then $e^{-rt}\pi(t)$ is equal to p_0 for all t: The present value of a unit extracted is the same in all periods if there is to be no gain from shifting extraction among periods. Equation (7.1) is obviously also valid for any storable good – whether exhaustible or not – sold under perfect competition.[2] It is worth noticing, though, that Hotelling interprets the price π as the *net* price received after paying the cost of extraction and placing it upon the market. This interpretation is especially to be kept in mind when comparing the economics of exhaustible resources with the economics of storable goods in general. In the latter, costs of production are, of course, not deducted.

Hotelling's rule was expressed in the preceding paragraphs as a condition of flow equilibrium in the market for the natural resource. Solow (1974) reformulated it as a condition of stock equilibrium in the asset market. What is the reason, he asks, for leaving a resource deposit in the ground? The only way that it can produce a current return for its owner is by appreciating in value. On the other hand, asset markets can be in equilibrium only when all assets in a given risk class earn the same rate of return. In equilibrium, the value of a resource deposit in the ground must therefore be growing at a rate equal to the rate of interest (which is the common rate of return in that risk class). And since the value of a deposit is also the present value of net revenues from future sales from it, the net price of the resource must be expected to increase exponentially at a rate equal to the rate of interest.

In the real world, competition is far from perfect, so that other market forms are likely to have more descriptive power. Hotelling considered the monopoly case, where a large firm[3] is capable of affecting the price by varying its rate of sales. Such a firm would want to maximize

$$\int_0^T e^{-rt}\pi q \, dt \tag{7.2}$$

subject to

$$\int_0^T q \, dt = \underline{a} \tag{7.3}$$

where $\pi = f(q, t)$ and is net of extraction cost, and $\underline{a}$ is the total supply of the resource.

Compare these equations with Equations (6.1) and (6.2). Setting the rate of production x equal to zero in the latter leads to the former, except that the total extracted is equal to a given magnitude $\underline{a}$ (rather than to cumulated output). The solution should be formally the same. Not surprisingly, Hotelling's rule becomes

$$e^{-rt}\left(\pi + q \, \frac{\partial \pi}{\partial q}\right) = \lambda \tag{7.4}$$

with λ a constant, which is the first half of the intertemporal discrimination rule. Discounted marginal revenues must again be equal over time. Remember, though, that marginal revenues of natural resources are net of extraction costs, so that it is discounted marginal *profit* that is being equated over time. Of course, if extraction costs were constant, both with respect to the rate of extraction and with respect to time, then the intertemporal discrimination rule would be applicable without reinterpretation. It is likely that Hotelling had such constant extraction costs[4] in mind.

The difference between the perfect competition case and the monopoly case can be illustrated with the help of Figure 7.1. It should be clear from our discussion of the storable goods case in Chapter 6 that the (net) price has to be sticky under monopoly: It is in the monopoly's interest to raise it by less than the rate of interest. Simultaneously, the monopoly finds it

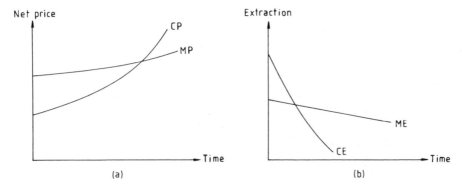

Figure 7.1. Price paths (a) and extraction paths (b) for competitive and monopoly cases. (CP = competitive price, MP = monopoly price; CE = competitive extraction, ME = monopoly extraction.)

profitable to extract the resource more slowly, which implies starting at a lower rate and going on a longer time (since the same amount is to be extracted by assumption).

These conclusions are not entirely general. Hotelling derived them on the basis of a numerical example, using a linear instantaneous demand curve. One can think of demand curves for which monopoly extraction is equal to competitive extraction or even faster, at least when extraction costs are zero.[5] An isoelastic demand function, for example, would lead to the same price and extraction paths, under perfect competition and under monopoly, because then price is proportional to marginal revenue. Intuition suggests, though, that these special cases are rather exceptional, the more so as they are based on the assumption of a zero extraction cost. In general, monopoly does lead to sticky prices and to too much con-servation.

Sticky prices, Hotelling's rule, and intertemporal welfare

To analyze the welfare aspect of intertemporal pricing, consider a producer who faces identical aggregate instantaneous (reciprocal) demand functions for a storable good

$$\pi_t = \alpha - \beta q_t \qquad (t = 1, \ldots, T) \tag{7.5}$$

for T time periods, where π_t is the future price. In this intertemporal framework, the sum of consumer surpluses over the planning period is

$$S = \frac{1}{2} \sum_{t=1}^{T} (\alpha - \pi_t) q_t \tag{7.6}$$

and the profit function is defined as

$$\Pi = \sum_{t=1}^{T} [\pi_t q_t - c_t(x_t)x_t - C(s_t)] \tag{7.7}$$

where c_t is average cost at time t, x_t is the rate of production in t, q_t is the rate of sales, s_t is the level of inventories, and $C(s_t)$ is the cost of storage. As such, Equation (7.7) does not imply intertemporal price discrimination, since there is a cost function for each time period. (In other words, intertemporal maximization of the objective in [7.7] leads to the same results as instantaneous profit maximization.) However, a correct description of the problem includes the constraint

$$\sum_{t=1}^{T} x_t = \sum_{t=1}^{T} q_t \tag{7.8}$$

which says that all new production has to be sold.

Maximization[6] of $\mu S + \Pi$ subject to Constraint (7.8) leads to

$$\mu \beta q_T + (\alpha - 2\beta q_T) + C_T' - \lambda = 0 \tag{7.9a}$$

$$-\left(c_T + x_T \frac{dc_T}{dx_T}\right) - C_T' + \lambda = 0 \tag{7.9b}$$

in period T. The multiplier λ is a constant and is associated with Equation (7.8). If $\mu = 1$, Equations (7.9) imply marginal-cost pricing or

$$\pi_T = c_T + x_T \frac{dc_T}{dx_T}$$

whereas with $\mu = 0$ the same equations imply

$$\pi_T + q_T \frac{d\pi_T}{dq_T} = c_T + x_T \frac{dc_T}{dx_T}$$

At period $t < T$, I find

$$(\mu - 2)\beta q_t - (\mu - 2)\beta q_{t+1} + C_t' = 0 \tag{7.10a}$$

$$\left(c_{t+1} + x_{t+1} \frac{dc_{t+1}}{dx_{t+1}}\right) - \left(c_t + x_t \frac{dc_t}{dx_t}\right) - C_t' = 0 \tag{7.10b}$$

Using the equilibrium conditions for $(t+1), \ldots, T$, I can rewrite (7.10a) and (7.10b) as

$$\mu \beta q_t + (\alpha - 2\beta q_t) - \lambda + \sum_{\tau=t}^{T} C_\tau' = 0 \tag{7.11a}$$

$$\lambda - \sum_{\tau=t}^{T} C_\tau' - \left(c_t + x_t \frac{dc_t}{dx_t}\right) = 0 \tag{7.11b}$$

from which I derive

$$\mu\beta q_t + (\alpha - 2\beta q_t) + \sum_{\tau=t}^{T} C'_\tau = c_t + x_t \frac{dc_t}{dx_t} + \sum_{\tau=t}^{T} C'_\tau = \lambda \qquad (7.12)$$

This is again a *generalized intertemporal discrimination rule.* Indeed, Equation (7.12) says that marginal revenue $(\alpha - 2\beta q_t)$ corrected for welfare maximization $(\mu\beta q_t)$ and for future marginal inventory costs $(\sum_\tau C'_\tau)$ must be constant over time and equal to marginal cost of production corrected for inventory costs. When storage costs reduce to interest costs and $\mu = 0$, Equation (7.12) specializes to the intertemporal discrimination rule.

To understand the implications of this rule, it is useful to notice that Equations (7.10a) and (7.10b) can be written when $\mu = 1$, as

$$\Delta\pi_t = C'_t = \Delta MC_t \qquad (7.13)$$

where $MC_t = c_t + x_t(dc_t/dx_t)$ and Δ designates the first differences between period $(t+1)$ and period t. When $\mu = 0$, we have

$$\Delta MR_t = C'_t = \Delta MC_t \qquad (7.14)$$

where $MR_t = \pi_t + q_t(d\pi_t/dq_t) = \alpha - 2\beta q_t$. According to (7.13), unconstrained welfare maximization implies that the marginal cost of storage should be fully reflected in price changes. According to (7.14), the discriminating monopolist "absorbs" part of the marginal cost of storage, since $\Delta MR_t = \Delta\pi_t + \Delta(\pi_t\eta_t)$, where η_t is the elasticity of the reciprocal demand function. When $0 < \mu < 1$, the absorption should be reduced (but not eliminated) and prices are less sticky (but without fully reflecting marginal costs).

Suppose, now, that $x_t = 0$ for all t, because the (storable) commodity is not reproducible, let there be a given stock, $\bar{s}_0$, so that Constraint (7.8) becomes

$$\sum_{t=1}^{T} q_t = \bar{s}_0 \qquad (7.8a)$$

and suppose π_t is the price *less extraction costs* (supposed constant for simplicity). Under these assumptions model (7.5)–(7.8) is nothing but a discrete version of the Hotelling (1931) model for natural resources. And $0 < \mu < 1$ implies that prices should rise by less than the rate of interest under constrained welfare maximization, since $\mu = 1$ corresponds to the Hotelling rule for perfect competition.

Asymmetric oligopoly

Further insights are obtained when one considers a situation "intermediate between monopoly and perfect competition, and more closely related than either to the real economic world" – to quote Hotelling again – in which there are a few competing owners of a natural resource. At this point, I could simply refer to the analysis of a noncooperative Nash solution in the case of a storable good, as carried out in the preceding chapter, and repeat the conclusions: As with a monopoly, the price of the resource will increase by less than the rate of interest, so that there will be more conservation than with perfect competition.[7]

The current interest in the price of oil calls for the analysis of a different type of oligopoly, namely the so-called asymmetric oligopoly. Indeed, the world's oil industry contains one cartel (OPEC) with more power than any other extractor, but other extractors do exist and have enough importance, collectively and perhaps individually, to restrain the full exercise of monopoly power. Neither the monopoly nor the (symmetric) oligopoly model are entirely appropriate: One wonders what the presence of a cartel that dominates other extractors because of its larger reserves implies in terms of price and extraction policies. This is exactly the question Salant (1976) answered in a most elegant way.[8]

Salant regards the world oil industry as a collection of firms having the same oil stock, the same cost function, and only one plant. Consumers purchase oil from these firms at the same price.[9] The OPEC cartel is treated as one firm controlling several plants: It is in the distinctive position of owning larger reserves than any other firm. If it is assumed that each firm has an upward-sloping marginal cost function, it is implied that OPEC can extract at the same rate as another firm for a smaller cost. In addition, Salant supposes that the rest of the world's oil stock is divided equally among a large number of small competitors (the competitive fringe) who take the price path of the cartel as given.

Under these assumptions, the competitive fringe chooses a sales path to maximize the sum of discounted profits, given the cartel's price path, whereas the cartel takes the sales path of the fringe as given and chooses a price path to maximize its discounted profits.

Suppose first that the marginal cost of extraction is constant, with the implication that the cartel's only advantage is to own more oil. (It cannot extract at the same rate as the competitive fringe at a lower cost.) Given the sales of the competitive fringe, the cartel has to maximize the sum of discounted revenues, under the constraint that total sales cannot exceed its initial inventory. This is exactly the monopoly problem as set up by Hotelling (or by Smithies, for that matter) except that here demand is defined as excess demand (in excess of what the competitive fringe sells at a given price at a given instant). The answer must be the same: The cartel must generate marginal revenues (derived from its excess demand curve) of the same discounted value in all periods in which the cartel sells.[10]

We also know the answer for the competitors' optimization problem. At equilibrium, the price must rise by the rate of interest. If it were to rise by more than the rate of interest, competitive speculators would enter and would attempt to make unlimited profits by buying now and selling later. If the price rises by less than the rate of interest, the competitive fringe will find it optimal to sell its inventory *before* this situation is reached. In any case, competitors will exhaust their stock.

What would be the properties of an uncooperative Cournot–Nash equilibrium, if it exists? We recall that any situation where each sector takes the optimal policy (path) of the other as given and where neither can increase its profits by altering its own strategy is such an equilibrium. In the circumstances just described, this equilibrium must imply that price rises at the rate of interest as long as the competitive fringe holds stocks. Afterward it can rise at a smaller or equal rate, never at a higher rate. As long as the cartel holds stocks, marginal revenue (derived from the excess demand curve) must also rise at the rate of interest. Afterward it can rise at a smaller or equal rate. Each sector ends by selling its entire stock.

When we put all these conditions together, it appears that the competitive fringe will at some point drop out and will abandon the market to the cartel. Before that point, at which the price is π^*, say, both price and marginal revenue grow at the rate r, so that t moments before $\pi(t)$ takes the form

$$\pi(t) = \pi^* e^{-rt} \quad \text{and} \quad \pi(t) + q(t) \frac{\partial \pi}{\partial q} = \left(\pi^* + q^* \frac{\partial \pi^*}{\partial q^*}\right) e^{-rt}$$

These conditions can be solved for the sales of each sector during the period before π^* is reached.[11] After the point π^*, price rises by less than r, since now it is only the marginal revenue of the cartel that has to rise at r. The cartel's stock is exhausted at the point where π is equal to the "choke price," that is, the vertical intercept of the instantaneous demand curve (at which buyers cease to buy). The equilibrium price path is thus as depicted in Figure 7.2.

Salant goes even further and is able to compare the price path (A) before the formation of a cartel with the paths followed after either some firms (path B) or all firms (path C) in the industry have joined it. Simple logic leads to Figure 7.3, which compares these three price paths. In a competitive world of many small extractors, prices rise along path A from an initial level p_0 at the rate of interest until the world inventory is exhausted. Each extractor receives a total discounted profit of p_0 times its initial stock, since selling a barrel of oil in any period has the same discounted value.

A number of extractors collude and form a cartel, whereas the others continue to behave competitively: This is the case described in Figure 7.3, so that the new path B has two phases. Path B must cross path A, since

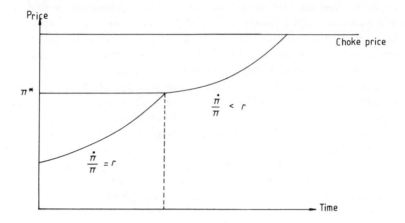

Figure 7.2. The price path in the dominant extractor model.

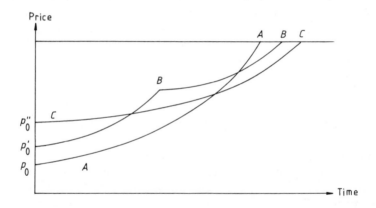

Figure 7.3. Comparison of price paths under different market structures.

cumulative sales must remain equal (the available stock has not changed), whereas the price rises at a slower rate during the second phase of path *B*. For this to happen, the new path must begin above p_0, say at p_0', must rise at the rate of interest during the first phase, and must then cross path *A* in the second phase.

The implications are two. First, each extractor gets a higher sum of discounted profits. Second, "the profits of every competitive firm jump by an *even larger percentage* than those of the cartel. This result arises here for exactly the same reason as in the theory of cartels selling an ordinary producible good" (Salant 1976, p. 1086). The competitive fringe enjoys the full benefit of the price rise, since it sells only during the first phase of path B, during which the discounted value of a barrel has the same value of p_0' in every period. The members of the cartel, to the contrary, must sell some of their stock during the second phase at discounted values which are smaller than p_0'. Path C corresponds to the case where all the extractors join the cartel. It must cut both path A and path B, again since cumulative sales must be equal along all three curves, while $\dot{\pi}/\pi$ is now always smaller than r. As a result, p_0'' must lie above p_0'. Path C must also terminate last.

It remains to ask[12] what happens when marginal extraction costs increase instead of being constant. Now the cartel has a cost advantage, if all firms have one plant and the same cost function. Under these assumptions, the equilibrium – though implying different numerical solutions – has the same basic properties as in the case of constant marginal costs. Readers are asked to verify this fact for themselves.

New durable goods

Storability and durability are related concepts. A durable good is – obviously – always storable. But storable goods are not necessarily durable: Oil does not strike me as being a durable good. Yet the two characteristics seem to be sufficiently close to suggest that durables may "behave" to some extent like storables. As an economist, I would not be surprised if prices of durables proved to behave according to some intertemporal discrimination rule. On the other hand, a quite different behavior (time shape) is to be expected, as durability suggests an eternal lifetime for a commodity, which is the opposite of exhaustibility (where a finite lifetime is implied).

Once durable goods have a well-established market, they normally behave like other storable goods: Their prices are fixed according to some normal-costing rule, as explained in Chapter 6. Our problem here is to understand how *new* durable goods are priced, *before* they have a well-established market. The cases discussed in Chapter 5 do suggest that (sometimes at least) a *decrease* in price over time is to be expected – the opposite of what is to be expected of the price of an exhaustible resource.[13]

To understand this phenomenon, we have to introduce an assumption, either that customers have different tastes or that they have different incomes. For the sake of clarity, I shall assume that all customers have the same tastes (or utility functions or demand curves), since the assumption proved very useful in earlier chapters, where it allowed me to concentrate on the effects of other sources of product differentiation. I shall therefore assume that (identical) consumers have different incomes – an assumption that will be further explored in Essay III, which is entirely

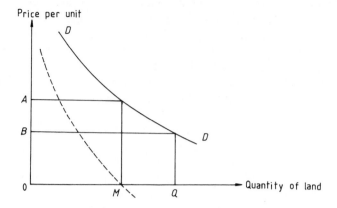

Figure 7.4. Coase's monopolistic landowner. (*Source:* Coase 1972, p. 144.)

devoted to the opportunities for price discrimination that result from income differences. Here I want to concentrate on the *temporal* aspects of pricing over different incomes. One thing is clear: A customer with a higher income is ready to pay a higher price for the durable good considered. (In a moment, I shall also consider the different assumption that the customer is ready to pay more to get the commodity more quickly.)

The best way to start this discussion is perhaps to take a closer look at the case of a monopolistic landowner, as discussed by Coase (1972). There is nothing more durable than land, after all. Coase imagines the following provocative situation:

> Assume that a supplier owns the total stock of a completely durable good. At what price will he sell it? To take a concrete example, assume that one person owns all the land in the United States and, to simplify the analysis, that all land is of uniform quality. Assume also that the landowner is not able to work the land himself, that ownership of land yields no utility and that there are no costs involved in disposing of the land. If there were a large number of landowners and the price were competitively determined, the price would be that at which the amount demanded was equal to the amount of land in the United States. If we imagine this fixed supply of land to be various amounts either greater or smaller, and then discover what the competitively determined price would be, we can trace out the demand schedule for American land. Assume that this demand schedule is DD and that from this a marginal revenue schedule, MR, has been derived. [1972, p. 143]

Both schedules are shown in Figure 7.4. The total amount of land in existence is *0Q*. The price, if it were competitively determined, would be *0B*.

What price will the monopolistic landowner charge for a unit of land? As you might expect by now, standard microeconomics again suggests the wrong answer: Make marginal revenue (*MR*) equal to marginal cost (here zero), and charge the price *0A*. Why is this the wrong policy? Because it implies selling only the quantity of land *0M*, that is, keeping the quantity of land *MQ* off the market. He could

> obviously improve his position by selling more land since he could by this means acquire more money. It is true that this would reduce the value of the land 0M owned by those who had previously bought land from him – but the loss would fall on them, not on him. If the same assumption about his behaviour was made as before, he would then sell part of MQ. But this is not the end of the story, since some of MQ would still remain unsold. The process would continue as long as the original landowner retained any land, that is, until 0Q had been sold. And if there were no costs of disposing of the land, the whole process would take place in the twinkling of an eye. [Ibid.]

To this point I entirely agree with Coase's analysis of the situation. Where I do not agree with him, though, is where he adds that the price for a unit of land is always going to be the competitive price *0B*, given that *0Q* is going to be sold, even if only one supplier owned the total supply of land. The landowner, he says, would find himself in the position that a price higher than *0B* would preclude any sale, for no buyer would be willing to pay more than *0B*.

I would expect the landowner to sell at decreasing prices at successive dates. The crucial necessary assumption is that some buyers are ready to pay a higher price in order to get the land earlier. Their reservation price is a function of time as such, in addition to being a function of income. It does not suffice that rich people are ready to pay more for Coase's conclusion to be invalidated, for rich people are not stupid and are always ready to pay, and are capable of paying, *less,* so that they would wait if waiting were costless (when they were offered a price above *0B*). When a buyer is impatient, the knowledge that other buyers will get a better price, *later,* does not prevent that buyer from paying the higher price. Notice that this tendency has nothing to do with the quality of information – it is always assumed that all economic agents considered know the landowner's price schedule: My argument relies entirely on the presence of time preference. Notice also that it is simply the passage of time that makes the price differences – price discrimination – possible.[14]

Land is an extreme case of durability and was chosen as a provocative example. Coase insists that his analysis is also applicable to reproducible durable goods. The same is true for my price-discriminating seller. Suppose, indeed, that this seller can produce a new durable at an average cost $c(x, t)$, when $\partial c/\partial x < 0$ (costs go down as the durable is produced

Price per unit

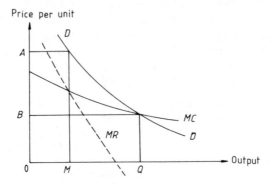

Figure 7.5. Coase's monopolistic producer of a new durable. (*Source:* Coase 1972, p. 146.)

in larger quantities) and $\partial c/\partial t < 0$ (costs go down over time because of "technical progress," whatever that may mean). My seller wonders what the time shape of the selling price $\pi(t)$ should be, as of the date $(t=0)$ when the durable is put on the market.[15] The seller knows that each potential buyer has a reservation price $R(t, t)$ with $\partial R/\partial y$ positive, since y represents income, and $\partial R/\partial t$ is negative, meaning that (all) buyers have (the same) time preference $(\partial^2 R/\partial y\partial t = 0)$. The income distribution is known to be $m(y)$.

In static terms, the situation is as depicted in Figure 7.5. Coase would argue, I suppose – although he did not consider this case explicitly – that no buyer would be ready to pay more than the competitive price $0B$, equal to marginal cost. I think Figure 7.5 is irrelevant.

A correct analysis could proceed along the following lines. On the assumption that each consumer buys one unit of the durable, to simplify, then

$$\int m(y)\, dy = \int x(t)\, dt \tag{7.15}$$

says that the total sold to the different income segments of the market must be equal to total production over the time period considered. Let us suppose that this time period has been determined together with total production, so that $\int x(t)\, dt = \bar{x}$.

Each consumer buys only if the difference between the reservation price R and the seller's price π is maximum. Necessarily, then,

$$\frac{\partial R}{\partial t} = \frac{d\pi}{dt} \tag{7.16}$$

an equilibrium condition that the seller must take into account. The seller's problem is therefore to maximize

$$\int_{\bar{y}}^{1} [\pi(t) - c(x, t)] m(y) \, dy \tag{7.17}$$

if y is distributed on the interval $[0, 1]$ and $\bar{y}$ is the largest income at which the durable is not bought. These profits are to be maximized subject to Equations (7.15) and (7.16). Differentiation of the Lagrangian with respect to time gives[16]

$$\left(\frac{\partial R}{\partial t} - \frac{\partial c}{\partial t} \right) M(y) = \lambda \tag{7.18}$$

or

$$\frac{\partial R}{\partial t} = \frac{d\pi}{dt} = \frac{\lambda}{M(y)} + \frac{\partial c}{\partial t} < 0 \tag{7.19}$$

where $M(y)$ is the cumulative distribution on the right.

The first result is again an intertemporal discrimination rule, expressed in terms of rates of change of reservation prices and marginal costs. The difference between these rates, weighted by $M(y)$, must be equalized over time. Equation (7.19) uses the fact that, for all buyers, $\partial R/\partial t = d\pi/dt$ and says that the slope of the temporal price schedule must be negative and inversely proportional to $M(y)$, that is, the number of people who have already purchased the good, when c is constant. (M measures total past sales, since my seller will first sell to the richest buyers.) When costs are not constant, it is profitable to decrease the selling price *faster*, as another negative element ($\partial c/\partial t$) is to be added.

I conclude that – contrary to what is generally taught and thought – technical progress is not the only explanation for the decrease of the price of new durables. To take away consumer surplus due to time preference by intertemporal price discrimination is another equally valid explanation. My guess is that the latter typically dominates in the early marketing stages and that technical progress comes in after some time has elapsed. It is illuminating to repeat the foregoing analysis in discrete time, especially to highlight the welfare properties of different time sequences of the prices.

Intertemporal welfare and skimming

Consider a monopolist who has decided to sell a reproducible new good over T future periods to N consumers, who each buy one unit during this time space.[17] The monopolist's problem is to determine the profit-maximizing time shape of the price of this new good, knowing that consumers have different reservation prices, depending upon their income and the date of purchase.

Indeed, there are n income classes, n indicating the highest income class, and R_t^i is the reservation price of all consumers in income class i for the purchase of one unit of the commodity in period t ($i=1,\ldots,n$; $t=1,\ldots,T$). Notice that $n=T$. Sales start at ($t=1$). Profits are maximized if prices are such that the highest possible consumer surplus is extracted. Reservation prices are known to increase with i (income) and to decrease with t (the date of purchase). More precisely, I suppose that

$$R^i < R^{i+1} \qquad (7.20\text{a})$$

for all t, that $\partial R^i/\partial t < 0$, and that

$$\left| \frac{\partial R^i}{\partial t} \right| < \left| \frac{\partial R^{i+1}}{\partial t} \right| \qquad (7.20\text{b})$$

so that richer customers are less ready to wait.

Obviously, the monopolist must fix prices in such a way that each income class buys in a particular period. The richest people must be persuaded not to wait at all, that is, the monopolist must make sure that income class n purchases the new good as soon as it is put on the market, that class ($n-1$) purchases not later than at ($t=2$), and so forth.[18] To make sure that class i buys in period t rather than in ($t+\tau$), prices π_t and $\pi_{t+\tau}$ must be such that

$$R_t^i - \pi_t \geqslant R_{t+\tau}^i - \pi_{t+\tau} \qquad (7.21)$$

Inequality (7.21) prevents shifts of demand to later periods.

The profit-maximizing prices are those that make Inequality (7.21) binding and extract most from those who are ready to pay most, that is, these prices "skim" the market. A lower bound is given by the reservation price of the poorest, who will have to buy last, or

$$\pi_T = R_T^1$$

To persuade class 2 to buy one period earlier, namely at ($T-1$), and to simultaneously extract the highest possible price, π_{T-1} has to be higher than π_T, but the difference ($\pi_{T-1} - \pi_T$) has to be just equal to ($R_{T-1}^2 - R_T^2$), that is, the difference between their reservation prices for delivery in ($T-1$) and in T, respectively. If the difference in prices were larger, class 2 would find it worthwhile to delay purchases until period T. If the difference were smaller, the seller would forgo some profit. In short:

$$\pi_{T-1} - \pi_T = R_{T-1}^2 - R_T^2$$
$$\pi_{T-2} - \pi_{T-1} = R_{T-2}^3 - R_{T-1}^3$$
$$\vdots$$
$$\pi_1 - \pi_2 = R_1^n - R_2^n$$

or

$$\pi_T = R_T^1 \tag{7.22}$$
$$\pi_{T-1} = R_{T-1}^2 - R_T^2 + \pi_T$$
$$\vdots$$
$$\pi_1 = R_1^n - R_2^n + \pi_2$$

and $R_{T+1}^i = 0$ for all i. This profit-maximizing time shape of the price can be summarized, in terms of reservation prices, as

$$\pi_{T-k} = \sum_{j=1}^{k+1} (R_{T-j+1}^j - R_{T-j+2}^j)$$

where $(k = i - 1)$. Associating i with the equation $t = T - k = T - i + 1$, I get

$$\pi_T = \sum_{j=1}^{i} (R_{T-j+1}^j - R_{T-j+2}^j) \tag{7.23}$$

Equation (7.23) allows us to introduce profit-maximizing discriminatory prices into aggregate welfare W, and to find the implications of constrained welfare maximization. Under the assumptions made, the monopolist's profit function is

$$\Pi = \sum_{t=1}^{T} N_t \pi_t - \sum_{t=1}^{T} N_t c(t)$$

where $c(t)$ is the average cost of production, N_t is the number of customers in an income class such that $i = T - t + 1 = n - t + 1$. The average cost is supposed to have a negative time derivative because of technical progress and/or because of economies resulting from increased production. The social surplus is

$$S = \sum_{t=1}^{T} N_t (R_t^t - \pi_t)$$

superscript t indicating the income class $i = n - t + 1$, whereas aggregate welfare, using Equation (7.23), is given by

$$W = \mu \sum_{t=1}^{T} N_t R_t^t + (1 - \mu) \sum_{t=1}^{T} N_t \left[\sum_{j=1}^{i} (R_{T-j+1}^j - R_{T-j+2}^j) \right] - \sum_{t=1}^{T} N_t c(t)$$

$$\tag{7.24}$$

Let the cumulative distribution on the right be

$$M_i = \sum_{j=i}^{n} N_j = \sum_{t=1}^{T-i+1} N_t = M_{T-i+1}$$

Then we can write

$$\sum_{t=1}^{T} N_t \left[\sum_{j=1}^{i} (R_{T-j+1}^j - R_{T-j+2}^j) \right] = \sum_{t=1}^{T} M_t R_t^t - \sum_{t=2}^{T} M_{t-1} R_t^{t-1}$$

whereas it is also true that

$$\sum_{t} M_t R_t^t = \sum_{t=1}^{T} N_t R_t^t + \sum_{t=2}^{T} R_t^t M_{t-1}$$

Substitution of these results reduces Equation (7.24) to

$$W = \sum_{t=1}^{T} N_t R_t^t + (1-\mu) \sum_{t=2}^{T} M_{t-1} R_t^t - (1-\mu) \sum_{t=2}^{T} M_{t-1} R_t^{t-1} - \sum_{t=1}^{T} N_t c(t)$$

$$(7.25)$$

which can easily be differentiated with respect to time.

For $(t=1)$ or $(i=n)$, differentiation gives

$$\frac{\partial W}{\partial t} = N_1 \frac{\partial R_1^n}{\partial t} - N_1 c'(1) = 0$$

or

$$\frac{\partial R_1^n}{\partial t} = c'(1) \qquad (7.26)$$

irrespective of the value of μ. Both unconstrained and constrained welfare maximization require cost savings to be immediately transformed into a price decrease, since $(\partial \pi_1 / \partial t = \partial R_1 / \partial t)$ maximizes the difference between the reservation price and the seller's price and is the condition at which income class n will actually buy in period 1. Even more surprising, perhaps, is the discovery that Equation (7.26) also implies that the monopolist's interest would be served by applying it, since it is valid when $\mu = 0$.

For $(t \geqslant 2)$ or $(i \leqslant n-1)$, the first-order condition leads to

$$\frac{\partial R_t^t}{\partial t} = \frac{N_t}{N_t + (1-\mu) M_{t-1}} c'(t) + \frac{(1-\mu) M_{t-1}}{N_t + (1-\mu) M_{t-1}} \frac{\partial R_t^{t-1}}{\partial t} \qquad (7.27)$$

Notice first, as a check on my derivations, that the unconstrained intertemporal optimum implies that $\mu = 1$ and therefore

$$\frac{\partial R_t^t}{\partial t} = c'(t)$$

so that any cost saving is fully reflected in the prices at all times. But the interesting question is to compare the constrained optimum with the profit-maximizing policy. The latter implies that $\mu = 0$ and therefore

$$\frac{\partial R_t^t}{\partial t} = \frac{N_t}{N_t + M_{t-1}} c'(t) + \frac{M_{t-1}}{N_t + M_{t-1}} \frac{\partial R_t^{t-1}}{\partial t}$$

so that the monopolist's prices change at a rate that is a weighted average of cost savings and properties of the reservation price of the *next* richer group. The constrained optimum, with intertemporal price discrimination, also admits both influences but attaches different weights. Given that $0 < \mu < 1$, more weight is given to cost savings and less weight is given to the structure of reservation prices.

All in all, the richest income group not only keeps the highest surplus (according to Equations [7.22]) but actually buys during the optimal time period – the first – during which the time shape of prices is the same as under marginal-cost pricing, even though the seller is discriminating. As of the next time period, or for the next (poorer) income class, profit-maximizing prices diverge not only from prices based on marginal cost but also from the prices that would be optimal under the circumstances. Does this statement mean that profit-maximizing prices go down too slowly? They certainly follow more closely the intertemporal structure of reservation prices as time elapses and are less and less influenced by cost savings. But the same is true for the optimal prices, although to a smaller degree. The ultimate time shape will therefore depend on the comparative speed with which costs and reservation prices decrease, and we can work out cases in which the profit-maximizing prices decrease faster than the optimal discriminatory prices.

These conclusions suggest that we should be careful, in empirical work, not to conclude that prices that decrease faster are *therefore* more competitive and reveal a higher rate of technical progress or that a reduction in the price decrease reveals some reduction in the competitive pressures. (The latter reduction may be due, simply, to a stabilization of R_t^{t-1}.)

Equation (7.27) also sheds light on the recurrent phenomenon of "sales" of clothing and shoes at the end of a season. As the seller approaches T, M_{t-1} – the volume of past sales – grows, and the seller therefore attaches more and more importance to the reservation prices of customers (and less and less to costs). At the limit, the seller is ready to sell at whatever price the "shopping ladies" – who specialize in buying only during sales because their time preference is so low[19] – are ready to pay. And if this price is below marginal cost, the sale will still be made, below marginal cost, at less than the socially optimal price (which might itself be below marginal cost).

CHAPTER 8

Nonstorable commodities

Most commodities produced by industrial firms are more or less storable. For some, the costs of storage are so high that the possibility of meeting demand shifts by varying inventory holdings can be ignored. Electricity is the classic example. Services are, by definition, not storable: Commercial transportation, hotel and motel rooms, car-rental services, theaters and movie houses, sports arenas, and so forth come to mind. In these service industries, demand often fluctuates over time, and the price responses to these intertemporal differences in demand are of interest to us, to the extent that they might be discriminatory.

Demand fluctuations may be certain or random. Over a day, the demand for electricity fluctuates in a periodic way that is related to the rotation of the earth. The electricity utilities know the differences, hour after hour, with what may be considered complete certainty, for practical purposes. Over a week or a year hotels and airlines know in advance how the tourist traffic will change from day to day or from month to month.

Random fluctuations are to be expected, though, even in the previous examples where the periodicity is known, as far as the *level* of demand in each period is concerned. This randomness[1] may itself be periodic, in the sense that this period's mean and/or variance of the probability distribution will be the same a day from now or a week or a month from now. Or it may be, as should generally be the case, that the randomness is nonperiodic; think of the situation of an ice cream producer in a region where the weather changes every so often. But even the rental of hotel rooms or cars is subject to unpredictable random fluctuations at any moment of time.

Certain demand fluctuations

Consider the certainty case first, and suppose, for simplicity, that two periods are involved: a known off-peak demand D_1, followed by a known peak demand D_2. What prices will a profit-maximizing firm, facing D_1 and D_2, announce?

Consider Figure 8.1, and suppose that marginal production cost of the nonstorable commodity is at level b. There is no reason to distinguish between the rate of sales, q, and the rate of production, x, as both must

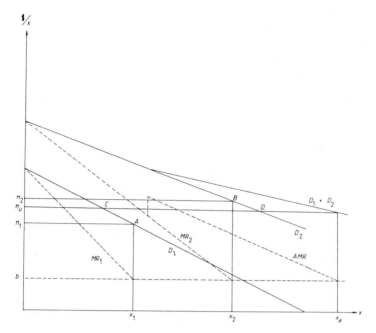

Figure 8.1. Discriminating monopoly pricing.

always be equal. (Why not, then, use x to designate both sales and production?) It is well known that intertemporal profit maximization leads to the same pricing policy as instantaneous ("myopic") profit maximization. In other words, the discrimination rule, which says that prices are such that off-peak marginal revenue MR_1 should be equal to peak marginal revenue MR_2 and both should be equal to marginal cost b, amounts to saying that marginal revenue and marginal cost should be equalized in each period myopically, that is, independently of the other periods. This is how π_1 and π_2 are determined, leading to off-peak production and sales x_1 and to peak production x_2. This would be the policy of a discriminating monopoly. It is also the so-called value-of-service policy, adopted by some electricity utilities in the United States before the Second World War: a clear case of third-degree price discrimination, since differences in demand intensities are used to increase profits, and price differences are in no way related to costs.

It might be of interest to have a quick look at the price level that would have come about if the firm, say the utility, had been obliged by law to charge the same price[2] to peak and off-peak customers, for example, on the basis of some equality principle (according to which everybody should pay the same price for what is after all the same electricity:

Why should an active worker who prepares his breakfast at rush hour – at 7:15 a.m. – pay more for energy than a retired worker who has tea at 11:00 a.m.?). Add D_1 and D_2 horizontally, to find the zigzag aggregate marginal revenue AMR and the point where it cuts the horizontal marginal-cost line. This intersection point determines π_u, the uniform peak–off-peak price, which is between π_1 and π_2 and "cuts the apple in two," so to speak.

Optimal peak-load pricing

What are the effects on sales of a uniform peak–off-peak price π_u? Compare points C and D (which determine off-peak sales and peak sales, respectively) with points A and B: Quite understandably, off-peak sales are reduced and peak sales are increased.

At first sight, these changes might compensate each other more or less, so that the overall effect on the firm's rate of production need not be dramatic. This reasoning neglects one important factor, though: Is there enough *capacity* to satisfy this increased peak demand? One thing is clear. The profit-maximizing prices π_1 and π_2 allow the firm not only to make more profit but also to invest less, since a smaller capacity, corresponding to point B, will do. This problem does not arise in the same terms in a spatial framework, where capacity must correspond to *aggregate* demand (e.g., $D_1 + D_2$). There one has to discuss changes in aggregate demand, as we did in Essay I. Here, capacity has to correspond[3] to *peak* demand, whatever the behavior of aggregate sales (in Figure 8.1, aggregate sales are identical under both pricing policies, since aggregate marginal revenue is identical in both cases). And in an intertemporal framework where inventories are possible, such as in the previous chapter, capacity is linked with the *current* rate of production x. Are any of the capacities corresponding to points B and D too high or too low? From the point of view of the firm, a smaller investment giving a higher profit is to be preferred: B is better than D. What can we say from the point of view of society? What is the socially optimal capacity?

We know that an unconstrained optimal allocation of resources implies prices that fully reflect costs of transportation over space or time. What is the corresponding cost here? This should be a cost to be added to the marginal cost of production (b), just as transport costs had to be added to marginal cost, which is incurred anyway at peak as well as at off-peak periods. The cost we are looking for is nothing but the marginal capacity cost, the cost of providing a unit of capacity. Let this cost be β, also constant with respect to the amount of capacity required. We thus have an off-peak marginal cost of b, and a peak marginal cost of $(b+\beta)$. The so-called peak-load problem is then to find the socially optimal peak and

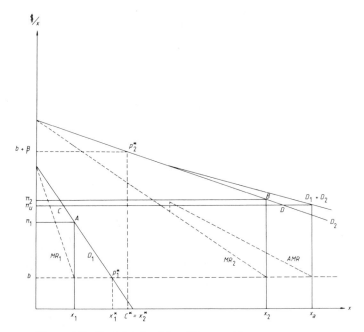

Figure 8.2. Peak-load pricing (firm peak).

off-peak prices such that capacity is optimal – such that the excess of expressed consumer satisfaction over the cost of resources devoted to production, that is, the social surplus, is maximized. The amount of capacity is to be determined *ab initio,* (i.e., with no given capacity to start with).

The correct answer to this problem is a particular application of the principle of marginal-cost pricing, and was found almost simultaneously but independently by Boiteux (1949) and Houthakker (1951) with important refinements by Davidson (1955), Steiner (1957), Hirschleifer (1958), and Williamson (1966). We will use Steiner's graphic device, which amounts to adding the two demand curves vertically rather than horizontally.

If quantity demanded were independent of prices charged for output in each period, there would be neither difficulty nor interest in the peak-load problem. The optimal solution (p_1^*, p_2^*) would simply mean that $p_1^* = b$ and $p_2^* = b + \beta$: Total costs would be covered, and all units sold would be paying the full marginal costs of their production. This solution would assure that no unproduced unit was capable of paying such costs.[4] When quantity demanded does depend on prices, the same answer may be correct, as can be illustrated with the help of Figure 8.2. The demand curves are drawn[5] in such a way that, when $p_1^* = b$ and $p_2^* = b + \beta$,

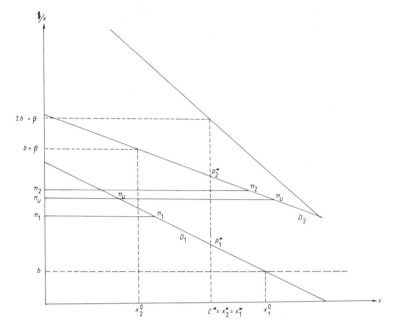

Figure 8.3. Peak-load pricing (shifting peak).

all costs $(2b + \beta)$ are covered, by definition. (Off-peak demand is small relative to on-peak demand.) The optimal capacity is the one determined by $p_2^* = b + \beta$, that is, C^*. Obviously the correction brought in by charging π_2 (and π_1) rather than π_u was not sufficient: By charging p_2^* (and p_1^*), capacity can be reduced from x_2 to C^*. It is true that aggregate sales are reduced from x_a to the sum of $x_1^* + x_2^*$. But this drop should not disturb us. Why should bigger (total) sales be better? Think about electricity: Why should a larger consumption of electricity be better? We are reasoning in terms of an optimal allocation of resources. The money not spent on electricity, when the tariff is (p_1^*, p_2^*) rather than (π_1, π_2) or π_u, can better be spent on some other commodity.

Suppose, however, that off-peak demand is large relative to on-peak demand,[6] as in Figure 8.1. Then the simple solution $p_1^* = b$ and $p_2^* = b + \beta$ will not do. To see this, reproduce the demand curves of Figure 8.1 as in Figure 8.3, together with the profit-maximizing prices π_1, π_2 and the uniform price π_u obtained in Figure 8.1. Notice that, if the off-peak price were equal to b, "off-peak" sales x_1^0 would be larger than the "peak" sales x_2^0 made at a price equal to $b + \beta$: the off-peak price would in fact be charged to units that make the *peak* demand upon capacity. More important, capacity costs of only x_2^0 units would be recovered, whereas x_1^0 units of capacity are required!

The correct solution can be found using the fact that demand for both periods combined can be satisfied at a cost of $2b$ per combined unit up to the capacity limit, and $(2b + \beta)$ per combined unit beyond that limit. On comparing the *vertical* sum of D_1 and D_2 with $(2b + \beta)$, one finds the point at which customers are ready to pay for the combined unit in both the peak and off-peak period: The optimal capacity is C^*.

This capacity must be used to its limit, so that the optimal prices are p_1^* and p_2^*. At these prices, $C^* = x_2^* = x_1^*$, so that peak and off-peak sales are equal. At these prices, total cost is covered, since $p_1^* + p_2^* = 2b + \beta$ by construction! Steiner concludes:

> To generalize the argument it is essential to recognize that a unit of capacity is justified if and only if (1) it is justified by the demand in any period alone *or* (2) it is justified by the combined demands in two or more periods. Once the appropriate capacity is determined, output in each period should be extended to that capacity unless additional units of output fail to cover the operating costs at an earlier output. Then given the optimal outputs in each period and the demand curves, it is routine to determine the optimal prices...
>
> These results are easily generalized to more than two periods, which may be mixed in the sense that among some subgroup of periods shifting peak relationships apply, yet between this group and the others a firm peak prevails... The essence of this solution is the same as for the two period case. The total capacity cost is borne by the periods which make the peak demand upon the capacity, and whose demands collectively justify the marginal unit of capacity. But the capacity charge among these periods is unequal; it is proportional to the strength of the effective demand for capacity. Fundamentally this charge is thus allocated according to demand, and is discriminatory. Output, among these periods, is equal notwithstanding differences in demand. [1957, pp. 589-90]

Can peak-load pricing be discriminatory?

Before confronting random demand fluctuations, we must ask whether and to what extent peak-load pricing is discriminatory, the more so as there is a famous controversy on this point with, as main opponents, Steiner (1957), on the one hand, and Hirschleifer (1958) – supported by Ekelund and Hulett (1973) and Demsetz (1973) – on the other hand.

To begin with, we must carefully distinguish between the two cases just discussed. In the first case, where off-peak demand is small compared with on-peak demand (with the result that, at $p_1^* = b$, demand remains off-peak), the situation is simple. Take Figure 8.2: The optimal "peak-load" prices p_1^* and p_2^* are nondiscriminatory, since $p_2^* - p_1^* = \beta$, the marginal cost of providing extra peak capacity. In other words, the off-peak net price $(p_1^* - b)$ is equal to the peak net price $(p_2^* - b - \beta)$, both being equal to zero. The profit-maximizing prices π_1 and π_2 are discriminatory, since the marginal capacity cost is not fully reflected in their difference. In fact, $\pi_2 - \pi_1 < \beta$: One could say that there is "capacity absorption," by analogy with the absorption of transport costs or storage costs discussed earlier. On-peak customers are being subsidized by off-peak customers, or – if you prefer – off-peak customers are being discriminated against. The uniform peak–off-peak price π_u is the *most* discriminatory of all, since it does not reflect any cost difference at all. This is also Davidson's conclusion in his path-breaking study *Price Discrimination in Selling Gas and Electricity:* "Peak–off-peak discrimination results from the absence of, or the use of inappropriate, differential rates for peak and off-peak service. Because of a reliance on a fallacious cost analysis, the significant variation of costs between peak and off-peak production of energy has not been recognized in general rate structures" (1955, p. 150).

The second case, where at an off-peak price equal to b, demand would become on-peak demand, is more delicate. In Figure 8.3, π_u is again the most discriminatory price, in the sense just defined. And the profit-maximizing prices π_1 and π_2 remain as discriminatory as before. However, the optimal peak-load prices p_1^* and p_2^* are now also discriminatory, though less than π_1 and π_2, since $p_2^* - p_1^* < \beta$. To some extent, the off-peak customers are paying for the on-peak customers. To make sure that total marginal costs are covered, use is made of the fact that a smaller (off-peak) demand is less elastic than a larger one, so that the former is asked to subsidize the latter. (The reader may check that the increase of p_1^* above b leads to a smaller reduction in sales $[x_1^0 - x_1^*]$ than the increase in sales $[x_2^* - x_2^0]$ due to the lowering of p_2^* below $[b + \beta]$.) Yet this discriminatory policy is the optimal thing to do, simply because differences in demand intensities are a fact of life and must be taken into account, even in a socially optimal solution.

Economists who tend to associate optimality with perfect competition find it understandably hard to accept the idea that optimal prices can be discriminatory. It is not surprising, therefore, to see that part of the profession follows Hirschleifer (1958) in his attempt to show that p_1^* and p_2^* are not discriminatory after all. Hirschleifer suggests that a true representation of marginal cost would make a horizontal line (at b) until C^*, rising vertically thereafter until either p_1^* or p_2^*. He justifies this idea on the grounds that b and $(b + \beta)$ are not the true marginal costs. By marginal cost he means, ultimately, the marginal *opportunity* cost – the value set upon the resource by the customer is the most valuable alternative use being sacrificed, that is, a price infinitesimally less than p_1^* or p_2^*. Steiner argues (correctly) that, in his view, "this neglects the fundamental discontinuity in the marginal cost function of a peak load problem, which leaves marginal cost undefined at $\bar{x}_0$ [i.e. my C^*]. Further, since we are concerned with a planning cost curve the use of a demand-determined optimal capacity as if it were a 'fixed cost' seems wholly unjustified'' (1957, p. 590).

In his reply to Hirschleifer, he adds rather pointedly:

> Since this issue does not affect the solution it would be both painless and gracious to accept Hirschleifer's definition of discrimination and to concede that the optimal solution is nondiscriminatory. His is a sophisticated definition and an intriguing one. It may even be right.
>
> I confess to some reservations. Marginal cost, Hirschleifer argues, should be interpreted as opportunity cost, the most valuable foregone alternative, including opportunities foregone in the same market. Under this interpretation it seems to me that (1) it is generally impossible to define marginal cost for a product independent of the demand function for that product, and (2) profit-maximizing marginal cost is in general always equal to (less only an epsilon) or *above* price. Has this definition saved the concept of price discrimination by annihilating the concept of marginal cost? [1958, p. 467]

Random demand fluctuations

Short-run demand fluctuations often occur in random as well as in periodic patterns. To what extent should price variations reflect these random patterns? Two approaches seem to be developing in the literature. Rather recent reasoning stresses the fact that randomness typically leads to excess demands, with the implication that some nonprice rationing method seems inevitable, such as queuing, priorities, quality deterioration, and so on. Different rationing schemes have been studied, such as serving first those customers who have the highest willingness to pay (Brown and Johnson 1969 and Visscher 1973), presetting a single price and capacity (Andersen 1974 and Sherman and Visscher 1977), or asking the customer to subscribe to a particular level of capacity in advance, above which further consumption will be curtailed automatically (see Panzar and Sibley 1978). On economic grounds, I find it hard to understand why a firm should not plan sufficient capacity to avoid rationing and should not let customers with random demands pay for the extra capacity cost due to their randomness. Only technical problems seem to explain rationing, for example, when "overloading" leads to system failure or congestion.[7] The alternative approach supposes, precisely, that sufficient capacity is available so as to have excess capacity rather than rationing. In fact, firms are supposed to build a sufficient *security margin* into a plant of fixed capacity. The problem is then to determine how randomness of a particular demand contributes to the cost of this extra capacity.

Boiteux (1951) stresses that the parameters of the probability distribution attached to a random demand are characteristics of the same nature as transportation or storage costs: They are characteristics of the good to be taken into account as elements of product differentiation. We should thus determine how, say, the mean and the variance of a random demand contribute to the cost of putting a commodity on the market.

Imagine, to that effect, that each consumer i has a random demand (at a given time and price) q_i, with known expected value $\bar{q}_i$ and variance σ_i^2. These demands are sufficiently analogous and independently distributed for aggregate demand to be approximately normally distributed with expected value $\bar{q} = \sum_i \bar{q}_i$ and variance $\sigma^2 = \sum_i \sigma_i^2$. We can then read the probability that aggregate demand will exceed a given level, say $(\bar{q} + k\sigma)$, from a table of the standardized normal density function. Conversely, to any probability ϵ there corresponds a level of aggregate demand $q(\epsilon)$ that has probability $(1 - \epsilon)$ of not being exceeded, namely $[\bar{q} + k(\epsilon)\sigma]$. The number $k(\epsilon)$ can be read from the same table [e.g., $k(.025) = 1.96$, $k(.005) = 2.58$, etc.].

The firm should build a plant of capacity $[q_c(\epsilon) = \bar{q} + k(\epsilon)\sigma]$. Let its short-run total cost function be

$$f(q_c, q) = \beta q_c(\epsilon) + \gamma q \qquad 0 \leqslant q \leqslant q_c$$
$$= \infty \qquad\qquad\qquad q > q_c$$

where β is marginal capacity cost and γ is short-term marginal cost of production. This cost function can be rewritten as

$$f[\bar{q}_c(\epsilon), q] = \beta[\bar{q} + k(\epsilon)\sigma] + \gamma q$$
$$= \beta\left[\sum_i \bar{q}_i + k(\epsilon)\left(\sum_i \sigma_i^2\right)^{1/2}\right] + \gamma \sum_i q_i^*$$

where q_i^* is actual sales to consumer i (there being no shortage). We have thus expressed total cost as a function of individual sales q_i and of two parameters of the density functions of individual demands: their mean $\bar{q}_i$ and their standard deviations σ_i (or their variances σ_i^2).

To find the "marginal cost" of actual sales *and* of each parameter, it suffices to differentiate the total cost function with respect to q_i^*, $\bar{q}_i$, and σ_i:

$$\frac{\partial f}{\partial \bar{q}_i} = \beta$$

$$\frac{\partial f}{\partial \sigma_i} = 2\sigma_i \frac{\partial f}{\partial \sigma_i^2} = \beta k(\epsilon) \frac{\sigma_i}{\sigma} \qquad \text{as} \qquad \frac{\partial f}{\partial \sigma_i^2} = \frac{\beta}{2} \frac{k(\epsilon)}{\sigma}$$

$$\frac{\partial f}{\partial q_i^*} = \gamma$$

Accordingly, pricing of all components (those that differentiate a good, including the mean $\bar{q}_i$ and the standard deviation σ_i) at marginal cost implies in this context that consumer i should be charged a sum equal to

$$\gamma q_i^* + \beta \bar{q}_i + \beta k(\epsilon)\frac{\sigma_i^2}{\sigma}$$

Total revenue to the firm is then

$$\gamma \sum_i q_i^* + \beta \sum_i \bar{q}_i + \beta \frac{k(\epsilon)}{\sigma} \sum_i \sigma_i^2 = \gamma q + \beta[\bar{q} + k(\epsilon)\sigma]$$

that is, equal to total cost, so that the firm breaks even.

The reader will have noticed that the firm would not break even if the "marginal cost of randomness" were defined with respect to the *variance* of individual demands σ_i^2 rather than with respect to their standard deviation σ_i. Indeed, differentiation of the same cost function with respect to the variance leads to a total revenue of

$$\gamma \sum_i q_i^* + \beta \sum_i \bar{q}_i + \frac{\beta}{2}\frac{k(\epsilon)}{\sigma} \sum_i \sigma_i^2 = \gamma q + \beta\left[\bar{q} + \frac{k(\epsilon)\sigma}{2}\right]$$

so that a deficit of $\frac{1}{2}\beta k(\epsilon)\sigma$ occurs: Only half of the costs brought about by the excess capacity (safety margin) $k(\epsilon)\sigma$ are covered. This is one of the reasons why Boiteux (1951) advocates the use of the standard deviation rather than the variance as the component that differentiates a good.

Drèze (1964) has shown that, quite to the contrary, it is the use of the *variance* that is to be advocated from the point of view of an efficient allocation of resources. Working with the standard deviation, he found that the marginal rate of transformation (of mean for variance) for the firm is *not* equal to the marginal rate of substitution (of mean for variance) for the ith consumer. When using the variance, these rates *are* equal, as required by Pareto optimality.

Whatever the pricing formula used, the practical implication should be clear. Reverting to the case of our travelers X, Y, and Z, who are flying on Apex, standby, and regular fares, respectively – as discussed in the introductory chapter – our initial intuition seems to be confirmed. Mr. X, who pays for his seat weeks in advance, has a zero σ_i^2 (or σ_i, for that matter). His fare should be lower than the one charged to the unpredictable Mr. Z, who has positive σ_i^2 and obliges the airline to offer extra capacity as a safety margin. As for the flexible student Mr. Y, who is ready to occupy an empty seat if there is one, but does not claim to find an empty one, it would not be absurd for a firm to offer him a very low standby or "super saver" fare, charging a price such that all remaining empty seats are just taken. In fact, it would – according to Boiteux (1951) – be the best thing to do. The difficulty, of course, is to work out the details in a practical case and to find the correct numbers!

Income differences

CHAPTER 9

Business practices

We have analyzed the possibilities for price discrimination that result from differences in location over space and time. In this third essay I consider possibilities resulting from income differences among customers. As before, taste differences are ignored. As for quality differences, I am aware of the fact that richer people often prefer to buy goods of better quality, so that there may be an additional possibility of discrimination. (The discriminating seller will have to take into account the circumstance that rich people can always buy lower-quality goods, whereas the reverse may not be true.) Problems related to quality differences are deferred to Essay IV, for the sake of clarity, so that I shall assume a homogeneous commodity throughout the present discussion of income differences.

The commodity sold will be supposed to be "normal," that is, to have a positive income elasticity. In other words, richer people will be supposed to buy and to consume larger quantities of the commodities considered than poorer people do. Across customers, therefore, income differences will be associated with differences in the quantities consumed, and the question will arise as to whether and how this circumstance gives rise to possibilities of surplus extraction, that is, is a new source of price discrimination.

The Belgian residential electricity tariff

We know, by now, that to ascertain the presence of price discrimination, price differences must be compared with cost differences. In considering the Belgian electricity tariff,[1] it is therefore of interest to record the essential characteristics of the cost of electricity generation and distribution, the more so as our preceding discussion of spatial and intertemporal pricing suggests that (unconstrained) optimal prices should reflect marginal costs. (You will not be surprised to discover that an [unconstrained] optimal electricity tariff would be as intricate as the cost structure.[2])

Total cost for residential users service includes (a) "demand-related" costs, (b) "customer-related" costs, and (c) "energy-related" costs. Demand-related costs are related to the "demand" or "capacity" at a given moment, that is, to the value of the power consumed at a given moment. It is expressed in kilowatts (kW) and gives rise to the peak-load

147

problem discussed in Chapter 8. I shall therefore ignore these capacity costs here. Customer-related costs are independent of the amount and timing of consumption. They include connection, maintenance, meter reading, and billing costs and could be directly related to a possible fee for connecting the customer to the system. Energy-related costs represent the cost of providing the customer with power (maintaining the necessary voltage in the circuit). They include transmission and production costs in the narrow sense (mainly operating and fuel costs) together with the related general costs and taxes. Energy-related costs are typically decreasing as production increases.

One problem is to see how customer- and energy-related costs are reflected in the connection fee and the electricity price for residential customers, and to what extent and why second-degree price discrimination arises. Another problem is whether third-degree discrimination results when connection charges and electricity prices vary between customer groups, for example, between industrial, commercial, and residential users. I shall limit myself here to the first question.

The present Belgian residential tariff goes back to the "Electricity Convention," held in 1955, the initial aim of which was to stimulate (*sic!*) national electricity consumption through a price reduction of electricity energy, obtained by rationalizing the entire sector. (You might think that today a national convention should be organized to *reduce* electricity consumption.) A regulatory committee, the "Comité de Contrôle de l'Electricité et du Gaz," was set up.[3]

Starting from 1957, a tariff identical over the entire country was introduced. Electric power was charged to residential customers according to a declining four-block tariff based on consumption in kilowatt-hours (kWh) which was converted to a three-block tariff in 1967.

The rate schedule prevailing in 1976 is shown below:

> for the first 450 kWh per year, 1.75 BF per kWh
> for the next 270 kWh per year, 1.10 BF per kWh
> for all excess over 720 kWh per year, 1.02 BF per kWh.

In addition, there was a fixed subscription charge of 240 BF per year.

If we ignore the fixed charge for customer-related cost, we can set the origin at 240 BF in Figure 9.1 and concentrate on the structure of the remainder of the schedule. One way of describing this schedule is to emphasize that charging a first-block price of 1.75 BF per kWh amounts to charging an "entrance fee" or tax for the right to buy at the lower second-block price. Indeed, the customer must spend a sum of $[450(1.75-1.10)\simeq]290$ BF before consuming more than 450 kWh at a price of 1.10 BF. The additional tax for access to the still lower third-block price is $[270(1.10-1.02)\simeq]21$ BF. These fees are to be distinguished

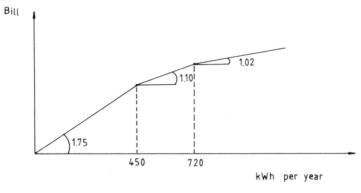

Figure 9.1. Residential tariff.

from the connection charge of 240 BF per year, to the extent that the former have nothing to do with costs of connection.

A declining block tariff implies an automatic decline in the average rate for increased use of electric power. Because customers with large incomes typically consume more electric power, the existing tariff was resented as unfair by some members of the regulatory commission. Accordingly, the structure of the tariff was changed in 1977, the aim being to reduce the bills for the low-income group. This seems to have been a typical income-distribution decision involving political and social judgments: A major trade union withdrew from the regulatory commission upon rejection of its proposal to introduce *increasing*-block pricing. Instead, a so-called uniform tariff was introduced. It included the following two tariffs:

> *Social tariff*
> Subscription charge: 200 BF per year
> Unit price: 4.810 BF per kWh per year
>
> *Normal tariff*
> Subscription charge: 1,300 BF per year
> Unit price: 2.752 BF per kWh per year

The "social" tariff is automatically applied as long as it is more favorable to the consumer than the "normal" tariff. The latter is automatically applied to customers finding no advantage in the social tariff (nor in the time-of-day tariff – the *tarif bihoraire* – which is available only on request).

In practice, the social tariff is charged to small customers with a consumption of as much as 570 kWh per year. Higher-income customers (with a consumption above 570 kWh per year) pay a smaller unit price but a much higher connection fee, although the costs of connection do not differ. This provision makes one wonder to what extent this new tariff is really uniform.

Let us compute the tax for access to the normal tariff as it would have been if all customers had been offered a two-block tariff, with a "social" first-block price of 4.81 and a "normal" second-block price of 2.752 BF. One finds that $570(4.81-2.752)=1.173\simeq1.100$! In other words, one finds almost exactly the difference between the social subscription charge and the normal subscription charge. The situation is the same as if the regulatory commission had continued to offer a block tariff to everybody (with two block prices, 4.81 BF and 2.75 BF, instead of three), plus a unique connection fee of 200 BF: The new tariff cannot be said to be uniform. Whether it is more advantageous or "fair" to low-income people therefore depends only on the values of the rates applied, not on its being more uniform.

This little story suggests that producers seem to find block tariffs more profitable than uniform pricing. (Although apparently satisfying the trade union's demand for uniformity, they managed to continue to price discriminate and to exact some consumer surplus from the rich through an increased connection fee.) We shall have to determine, in the following chapters, whether this impression is correct.

Two-part tariffs

We have discovered that a block tariff can be described as a series of two-part tariffs whose first part is an entrance fee (or tax) giving access to the second, lower-priced part. We have also noticed that, in addition, an entrance fee aiming at covering costs of connecting a customer to a network may be charged. These two types of fees are very different: The former are not based on any costs and simply aim at extracting more consumer surplus.

The time has come to record business practices in which the former type of entrance fee is charged explicitly in addition to a unit price. Amusement parks charge an entrance fee before any service is offered, although there is no connection cost involved in letting a customer enter the park. Exhibitions (Expo 58, World Fairs, etc.) charge an entrance fee, with reductions for senior people, students, military, and groups. Once people are inside the exhibition halls, the price is the same for everybody. Car-rental firms have a similar policy. There is a fee for the rental of the car that differs, depending on the number of days that you want to use the car. However, there is the same (small) unit price per mile.

Tie-ins

Block tariffs have another feature worth emphasizing: They leave the customers free to decide which block(s) they want to be in and thus which price(s) they are ready to pay. Offering a block tariff is much more elegant than directly charging different prices to different individuals. It is also a way of having customers *reveal* how much they are ready to pay. This information may not be available otherwise.

A similar reasoning leads to another type of price discrimination, the so-called tie-in sales. The classic example is a practice followed by International Business Machines (IBM) before its condemnation in 1936 (*International Business Machine Corp.* versus *United States,* 298 U.S. 131 [1936]). The case is described as follows by Telser:

> IBM had a monopoly on certain kinds of tabulating equipment, and it required its customers to purchase all of their tabulating cards (on which it held no monopoly) from itself. Some would interpret this as IBM's attempt to extend its monopoly from tabulating equipment to tabulating cards. A more plausible explanation is that the customers' rate of use of the cards measured their rate of use of the equipment. Hence, by charging a price for the cards in excess of their cost, IBM was able to discriminate among its customers according to the intensity of their demand for tabulating equipment. If customers had been allowed to purchase cards from sources other than IBM or from each other, IBM could not as easily have obtained the additional profits of price discrimination. [1965, p. 490]

By determining the number of cards used, customers in fact fix their total expenditure and thus reveal the intensity of their demand for tabulating *equipment*.

Still another way of describing this practice is to interpret it as a two-part tariff, in which the rental price for the equipment is the entrance fee. Instead of varying, though, as in the case of an amusement park, the rental fee is the same for all customers. The surplus is extracted by varying the receipt from the sale of punch cards. And this is possible, notwithstanding the fact that the unit price per card is the same for all, because the customers themselves decide how many cards to use. The only difficulty is to make sure that the customer will not use cards bought from competitors. Hence the tie-in.

Xerox versus Electrofax

Xerox's price policy in the early 1960s was similar to IBM's, although xerography uses ordinary paper. Instead of trying to control the use of paper – an obviously impossible task – it exploited the fact that the intensity of use of a copying machine can be metered. As a result, Xerox only leased its machines but priced them on a per copy basis. Blackstone describes its pricing policy as follows:

> At the time Xerox charged $25 + 0.035 per copy for a minimum of 2,000 copies per month. Since the marginal cost per copy to Xerox was much less than $0.035, its profit was greater as the intensity of use was greater. For example, a firm making 2,000 copies per month paid Xerox $1,140 per year while a firm making 20,000 copies per month paid $8,700. Over the lives of the two machines the prices amounted to $5,700 and $43,000, respectively. If leasing and metering were impossible (and assuming for illustration a market of two firms) Xerox would have only two choices. It could price at $5,700 and sell two machines, and in so doing sacrifice $37,800 that the more intensive user would be willing to pay, or it could charge $43,500 and sell one machine, and thereby lose the profit from the user willing to pay $5,700. With a reported manufacturing cost for a Xerox machine of $2,500, the policy of leasing and metering would yield a profit of $44,200 compared to a maximum profit of $41,000 from selling the machine outright and without discrimination. The policy of market segmentation and pricing on the basis of intensity of use was apparently highly profitable, as evidenced both by Xerox's reluctance to sell its machines – it did not establish a price until 1962, two years after its machines have been on the market – and by the price then set of $29,500, which was obviously not designed to encourage purchase. [1975, pp. 190–1]

In those days, the alternative to xerography was the Electrofax copying process, the key distinction being the latter's use of special coated paper, which is heavier than ordinary paper and has a waxy coating. The Electrofax producers tried to use Xerox's selling method, although they did not enjoy its market power. They succeeded, because they could use the sale of the special coated paper to segment the market and could meter the usage. Being few in numbers, each possessed some market power; the value of the machine differed significantly among the users; and very few sources existed from which to purchase the paper. In fact, each firm was initially a monopolist in supplies, since the supplies were not perfectly interchangeable among different firms' machines. The prerequisites for discriminatory pricing were thus satisfied.

The Electrofax producers priced the paper initially at $0.04 per sheet, which implied a net markup of about 200%, whereas the markup on the copying machines was only 25%. Blackstone rationalizes this policy of pricing machines much closer to marginal costs than supplies as follows:

> The advantage of the policy, which is the equivalent of Xerox's leasing and metering, can be seen by a simple numerical example. Suppose that with a paper price of $0.04, one user would make 2,000 copies per

month and the only other user, 10,000 copies, The marginal and average cost per copy of the electrofax paper is $0.01. Now suppose that the $1,000 machine price includes $200 supernormal profit. The user who makes 10,000 copies contributes in the first year $200 + (10,000 × 12 × $0.03) or $3,800 of supernormal profit and the user who makes 2,000 copies adds $920. The firm is clearly segmenting the market and engaging in price discrimination, since effectively different monthly or annual prices are charged for the machines; or, what amounts to the same thing, different levels of supernormal profit are earned on the basis of intensity of use. If the firm had instead a simple monopolistic pricing rule, with the same price for all users, it could not simultaneously have earned a small profit from a low volume user and a much greater profit from a high volume user. Its total would then have been lower. Without metering through supplies, price discrimination would have been impossible. First, the firm could not have known beforehand the purchaser's intensity of use. Second, even if one could know, one could not have prevented a lower volume user from selling the machine to a higher volume user. Pricing on the basis of use of supplies solved both of these problems, at least temporarily. [1975, pp. 192–3]

The supernormal profits earned on the sale of Electrofax paper soon drew a substantial number of paper firms into competition with the equipment firms. The latter responded to the entry threat in two ways. First, they raised machine prices, whereas paper prices were cut. Second, some firms attempted to maintain the original pricing policy by tying, among other things, the rental of their machines to the use of their paper. Since they had lost their monopoly power over supplies, continuation of the previous policy required an explicit tie-in.

The *Northern Pacific* case

Another famous case of tying contracts – which actually led to a decision in court[4] – involved the Northern Pacific Railway. The alleged violations of sections 1 and 2 of the Sherman Act involved Northern Pacific's use of contracts that generally required lessees and, in some cases, buyers of its land to ship commodities produced on those lands via Northern Pacific unless lower rates or better services were available from competing lines.

Cummings and Ruhter (1979) reexamined the case and quote the following typical provision that was found in almost all of the land sales contracts:

The purchaser agrees as one of the material considerations of this contract that rates being equal it will ship via the Northern Pacific Railway Company all logs, poles, timber and other products manufactured by it from the timber cut under this contract... Where the destination of the manufactured product is not on the line of the Northern Pacific Railway

Company, such shipments shall be routed to favor said Railway Company with the longest haul, if the expense to the purchaser is not increased over the cost of shipment over another rail line. The purchaser shall make monthly reports to the vendor of shipments under this provision, and shall permit the vendor to examine the purchaser's records at any convenient time or place for the purpose of verifying such reports. [1979, p. 330]

Several possible explanations for these practices are discussed in Cummings and Ruhter (1979). The one that is relevant here is the metering argument. Could it be that Northern Pacific was facing buyers and lessees who placed differing values on the land and therefore sold the land at a low price (as the Electrofax producers did with their machines) while extracting consumer surplus via high rail rates, which supposedly revealed the land users' valuations of the land? The argument seems farfetched. First, because there is no evidence that Northern Pacific offered its land at a price below the market price, the more so as it did not sell land with particular properties on which it would have had a monopoly. In addition, it did give land users opportunities to ship with other carriers, if these offered lower rates. Only one explanation seems to be compatible with the facts, and it is a rather surprising one: Given that competitors are not allowed to exchange information about their practices directly among themselves in the United States, these tying provisions simply aimed at forcing the buyers to provide information on the rates (possibly secret rates) offered by competing railways.

Leaving aside the question of whether there was "tacit collusion" among railroad companies, I want to emphasize that sellers must be informed[5] about their competitors' prices, even if these sell at published or "list" prices. And they have to be informed about true *transaction* prices, since published prices are not necessarily adhered to, together with elements other than the nominal price, such as the quality of service, which also determine the true price. Furthermore, sellers must know how customers react to prices and services offered by competitors.

Northern Pacific's tying contracts provided precisely this sort of information, especially through the escape provisions that permitted buyers and lessees to ship on other carriers. Cummings and Ruhter (1979) note several particular features and circumstances. First, when buyers or lessees did *not* use Northern Pacific, the contract compelled them to disclose the lower rate or better service offered elsewhere. Second, Northern Pacific had grounds for legal action when buyers or lessees were uncooperative in *reporting*. And some contracts required them to keep records of production and shipments. Finally, Northern Pacific relied on the buyer's or lessee's judgment in determining whether a competing railway was offering a better price or better service, given the difficulty of determining the actual cost of a particular shipment between two specific points. In general, shippers indeed have better information on the market for their particular product and on the value of differing services than the carrier does. The tie-in can be rationalized as a device to reduce the cost of information.

But why a *tying* arrangement, if it is the escape clause that leads to the information one is after? Simply because buyers may view the gains from reporting competing offers as being not worth the trouble, especially where infrequent shipping (e.g., by truck or ships) is involved, or where transportation costs are small, or where regulation would prevent Northern Pacific from reacting rapidly and giving similar price reductions.

The *International Salt* case

In 1947, the U.S. Supreme Court[6] found a tying clause used by the International Salt Company illegal, primarily because it prevented other firms from directly supplying salt for use in a machine called a Lixator. International Salt owned patents on this machine, which dissolved rock salt into brine for use in a variety of industrial processes, only leased it, and required salt used in it to be purchased from International.

Again, the tie looks like a price discrimination device, the more so as more or less intensive uses of durables are involved. Yet, Peterman (1979) found good reasons to cast doubt on this metering explanation. Indeed, the Lixator leases contained a clause allowing lessees to buy salt on the open market whenever International failed to meet competitive prices for a competitive grade of salt. One possible explanation is, again, that the tie-in was meant to provide information on the extent of secret price cutting by competitors. Whether this explanation implies that there was a (secret) price agreement among salt producers is doubtful, in view of our discussion, in Chapter 3, of tacit collusion and imperfect information.

Commodity bundling

When no durable equipment is involved, offering a "commodity bundle" together with the individual commodities is the simplest way to solve the problem of having the customers themselves select the discriminatory price they want to pay.

Examples are very numerous indeed. Why do concert halls offer subscriptions to concert series while simultaneously permitting people to buy a ticket for a particular performance right on the spot, a couple of hours before the concert starts? Why do restaurants offer complete meals with several courses at a bargain price (the so-called menus in France) while simultaneously giving you the possibility of ordering your preferred dish (steak béarnaise, no doubt) at the "regular" price printed on the menu? Why did Coca-Cola put the huge "family" bottles on the market, at a "family" price, while simultaneously maintaining the much-higher-priced small bottles (anyone can compute the price per ounce to check that the small bottles are more expensive)? Why are the famous Belgian chocolate bars "Côte d'Or" also offered in a plastic bag with *three* bars in it?

Obviously, each of these examples implies that a quantity discount is given to those who consume more. There is thus an analogy, again, with block tariffs in which large consumers also get lower prices. On the other hand, there is an analogy with tie-ins, to the extent that the successive concerts, dishes, and so forth are tied together.

Block booking

Block booking is a type of tie-in that involves no metering, and its profitability crucially depends on the variation among the buyers of their valuation of the bundle being offered. It occurs frequently in the film industry, when only a combined assortment of movies (the "bundle") is offered by the film maker to an exhibitor. It was outlawed, in *United States* v. *Loew's, Inc.*[7]

In his amusing "Note on Block Booking," Stigler gives the following example:

> One film, Justice Goldberg cited *Gone with the Wind,* is worth $10,000 to the buyer, while a second film, the justice cited *Getting Gertie's Garter,* is worthless to him. The seller could sell the one for $10,000, and throw away the second, for no matter what it costs, bygones are forever bygones. Instead the seller compels the buyer to take both. But surely he can obtain no more than $10,000, since by hypothesis this is the value of both films to the buyer. Why not, in short, use his monopoly power directly on the desirable film? It seems no more sensible, on this logic, to block book the two films than it would to compel the exhibitor to buy *Gone with the Wind* and seven Ouija boards, again for $10,000.
>
> The explanation for the practice must lie elsewhere. The simplest plausible explanation is that some buyers would prize one film much more relative to the other. Consider the two buyers:
>
> *A* would pay $8,000 for film *X* and $2,500 for film *Y*.
> *B* would pay $7,000 for film *X* and $3,000 for film *Y*.
>
> If the seller were to price the two films separately, he would receive:
>
> 1. $5,000 for the sale of *Y*, at $2,500 per buyer. A higher price would exclude *A* and reduce receipts.
> 2. $14,000 for the sale of *X*, at $7,000 per buyer on the same logic.
>
> The total received is $19,000. But with block booking, a single price of $10,000 can be set for the pair of films, and $20,000 will be received.

> On this approach, block booking is a method of selling calculated to extract larger sums than otherwise would be possible. [1968, p. 165]

I might add that, for block booking to be profitable, the variation of the reservation prices for the bundle should not be too large. In Stigler's example, A was ready to pay \$10,500 for the bundle, which is rather close to the \$10,000 B would pay. Furthermore,[8] there should be an inverse relation, as in Stigler's example, between the value of the two films, so that film X is most valuable where film Y is valued less, and vice versa.

CHAPTER 10

Two-part tariffs and
quantity-dependent prices

First-degree price discrimination

First-degree price discrimination is often, understandably, called "perfect" discrimination. On the one hand, it is the most profitable form of discrimination, since it extracts the entire consumer surplus. On the other hand, it has optimality properties that the other forms of price discrimination do not have. Indeed, under perfect discrimination each buyer is able to buy the product he or she wants to buy. And for each unit bought, buyers pay the highest price they are ready to pay and thus entirely reveal the value the commodity has for them. The producer produces more than he or she would have otherwise and earns the highest possible profit. In short, if a firm has the possibility of discriminating, perfect discrimination is the best type of discrimination to use.

It is often said that perfect discrimination cannot be realized in real life situations. Pigou (1920) stressed the fact that the seller would have to discuss each price separately with each individual customer, for each unit sold. This would be an expensive and laborious sales procedure. Furthermore, these discussions (around a dinner table?) create opportunities for briberies that the seller's sales agents could hardly resist. Yet recent scandals in the aircraft industry, where buyers are few and one unit of the product costs a fortune, *do* seem to provide examples of perfect price discrimination. Explicit price discrimination that looks very much like first-degree discrimination has also been common practice among railroads. Under the euphemism of "value of service" pricing, it frequently goes as far as to discriminate between identical items of freight intended for different uses. (Individually bargained reductions in freight rates are the most frequently used technique.)

D. Friedman (1979) provides[1] a fascinating graphic illustration – reproduced in Figures 10.1 and 10.2 – of how perfect discrimination might work in an extreme and long-since-prohibited "long-haul/short-haul" discrimination case. It shows how to make sense of a practice of charging higher rates for carrying passengers (or freight) between two intermediate points on a line than for carrying the same people the full length of the line, including the intermediate section. (I have often heard people com-

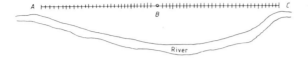

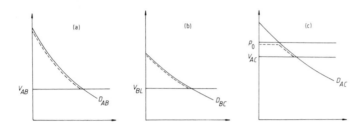

Figure 10.1. Shipping by rail and by water. (*Source:* D. D. Friedman 1979, p. 707.)

Figure 10.2. Long-haul/short-haul discrimination. The broken line indicates a discriminatory price schedule. See text. (*Source:* D. D. Friedman 1979, p. 707.)

plain [!?] that it is cheaper to fly from Brussels to New York than from Brussels to London.)

Suppose a railroad has a monopoly on the short haul but is competing with a perfectly competitive shipping industry on the long haul. It is running from point A to point C via B while ships carry goods between A and C along the river, as shown in Figure 10.1. The marginal cost of shipping is equal to average cost and to the price p_0. The railroad's cost structure consists of a sunk cost ($C_{AC}=C_{AB}+C_{BC}$) (the sum of costs from A to B and from B to C) plus a constant variable cost ($V_{AC}=V_{AB}+V_{BC}$). In Figure 10.2, D_{AB} is the demand for transport from A to B and similarly for D_{BC} and D_{AC}. (D_{AC} is *not* the sum of D_{AB} and D_{BC}.) The transport services provided by rail and by water are identical.

The best thing to do, for the railroad, is to charge discriminatory prices that exactly follow D_{AB} and D_{BC} down to the point where they cross V_{AB} and V_{BC}, for transport from A to B and from B to C, respectively. For transport from A to C, p_0 is a ceiling above which it cannot go, for otherwise customers will ship by water. But additional consumer surplus can be extracted by charging a schedule running down from p_0 to V_{AC}. If p_0 is lower than the intercept of either D_{AB} or D_{BC}, long-haul/short-haul discrimination occurs: For some passengers the price for the long haul is lower than for the short haul.

Following Coase (1946 and 1947), Friedman (1979) argues that this type of discriminatory pricing gives the railroad the correct incentives for deciding what rail lines to build and should therefore not have been prohibited. The return the railroad can expect, he says, is the area under the demand curves D_{AB} and D_{BC}, plus the area under D_{AC}, *given* the existence of water transport, that is, below p_0. And this return is precisely the social value of building and operating such a rail line (no producer surplus is lost if water transport is eliminated, given that it is perfectly competitive and uses factors that are available at constant cost). The railroad will build the line if and only if its social value covers the actual costs (fixed plus variable). The same is true for each segment *AB* and *BC* separately. The conclusion is: "If the railroad were forbidden to charge a higher price for the short haul than for the long, it would either have to give up some of the business it might have carried on the long haul, or fail to capture some of the consumer surplus it generates on the short haul; in either case its incentives would be distorted in such a way as to discourage the building of some desirable lines" (p. 708).

When direct first-degree price discrimination is impossible (e.g., because buyers are too numerous and the unit value of the product is low), the consumer surplus can often be extracted in an indirect way, using some rather simple practices such as two-part tariffs and block tariffs. Given that these practices are substitutes for first-degree price discrimination, we should not be surprised to discover that they share the latter's optimality properties (with the implication that the new electricity tariff structure in Belgium, e.g., with its *non*uniform character – the official terminology notwithstanding – may be preferred to a truly uniform price for electricity).

Two-part tariffs are likely to be feasible if the product cannot be resold at a reasonable cost among consumers. Most service industries meet this requirement. Two-part tariffs are easy to implement when a connection fee can be charged in addition to a price per unit consumed. Indeed, they imply that a lump sum fee must be paid for the right to buy a product. A two-part tariff is the simplest form of a "nonlinear" or quantity-dependent price. This chapter will therefore start with simple two-part tariffs, will then consider block tariffs, and will end with a discussion of nonlinear pricing in general.[2]

Discriminatory two-part tariffs

Consider the case of Disneyland: the product offered is typically a ride in the amusement park. Oi (1971) introduces his analysis of the case with the following remarks:

If you were the owner of Disneyland, should you charge high lump sum admission fees and give the rides away, or should you let people into the amusement park for nothing and stick them with high monopolistic prices for the rides? Received theories of monopoly pricing shed little light on this question. The standard model that appears in almost every text assumes that the monopolist sets a single price for his product. The third-degree price discrimination model due to A. C. Pigou still presumes that a single price prevails in each segregated market. Pricing policies that involve tying arrangements (like those examined by M. L. Burstein and W. S. Bowman, Jr.) and the multi-part tariffs of Pigou's first- and second-degree discrimination models come closer to the goal of maximizing the ill-gotten gains of monopoly power. The intricate pricing schemes reported in the antitrust literature are testimony to the fact that the imagination of the greedy entrepreneur outstrips the analytic ability of the economist. [1971, p. 77]

Suppose, then, that customers are asked to pay a lump sum entrance fee of T dollars for the right to buy rides at a uniform price p per ride. Such a two-part tariff introduces a discontinuity in the customer's budget equation:

$$qp + y = Y - T \quad \text{if} \quad q > 0$$
$$y = Y \quad \text{if} \quad q = 0 \tag{10.1}$$

where q is the number of rides and Y is income measured in terms of y, which serves as numeraire. The variable y represents all other goods and thus has a price equal to one.

Customers maximize their utility $u = u(q, y)$ subject to Equation (10.1). At equilibrium they therefore equate their marginal rate of substitution between q and y with the price p. Indeed, the fact that a person has entered Disneyland is supposed not to produce any utility as such. On the other hand, refusing to pay the entrance fee, with the implication that $q = 0$ and $y = Y$, is optimal only if the person's marginal rate of substitution is smaller than the price p. What the lump sum fee does is therefore to extract part of the consumer surplus from rides, thereby transferring incomes from consumers to Disneyland. T appears as a purchase privilege tax.

The customer's demand for rides is a function of p and of the difference $(Y - T)$, or

$$q = q(p, Y - T) \tag{10.2}$$

Indeed, an increase by the same amount of Y and T does not affect the budget constraint (please examine [10.1]). Hence

$$\frac{\partial q}{\partial Y} = -\frac{\partial q}{\partial T} \tag{10.3}$$

What is the profit-maximizing T? And the profit-maximizing p? To simplify matters, suppose first that there is only one customer (or that all customers are identical, so that they have the same utility functions and the same incomes). Total profits are

$$\Pi = qp + T - C(q) \tag{10.4}$$

$C(q)$ being the total cost function. Differentiation of Π with respect to T yields

$$\frac{\partial \Pi}{\partial T} = 1 - (p - C') \frac{\partial q}{\partial Y} = \frac{\partial y}{\partial Y} + C' \frac{\partial q}{\partial Y} \tag{10.5}$$

given that $p(\partial q/\partial Y) = 1 - (\partial y/\partial Y)$, according to Equation (10.1). Commodity y (all other goods!) cannot be an inferior good, so that $\partial y/\partial Y$ is positive. We decided to consider normal goods in this essay, so that q also has a positive income derivative. With C' positive as well, Equation (10.5) shows that an increase in the entrance fee increases profits; this is true as long as the customer is ready to pay an entrance fee. The highest possible entrance fee, say T^*, is therefore just equal to the consumer surplus enjoyed by the customers (in their consumption of q), when they consider specializing their purchases to good y because they would be better off not to enter Disneyland. In other words, T^* is the area between the price line at p (to be determined) and a demand curve $q = \psi(p)$ such that the customer would be better off to withdraw from the market for q. This area can be measured[3] by the integral over p, so that the derivative of T^* turns out to be $dT^*/dp = -q$. This result will be used to find the optimal uniform price p.

To find the optimal p, differentiate Π with respect to p, after replacing T by T^*, and replace dT^*/dp by $-q$. You will find that

$$\frac{\partial \Pi}{\partial p} = (p - C') \frac{\partial q}{\partial p} \tag{10.6}$$

so that, on equating this expression to zero, we have $p - C' = 0$. The price for a ride must be set equal to the marginal cost of a ride!

To sum up, the best way to make profits is to make them *at the entrance*, by charging a T^* equal to the customer's consumer surplus. Once inside the amusement park, the price should not be higher than the marginal cost of a ride. If this cost is constant (and therefore equal to average variable cost), no profits are made on the rides. There is no point in raising the price inside the park, since doing so would decrease the consumer surplus and therefore the entrance fee.

In the real world, customers are probably different. One then has to add up the individual (constant utility) demand curves $q_j = \psi_j(p)$ over all customers, to find the intersection of aggregate demand and marginal cost, which determines p. Given p, each consumer is then charged a T_j^* equal to his or her consumer surplus. This is first-degree price discrimination, but with a drastic simplification: Instead of discussing the price for each possible value of q, the problem is simplified to finding the single highest possible entrance fee each customer is ready to pay. In practice this will probably still be too difficult to implement, so that the owner of the park will have to determine a set of entrance fees by second-degree discrimination. Very often the owner will announce a "normal" entrance fee and then will give "special" reductions to children, elder people, military, small groups, large groups, and whatnot. An alternative way of obtaining the same result is to charge a "basic" lump sum (monthly or yearly) rental for the right to buy machine time from a computer or a copying machine, as much as q^* hours of machine time, but to add a volume surcharge for, say, each additional hour. In this way, the lessees are partitioned into subgroups, with a different entrance fee (rental charge) for each subgroup.

Although it is discriminatory, Oi's two-part tariff is Pareto-optimal. To see that this is so, remember that the marginal rate of substitution in consumption is equal to p and therefore to C'. But C' is the marginal rate of transformation (the ratio of the marginal costs of q and y) where the marginal cost of y is assumed equal to one. As always, this optimum is defined for a given distribution of income.[4] It is also defined for a given monopoly. If Disneyland ceased to be a monopoly – two amusement parks facing each other – other prices might be Pareto-optimal.

Uniform two-part tariffs

The optimality of the two-part tariffs may not be perceived by the legislator. Or other criteria, such as social justice, may be used. Whatever the reason, suppose the antitrust law prohibits unequal treatment of customers, so that Disneyland feels compelled to charge the same uniform entrance fee to all. What would the optimal T and p be under this constraint?

Suppose first that Disneyland is also obliged to fix its prices in such a way that all customers remain in the market, that is, that none is priced out of the market. In a spatial context, the analogous restriction is to suppose that the seller must serve the entire geographical market, as discussed in Chapter 2. Let there be two customers, with constant utility demands ψ_1 and ψ_2 as represented in Figure 10.3 (taken from Oi 1971).

When the price per ride is equal to marginal cost C' (supposed constant per ride), the surplus enjoyed by the first consumer is equal to the area of the triangle ABC'. The second consumer enjoys a surplus of $A'B'C'$. The highest entrance fee that can be charged is equal to ABC',

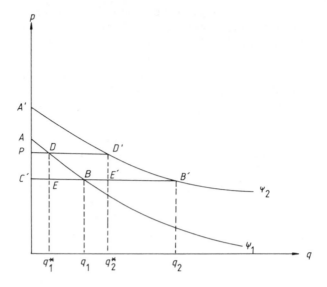

Figure 10.3. A uniform two-part tariff. (*Source:* Oi 1971, p. 82.)

for any higher T would eliminate the first consumer from the market. Total profit is then $2(ABC')$, since no profit is derived from the rides, the marginal cost of production being constant.

Is this the best Disneyland can do under the constraint of uniform treatment of all customers? Obviously not. It might be more profitable to *reduce* the uniform entrance fee and to raise p above marginal cost. Consider a raise of p to the level P, at which the first consumer demands q_1^* rides (instead of q_1) and is willing to pay an admission tax of no more than ADP. The profits extracted from this first consumer are reduced by DBE. The second consumer now pays the same reduced entrance fee of ADP and contributes an additional sum of $PD'E'C'$ (for q_2^* rides) to Disneyland's profits. Compared with ABC' (the consumer's contribution to profits when $p = C'$ and $T = ABC'$), there is an increase of $DD'E'B$. On balance, profits are increased if the area of the quadrangle $DD'E'B$ exceeds that of the triangle DBE, as is the case in Figure 10.3. And the optimal price p is the one that maximizes the difference in the areas of the quadrangle and triangle.[5]

It should be clear that Disneyland may have an interest in restricting the number of visitors, just as a spatial monopolist may find it profitable to reduce the geographical size of his market when obliged to sell at a uniform delivered price. A spatial monopolist would do this by refusing to sell above a certain distance from its plants. Disneyland can force the first consumer out of the market by raising the lump sum entrance tax

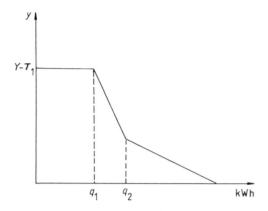

Figure 10.4. A block tariff.

above ABC' and charging $A'B'C'$ – thus extracting the second visitor's surplus. More generally, profits can be maximized with respect to the number of visitors, subject to the condition that they pay the same entrance fee. One finds that the optimal number of visitors is then such that

$$\frac{\partial \Pi_A}{\partial n} = \frac{\partial \Pi_B}{\partial n} \tag{10.7}$$

where $\Pi_A = nT$ is the profit due to the (uniform) entrance tax paid by the n visitors and $\Pi_B = (p - C')q$ is the profit made on the rides. In practice, this optimal number of visitors could be found by iteration, trying out successively higher entrance taxes and successively lower prices per ride.

Block tariffs and quantity discounts

We know that many public utilities use block tariffs, in which marginal prices go down as quantity consumed goes up. Tariffs for the domestic use of electricity typically take the following form:

> The first q_1 kWh or less cost the lump sum T_1 (when $q_1 = 0$, T_1 is the connection fee discussed in Chapter 9).
> From q_1 to q_2 kWh, the price is p_1 per kWh.
> More than q_2 kWh cost p_2 per kWh, where $p_2 < p_1$.

Taylor (1975) notices that this sort of tariff leads to a nonlinear budget constraint such as the one represented in Figure 10.4. The horizontal segment corresponds to $(Y - T_1)$ (see Equation [10.1]). The linear segment between q_1 and q_2 has a slope of $-p_1$. To the right of q_2, the slope is $-p_2$. Again, y (all other goods) is the numeraire.

A situation such as the one depicted in Figure 10.4 could be described as a *three*-part tariff, or as a series of two successive two-part tariffs.

The public has to pay a tax of T_1 for obtaining the privilege of purchasing a quantity above q_1. Those who want to consume more than q_2 pay a second tax $[T_2 = (q_2 - q_1)(p_1 - p_2)]$ for the right to purchase quantities above q_2 at the marginal price p_2. In this way (part of) the surplus of the big customers (the "rich") is extracted.[6]

Still another way of presenting the same block tariff is to say that big customers get a volume discount (or quantity discount) in the form of a lower marginal price ($p_2 < p_1$). Buchanan (1952–3) was the first to recognize that quantity discounts are surplus-extracting devices, whereas Oi (1971) emphasized their interpretation as two-part tariffs. Oi also distinguishes these quantity discounts, implying marginal price discounts, from "average price discounts," in which p_2 (smaller than p_1) applies to *all* units bought including the previous block of q_2 units, if demand is higher than q_2. Here the big consumer, who demands enough to get the lower price p_2, is rewarded by getting an implicit *rebate* of $(q_2 - q_1) \cdot (p_1 - p_2)$.

We are now well equipped to revisit the case of the Belgian tariff for residential electricity discussed in Chapter 9 and to evaluate the trade union's criticism of the block structure. First of all, I would stress the fact that *marginal* price discounts are involved, with the implication that it is the *big* customer, who consumes more than q_2, who pays the implicit entrance tax $(q_2 - q_1) \cdot (p_1 - p_2)$, not the small one. Second, this statement holds true for both the old pre-1977 block tariff and for the new "uniform" tariff, given that the new "normal" tariff is implicitly a two-block tariff plus a connection charge. Third, from the point of view of Pareto optimality, it is fortunate that the Belgian regulatory committee did not introduce a truly uniform price, given that the new "normal" tariff is also a two-part tariff. This last conclusion relates only to the structure of the tariffs involved, not to the numerical values of the prices charged, obviously. It will also emerge in our discussion of nonlinear prices in general, to which we now turn.

Nonlinear prices and welfare

I define "nonlinear prices" as prices that are quantity dependent.[7] Any tariff (or list of prices) according to which various quantities may be purchased from a seller at various *average* prices is therefore "nonlinear." Two-part tariffs, block tariffs, marginal quantity discounts, and – a fortiori – average quantity discounts are well-known cases of nonlinear prices. To illustrate, consider the outlay schedules (which relate the total "bill" and the corresponding quantities bought) reproduced in Figure 10.5.

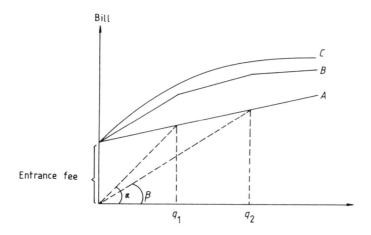

Figure 10.5. Nonlinear outlay schedules.

Schedule A results from the application of a two-part tariff. The intercept is the entrance fee (right-to-purchase tax), whereas the slope is equal to marginal cost (in turn equal to the uniform marginal price per ride). Although the marginal price is constant, the average price is not: At q_1, the average price is measured by α: at q_2, the average price is β. In fact, to *each* point on the schedule corresponds a different average price. For average price to be constant, that is, to have the usual uniform price, the outlay curve must be a straight line through the origin.

Schedule B results from the application of a three-part block tariff. As with schedule A, to *each* quantity (not only q_1 and q_2) corresponds a different average price. Schedule C represents the extreme case where an infinitely small quantity increase leads to a corresponding decrease in the marginal price.[8] Its only advantage is that it allows the use of calculus techniques: Both A and B are already "nonlinear" in the sense that any quantity increase implies a decrease in the average price. To study nonlinear pricing rules, one can thus use a discrete presentation, as in schedules A and B, or calculus methods on outlay schedules like C. In principle, both are equally valid. And conclusions that are valid for nonlinear prices in general[9] must also apply to special structures or practices such as two-part tariffs, block tariffs, and quantity discount schemes – and vice versa.

I shall first determine how a consumer makes his choice when confronted with a nonlinear price schedule, to derive possible constraints on the form of the schedule that a profit-maximizing seller will select.

Armed with this knowledge, we shall then proceed to an analysis of the welfare properties of nonlinear prices as compared with a uniform price.

Suppose $R_i(q)$ is the maximum amount a consumer of type i is ready to pay for q units of the commodity. (Instead of working with reservation prices for one unit of the commodity,[10] I am here using subjective "reservation outlays" for different *numbers of units*.) Let q_i be the number of units bought by the consumer of type i: Confronted with a nonlinear price schedule, the consumer must determine this number and must thereby choose a point on the schedule. To this point corresponds a "bill," or total outlay, of Y_i (a point on the corresponding nonlinear outlay schedule). What will make consumer i prefer the combination (q_i, Y_i) to all other options (q_j, Y_j), given that $i = 1, \ldots, n$ (there are n consumer types and n possible quantities) and $j \neq i$? The answer is very simple: The difference in outlay between quantity i and quantity j should not be larger than the difference between what the consumer was ready to pay for the two quantities. In other words, the increase in expenditure implied in buying a larger quantity should not exceed the difference in reservation outlays, or

$$R_i(q_i) - R_i(q_j) \geqslant Y_i - Y_j \qquad (10.8)$$

Consider now what this statement implies for a seller who wants to maximize profits. The highest surplus is extracted (and profit is maximum) if the seller can persuade the richest customers – who have the highest reservation outlays – to buy the largest quantities. This will be true if, indeed, higher incomes correspond to higher reservation outlays for the same number of units *and* if a higher income implies that an additional unit is worth more. Then we have

$$R_i(q) < R_{i+1}(q) \qquad \text{for all } q$$

and

$$R_i'(q) < R_{i+1}'(q) \qquad \text{for all } q$$

A curve representing $R_{i+1}(q)$ as a function of q would lie above a curve representing $R_i(q)$ *and* would have a steeper slope (so that the two could never cross). Obviously, to maximize profits under these conditions, a seller must simply (a) prevent groups with higher indexes from buying too little and (b) charge the highest possible price (outlay). Condition (a) is satisfied as long as Inequality (10.8) is satisfied. Condition (b) makes Inequality (10.8) binding, that is, implies charging prices such that

$$Y_i - Y_j = R_i(q_i) - R_i(q_j)$$

or Y_i just equal to

$$Y_i = R_i(q_i) - R_i(q_j) + Y_j$$

The profit-maximizing outlays are thus determined, given the quantities $(q_1, \ldots, q_n)$ and the reservation outlays. Indeed, starting with the lowest income class 1, such that $q_0 = 0$ and $R_i(0) = 0$ for all i, the entire profit-maximizing outlay schedule is determined as follows:

$$Y_1 = R_1(q_1)$$
$$Y_2 = R_2(q_2) - R_2(q_1) + Y_1$$
$$\vdots$$
$$Y_i = R_i(q_i) - R_i(q_{i-1}) + Y_{i-1}$$
$$\vdots$$
$$Y_n = R_n(q_n) - R_n(q_{n-1}) + Y_{n-1}$$

The entire schedule can be summarized as

$$Y_i = \sum_{j=1}^{i} [R_j(q_j) - R_j(q_{j-1})] \tag{10.9}$$

We may now ask which quantities q_i the seller will offer, given these outlays and which quantities the seller *should* offer from a welfare standpoint. Suppose there are N_i customers in each income class i. Then the social consumer surplus is

$$S = \sum_i N_i [R_i(q_i) - Y_i]$$

the sum of the individual surpluses. Notice that the poorest consumers have no surplus left, since $Y_1 = R_1(q_1)$ in Equation (10.9). For the next income group, there is a surplus of $R_2(q_2) - Y_2 = R_2(q_1) - Y_1$, namely the difference between the bill for quantity q_1 and what type 2 consumers would be ready to pay for it. Given our assumptions about the reservation outlays (a higher income implies a higher reservation outlay for the same quantity), the consumer surplus becomes bigger and bigger, the higher the income.

On the other hand, the profits of the seller are

$$\Pi = \sum_i N_i Y_i - C\left(\sum_i N_i q_i\right)$$

$C(q)$ being the cost function of the commodity. The problem of welfare maximization is then to find the quantities that, given Y_i, maximize $S + \Pi$, subject to the condition that profits are nonnegative. Alternatively, one could say that the problem is to maximize

$$W = \lambda S + \Pi$$

When $\lambda=1$, this is the so-called unconstrained welfare maximization problem, where real world imperfections are not taken into account. When $0<\lambda<1$, the maximization is constrained, and some appropriate λ (such that profit is nonnegative) must be chosen. When $\lambda=0$, we have profit maximization.

Before maximizing W, Spence (1980) writes it out in full:

$$W = \lambda \sum_i N_i[R_i(q_i) - Y_i] + \sum_i N_i Y_i - C\left(\sum_i N_i q_i\right)$$

$$= \lambda \sum_i N_i R_i(q_i) + (1-\lambda) \sum_i N_i Y_i - C\left(\sum_i N_i q_i\right) \quad (10.10)$$

Next Spence defines M_i:

$$M_i = \sum_{j=i}^{n} N_j \quad i = 1,\ldots,n$$

M_i thus measures the cumulative upper part (from i to n) of the distribution of types of consumers. Substituting for Y_i in Equation (10.10) using Equation (10.9), Spence rewrites W in terms of quantities alone as[11]

$$W = \sum_i [N_i + (1-\lambda)M_{i+1}]R_i(q_i) - (1-\lambda) \sum_{i=1}^{n-1} R_{i+1}(q_i)M_{i+1}$$

$$- C\left(\sum_i N_i q_i\right)$$

Everything is now ready for W to be maximized with respect to q_i. Differentiating and setting the result equal to zero, one gets

$$\frac{\partial R_i(q_i)}{\partial q_i} = \left[\frac{N_i}{N_i + (1-\lambda)M_{i+1}}\right] \cdot C'(q_i)$$

$$+ \left[\frac{(1-\lambda)M_{i+1}}{N_i + (1-\lambda)M_{i+1}}\right] \frac{\partial R_{i+1}(q_i)}{\partial q_i} \quad (10.11)$$

for $(i=1,\ldots,n)$. Notice that $M_{n+1}=0$ by convention and that $\lambda<1$, to take real world imperfections into account.

What is the quantity q_n that should be offered to the richest customers at a total outlay of Y_n? As $M_{n+1}=0$, Equation (10.11) reduces to

$$\frac{\partial R_n(q_n)}{\partial q_n} = C'$$

so that the highest value users should purchase the quantity they would select if the good were priced at marginal cost. All customer groups with lower incomes, however, should be offered quantities for which the implicit marginal price $\partial R_i(q_i)/\partial q_i$ is *above* marginal cost. Indeed, this marginal price is seen to be a weighted average of the marginal cost and the marginal value placed on the commodity by the *next* group, $\partial R_{i+1}(q_i)/\partial q_i$. (Again, in the abstract unconstrained case where $\lambda=1$, welfare maximization would imply that all income groups got quantities priced at marginal cost, since the second term in [10.11] would drop out for *all* income groups, whereas the first term would reduce to C'.)

What will a profit-maximizing seller do in this situation? When $\lambda=0$, the seller's profit-maximizing conditions reduce to

$$\frac{\partial R_i(q_i)}{\partial q_i} = \left[\frac{N_i}{N_i + M_{i+1}}\right] \cdot C'(q_i) + \left[\frac{M_{i+1}}{N_i + M_{i+1}}\right] \frac{\partial R_{i+1}(q_i)}{\partial q_i}$$

(10.12)

Compared with the welfare-maximizing conditions (10.11), these equations attach more weight to the second term: The marginal value for the *next* group in the income scale is relatively more important than marginal cost. To extract more profit, one must attach more importance to high-value users. The remarkable thing, though, is that a profit-maximizing seller will provide the optimal quantity to the richest customers. For $i = n$, the first-order condition is the same, whether $\lambda = 1$, $\lambda = 0$, or $0 < \lambda < 1$!

Pareto-superior nonlinear outlay schedules

As long as there is no constraint on profits ($\lambda=1$) – as long as profits can be negative – the best thing to do is to use a uniform average price (or linear outlay curve through the origin) equal to marginal cost. But as soon as profits have to be nonnegative ($\lambda<1$), we have just discovered, nonlinear prices are better. In a world in which private firms are maximizing profits, it makes little sense, therefore, to talk about marginal-cost pricing as the best thing to do. (The same is true for a world of public utilities that are not allowed to make losses.) Suppose, then, a uniform average price, unequal to marginal cost (e.g., because private firms are maximizing profits or because utilities avoid making losses). Could one argue that a nonlinear price schedule, such as a two-part tariff or a quantity discount scheme, is Pareto-superior? The answer is yes, with some qualifications.

One can analyze the effects of moving from a uniform price to a nonlinear price from two different points of view: with respect to *aggregate* welfare (measured by the total money equivalent of the price changes to all the consumers of the commodity) and with respect to the preferences of *each individual* agent (consumers and sellers). Leland and Meyer (1976), Littlechild (1975), and Ng and Weisser (1974) have shown that the

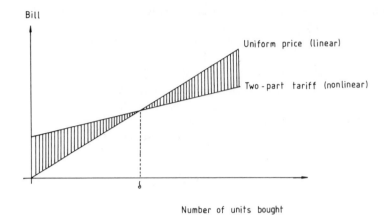

Bill

Uniform price (linear)

Two-part tariff (nonlinear)

Number of units bought

Figure 10.6. A linear outlay schedule versus a nonlinear outlay schedule.

move benefits consumers in the aggregate, with the gainers able to compensate (in principle) those who lose. Willig (1978) and Spence (1980) show that for any uniform price different from marginal cost, there is a change to a nonlinear outlay schedule that directly benefits all consumers through the market, without the need for transfers effected outside the market.

The argument from the aggregate point of view is easy to understand. Given a straight line through the origin (total outlay under uniform pricing), it is always possible to find another straight line with a positive intercept (total outlay under a two-part tariff) such that those customers who buy more than δ units (where the two outlay curves cross – see Figure 10.6) gain more than is lost by those who buy less than δ units. The area between the two curves to the right of δ can always be made larger than the area between the two to the left, by a suitable choice of the intercept (the entrance fee) and of the slope (the marginal price) of the two-part tariff. The same is true for a block tariff or quantity discount scheme, obviously.

The argument from the individual point of view is less obvious and perhaps more important. Remember, first, that the aggregate consumer surplus criterion just used gives an equal weight to an extra dollar no matter who spends it. It is therefore supposed that the distribution of income is optimal – that is, that an extra dollar has the same marginal social utility for smaller as for bigger consumers. That statement may, in fact, not be true: It may be desirable to weigh smaller consumers' surpluses more heavily. If so, one may object to the move from a linear to a nonlinear price schedule, given that it is precisely the poorer households

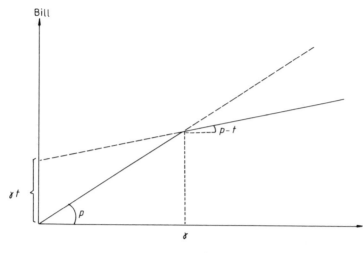

Number of units bought

Figure 10.7. Option between a uniform price and a two-part tariff.

(those at the left of δ) that lose and the rich households that gain. To avoid these skewed and possibly undesirable income distributional effects, one can offer individual consumers a choice between a uniform price and a two-part rate. The surprising fact, discovered by Willig (1978), is that is is always possible, given a uniform price above marginal cost, to find a combination of a uniform price and a two-part rate such that all consumers will be better off *and* the seller's profit is increased. Even more remarkable, perhaps, is the historical fact that the Belgian regulatory commission for electricity and gas realized this combination in 1977 in practice, when it implemented its new tariff structure – which implies precisely a choice[12] between a uniform price (the "social" tariff where the connection fee is negligible) and a two-part tariff (the "normal" tariff).

Consider first the case where, given a uniform price p, customers also have the option of paying a fixed charge $T_1 = \gamma t$ for the right to buy at the lower price $(p-t)$. The linear outlay curve pq intersects the nonlinear curve $\gamma t + (p-t)q$ where $\gamma t = qt$ or $q = \gamma$. For small t, consumers select the uniform price when their demands are smaller than γ, and the two-part rate when their demands are larger than γ. The situation is depicted in Figure 10.7. (In Belgium, γ is fixed at 570 kWh, and $t = 4.810 - 2.752 = 2.058$.) The solid lower envelope Pareto-dominates the straight line through the origi... It is the equivalent of a two-block tariff. Consumers with demand above γ are better off. And so is the seller, whose profit is

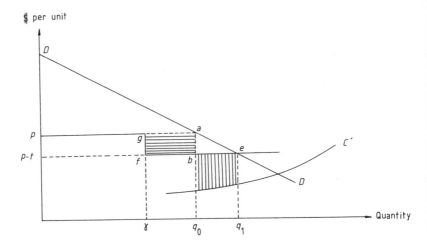

Figure 10.8. Pareto-superior nonlinear price.

larger (since the seller is in fact using a block tariff). However, those with demands smaller than γ are unaffected by the shift from p to the option between p and the two-part rate.

It might be illuminating to illustrate this point further by considering the consequences of the option when only one consumer uses it – that is, when only one consumer benefits from the lower price $(p-t)$. Figure 10.8, also taken from Willig (1978), represents this consumer's demand curve DD, the uniform price for purchases smaller than γ, and the lower price $(p-t)$ valid for units purchased additional to γ. In response to the shift to $(p-t)$, the consumer expands his or her purchases from q_0 to q_1. The resulting net welfare gain, in money units, is the area $gaef$. The change in the seller's profit is the profit on the newly purchased units, the vertically shaded area, minus the loss in revenues from the first q_0 units sold to this consumer, the horizontally shaded area. The vertically shaded area is positive as long as t is smaller than $(p-C')$. An increase in γ reduces the horizontally shaded area. With t small enough and γ large enough it must be that both the seller and the larger consumers are happier with the nonlinear outlay schedule than they are with the uniform price $p > C'$.

To construct a Pareto-dominating outlay schedule such that all consumers benefit, one needs only feed back some of the gain in vendor profit by means of a decrease in p. Given that the Belgian electric utilities were very profitable, it is likely that the "social" tariff was Pareto-dominated by a price p lower than 2.752 BF when it was initiated. Yet it is also clear that giving a choice between a "social" and a two-part "normal" tariff - with the implied block-tariff structure - was a better thing to do than to impose a single uniform price on all electricity users.

Vertical production relationships and competition

For the Willig (1978) argument to work, it is necessary that a lowering of the marginal price offered leads to larger total sales. (Similarly, freight absorption increases profits through an enlargement of the spatial market area.) For this result to follow, it suffices that buyers have downward-sloping demand curves - if buyers are final customers. However, this condition is no longer sufficient if buyers are themselves firms (manufacturing businesses or distributors) who use the good under consideration as an input. When such vertical production relationships exist, it may be impossible to construct any nonlinear price schedule which is Pareto-superior to a (profit-maximizing) uniform price.

Ordover and Panzar (1980 and 1981) have analyzed the case where total sales (here intermediate demand) cannot be expanded because they are determined by total sales in the final product market. If this market is competitive, the final price will be determined by the minimum point of the average cost curve of the small, less efficient firms. There is no reason, then, for the seller of the input to offer quantity discounts: Offering discounts to the more efficient larger firms will expand their sales and will *therefore* reduce the market share of (and sales to) the less efficient firms. Indeed, total final sales remain unchanged, since the cost of the inefficient firms and therefore the final price remains unchanged. Offering the discount to larger firms therefore merely converts some high-price sales into low-price sales, resulting in lower profits. Lowering the (uniform) price facing small firms would, of course, expand total final output but would also lower profits (since the uniform price Willig refers to is already profit maximizing).

CHAPTER 11

Multiproduct pricing

Nonlinear prices were discussed above on the assumption that one product was offered for sale. We can now consider some more complicated cases in which several products are offered together by the same seller with the purpose of extracting more consumer surplus. Some particular practices such as commodity bundling, tie-ins, block booking, and packaging are analyzed.[1] We shall maintain the assumption that reselling implies a prohibitive cost.

Commodity bundling

The examples given in Chapter 10 suggest that firms often sell their goods in packages. The practice of package selling is referred to in Adams and Yellen's (1976) seminal article as "commodity bundling." Why is it such a prevalent marketing strategy? One could focus on cost savings in production, transactions and information, as Coase (1960) and Demsetz (1968) do, or dwell on the complementarity in consumption of bundle components. Adams and Yellen instead demonstrate[2] that commodity bundling can be profitable because of its ability to sort customers into groups with different reservation price characteristics and hence to extract consumer surplus. This is particularly the case when reservation prices of specific customers are unknown and/or when overtly discriminatory practices such as first-degree discrimination or quantity discounts are illegal.

To clarify the analysis, consider three types of marketing strategies:

1. *simple monopoly pricing,* which is to set, on each commodity separately, the single price $(p_1, p_2, \ldots)$ that yields the greatest profits;
2. *pure bundling strategy,* in which only a package (composed of one unit of each commodity) is offered for sale at the price p_B chosen so as to maximize profits;
3. *mixed bundling strategy,* in which strategies 1 and 2 are combined by offering each commodity separately and also a package of both at a set of prices $(p_1, p_2, \ldots, p_B)$ that maximizes overall profits.

Suppose, then, that a firm sells only two products. The marginal cost of producing each is invariant with respect to output, and the marginal cost of supplying the two products in a bundle is equal to the sum of the

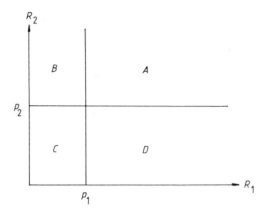

Figure 11.1. Simple monopoly pricing.

two component costs ($C'_B = C'_1 + C'_2$). There are no fixed costs. The reservation price for a bundle comprised of one unit of each commodity (R_B) is equal to the sum of their separate reservation prices ($R_B = R_1 + R_2$). Each customer buys at most one unit of either good. These assumptions exclude both economies in the bundling process and complementarity in consumption so that, if bundling is found to be profitable, it cannot be explained by these phenomena. Notice also that since the value of a bundle is no greater than the value of its components, mixed bundling is a distinct strategy only if the package is sold at a discount relative to its components. (When the two goods are identical, commodity bundling is then simply a form of quantity discount.) The firm knows the distribution of reservation prices in the population. The following three cases occur.

If simple monopoly prices p_1 and p_2 are set for each commodity separately, then the market is segmented into four groups, as represented in Figure 11.1. The A customers, with reservation prices $R_i \geqslant p_i$ ($i = 1, 2$), buy both products. The B and D customers, who have reservation prices larger than or equal to the prices of one of the two products, buy products 2 and 1, respectively. The C group does not buy any product, as their $R_i < p_i$ ($i = 1, 2$). With pure bundling, however, the market is segmented into two groups only. In Figure 11.2, group E has a reservation price larger than or equal to the price of the bundle. The rest of the market has a reservation price for the bundle that is smaller than p_B, and it does not purchase the bundle. The bundle price appears as a straight line with both intercepts equal to p_B and hence with a slope of minus one. Third, consider a mixed bundling strategy. Now the market is again segmented into four parts, but these are different from the four groups

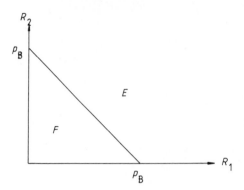

Figure 11.2. Pure bundling strategy.

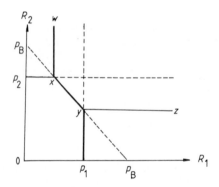

Figure 11.3. Mixed bundling strategy.

obtained with simple monopoly pricing (although the distribution of the reservation prices is unchanged). Figure 11.3 represents these four groups and is drawn on the assumption – just discussed – that $p_B < (p_1 + p_2)$ and that these three prices together maximize overall profits.

The customers located in area $0p_2 xyp_1$ (not including the boundaries) purchase nothing: They have $R_1 < p_1$, $R_2 < p_2$, and $R_B < p_B$. Those located in the triangle $p_1 yp_B$ have $R_1 \geqslant p_1$, $R_2 < p_2$ and $R_B < p_B$, so that they purchase product 1. What about those in the triangle $p_B yz$? They can certainly buy product 1. But they could also buy the bundle, as $R_1 + R_2 = R_B \geqslant p_B$. In fact, they will prefer to buy product 1, since they derive more surplus from it $(R_1 - p_1)$ then from purchase of the bundle $(R_1 + R_2 - p_B)$. Indeed, $R_1 - p_1 > R_1 + R_2 - p_B$, or $R_2 < p_B - p_1$ inside the area $p_B yz$, since along the segment yz we have $R_2 = p_1 y = p_1 p_B = p_B - p_1$. Putting the two triangles together, we conclude that all customers in area $p_1 yz$ consume only good 1. By a similar reasoning, all those located in area $p_2 xw$ consume only good 2. Finally, the fourth group in $wxyz$ (including the boundary) consumes the bundle, since $R_1 + R_2 \geqslant p_B$, *and* furthermore $R_2 \geqslant p_B - p_1$ and $R_1 \geqslant p_B - p_2$: They not only derive positive surplus from the bundle but also *more* surplus from it than from any of the two products separately.

Compare the four groups in Figure 11.3 with those in Figure 11.1. The C area is reduced: Part of these customers, who bought nothing under simple monopoly pricing, now buy the bundle. The same is true for the B and D areas. Part of those who bought only one product under simple monopoly pricing buy both under mixed bundling. Those in area A, who bought the two products under simple monopoly pricing, continue to purchase both, but at a discount. The final result is that production of both products is increased. The same conclusion is reached when Figures 11.3 and 11.2 are compared. With a given distribution of reservation prices, mixed bundling leads to higher sales than does pure bundling or simple monopoly pricing.

Mixed bundling can also give the highest profits. In fact, the relative profitability of the three strategies depends on the distribution of consumers in reservation price space and the structure of costs. The following numerical example, based on the assumptions made, shows how mixed bundling can succeed in giving the same profit as perfect price discrimination.

Suppose a firm has four customers A, B, C, and D. They have the same reservation price $R_B = 100$ for the bundle. Their reservation prices for the separate products are as follows:

for individual A, $R_1 = 10$, and $R_2 = 90$;
for individual B, $R_1 = 45$, and $B_2 = 55$;
for individual C, $R_1 = 60$, and $R_2 = 40$;
for individual D, $R_1 = 90$, and $R_2 = 10$.

The marginal costs of production are $C_1' = 20$ and $C_2' = 30$. These assumptions are reproduced in Figure 11.4.

Under simple monopoly pricing, profits are maximized[3] (and equal 140) when $p_1 = 60$ and $p_2 = 90$. These two prices are higher than the corresponding marginal costs. However, customer D derives a surplus of $90 - 60 = 30$, whereas customers A and B are excluded from the market for product 1. Furthermore, B, C, and D do not have the possibility of buying product 2. This situation is far from being optimal. Under perfect price discrimination, the four customers would have had the possibility of buying at least one product, and none of them would have kept any surplus.

If the firm moves to a pure bundling strategy, it will offer the bundle at the price $p_B = 100$. Each of the four customers will buy one bundle and the profits will be $100 \times 4 - [(20 + 30) \times 4] = 200$. We are coming closer to perfect price discrimination, since all customers can now buy the

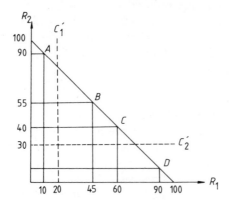

Figure 11.4. An example of profitable mixed bundling.

desired products and nobody keeps a surplus. There is one difference, though: Although A and D have a reservation price for a particular product that is below its marginal cost, they can nevertheless buy these products. Such a possibility would not have existed under simple perfect price discrimination. (It is clear that these possibilities are the more frequent the higher are marginal costs.)

The mixed bundling strategy is even more profitable in this example. Now the firm has four categories into which to sort its clients. It can sell product 1 at $p_1 = 90$ to D, product 2 at price $p_2 = 90$ to customer A, and the bundle at $p_B = 100$ to customers B and C. Profit climbs to 230; $(90 - 20) + (90 - 30) + [(100 - 50) \times 2] = 70 + 60 + 100 = 230$. No customer keeps any surplus. In addition, A and D cannot buy the product for which their reservation price is below the marginal cost of production.

In general, mixed bundling turns out to be the most profitable strategy to follow when certain customers have reservation prices that are below marginal cost for a particular product. One should not infer from the example, though, that all customers with this characteristic will be excluded from the market of the relevant product. A compromise is often necessary: The most profitable strategy may be to exclude only *some* clients[4] (to minimize the surplus left to the nonexcluded).

This reasoning suggests that the variance of the reservation prices, inside the market segments, is important. You will have noticed that, in this example, B and C (who are the bundle-buying group) were given rather similar (high) reservation prices for individual products. It turns out that mixed bundling is in general more profitable than pure bundling or simple monopoly pricing when those who have high reservation prices for the bundle evaluate the individual products in a similar way. Then the firm does indeed use the bundle to extract the surplus of those who appreciate it most and the separate products to extract the surplus of those who appreciate only one of the separate products.

We are now in a position to understand why restaurants simultaneously offer complete dinners as well as an à la carte menu. The reader has no doubt often verified that exactly the same dish costs more when ordered separately than when included in a complete dinner. There are no economies of scale in preparing several dishes in the preset order of the complete dinner rather than according to the personal choices of a diner who orders à la carte. Adams and Yellen correctly argue:

> Some people value an appetizer relatively highly (soup on a cold day), others may value dessert relatively higher (Baked Alaska, unavailable at home), but all may wish to pay roughly the same amount for a complete dinner. The à la carte menu is designed to capture consumer surplus from those gastronomes with extremely high valuations of particular dishes, while the complete dinner is designed to retain those with lower variance (1976, p. 488).

Similarly, we see why Coca-Cola launched large "family" bottles in addition to the usual small bottles. To understand why this is a case of mixed bundling, it is necessary to interpret the large bottle as a bundle containing the equivalent of, say, two ordinary bottles. In addition, one should interpret the first separate product as corresponding to the consumption of one ordinary bottle, whereas the product whose reservation prices are measured on the other axis is the consumption of a second bottle, *given* that the customer has emptied the first one. Although there is discrimination in favor of the large families (a family bottle costs less than two ordinary ones), the purpose of it is to capture their consumer surplus, since they have almost equal valuations of successive units (each of the children badly wants a Coke) and therefore have more elastic demands, while appreciating the bundle most. The small bottles are there to capture the surplus from those individuals with high reservation prices for the first bottle and low reservation prices for the second bottle, who therefore have less elastic demands.

Adams and Yellen's model also provides a plausible explanation of how price discrimination can occur under horizontal product differentiation, namely when a firm sells different varieties of the same commodity. I shall return to this question in Essay IV, devoted to quality differences.

Commodity bundling and welfare

In the absence of product differentiation (as in the Coca-Cola case, where the two products are identical, or in the restaurant case, where the two products are complementary and different, not two varieties of the

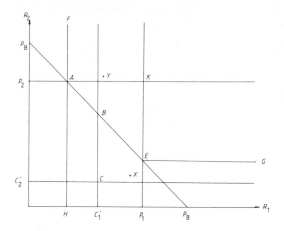

Figure 11.5. Commodity bundling and welfare.

same commodity), commodity bundling is not Pareto-optimal. Yet, it should Pareto-dominate simple monopoly pricing, given that it is, after all, a form of nonlinear pricing, so that the conclusions of the preceding chapter should apply. Pareto optimality requires equality of marginal rates of substitution among consumers, so that no mutual gains from trade are possible. It also requires equality of marginal rates of substitution and marginal rates of transformation, with the implication that output of each commodity should be just sufficient to supply all consumers with reservation prices at least equal to the marginal cost of that commodity.

Adams and Yellen show that neither of these conditions is satisfied – as can be seen from Figure 11.5, which is analogous to Figure 11.3 except that marginal costs of production are added. The reader should have no difficulty in identifying the four market segments. Compare individuals X and Y. Mr. X cannot buy good 1, yet he values it more than Mr. Y, who can buy it (through the purchase of the bundle). Thus, mutual gains from trade of product 1 between X and Y are possible. (Mr. Y cannot resell product 1, since by assumption we still suppose reselling is impossible. In the Coca-Cola case, this assumption is not entirely valid. When you order a Coke in a bar, a clever barman will serve you a glass from a family bottle.) The reader should have no difficulty in pinpointing individuals in Figure 11.5 for whom gains from trade in product 2 are possible.

On the other hand, all customers located east of C_1' should consume product 1. Under mixed bundling, those located northeast of $FAEp_1$ consume product 1. In general, the two areas are not equal. As Figure 11.5 is drawn, product 1 is undersupplied, since the area north of the segment *AB* is smaller than the area south of the segment *BE*. But the reverse may be true. The same logic applies to product 2.

Compared with simple monopoly pricing, though, commodity bundling is doing better. We already saw that production is larger: The area *AEK* includes those who are given access to the market, as a result of commodity bundling. In addition, the area north of segment *AK* is added to the production of product 1 and the area east of segment *KE* is added to the production of product 2. In all three areas, the consumers derive additional consumer surplus.

Tie-in sales

With mixed commodity bundling, the customer has a choice between buying the bundle or buying its components separately. We now consider cases of pure bundling where the customer is offered the bundle only, namely the so-called tie-in sales.[5] Pure bundling may be more profitable than mixed bundling, when reservation prices for particular components are relatively uniform among customers.[6] This may be expected to be the case for the components (ink and paper) needed to photocopy an article or for the punch cards needed to feed data into a computer.

In a tie-in sale, sellers of product 1 require their customers to make all of their purchases of one or more complementary products from them. Any buyer who wants product 1 must also buy product 2, say, from the same seller, who is thus offering a composite good. Buyers are of course free to buy as many units of product 2 as they want, so that the proportions of products 1 and 2 can vary from customer to customer. (For price discrimination to occur, the last condition is indeed essential.)

Suppose that customer i combines these two products in the nonnegative proportions a_{i1} and a_{i2} and that types of consumers differ with respect to the magnitude of these proportions. The price of the composite good is therefore, for consumer i,

$$p_B^i = a_{i1}p_1 + a_{i2}p_2 \tag{11.1}$$

where p_1 and p_2 are the prices of products 1 and 2. Suppose the demand for the composite good is linear:

$$q_B^i = b_{0i} - b_{1i}p_B^i \tag{11.2}$$

when $b_{0i} > 0$ and $b_{1i} > 0$. Suppose finally that the marginal cost of producing q_j [where $(j = 1, 2)$ indicates the products] is the constant c_j, so that tie-ins have no cost advantages for the producer, and that there are no fixed costs. Under these assumptions,[7] Telser (1979) is able to show that tie-in sales of q_B^i can be more profitable than separate sales of q_j

when the slopes b_{1i} of the demands for the composite good (q_B^i) differ –
on the condition, though, that the composite good be sold separately to
each type of customer at a special price p_B^i. (Without tie-ins the components would be sold separately at a price p_j, common to all consumers
of product j.)

Reverting to the example of IBM's requiring its customers to purchase
all of their tabulating cards (see Chapter 9) from itself, p_1 is the unit
rental of the tabulating machine, and p_2 is the price per card, so that a_{i2}
is simply the number of cards used by consumer i per unit of time,
whereas $a_{i1} = 1$. The effective price paid for the combined good (tabulating equipment) is $p_B^i = p_1 + a_{i2} p_2$, the rental price of the machine plus
the cost of the cards. The latter cost depends upon the number of cards
used, which reveals the intensity of consumer i's demands for *tabulating
equipment*. By fixing the number of cards used, each customer thus fixes
the special price p_B^i that customer must pay for the package offered by
IBM. This enables IBM to extract more surplus from each customer than
if it had not tied the purchase of cards to the rental of the equipment. An
alternative discrimination device would have been to charge different
rentals (or purchase prices) to each customer, without tying the purchase
of cards. The fact that IBM did not do so suggests that it did not have the
information necessary to discriminate in rental rates. The missing information is provided precisely by the trick of letting each customer choose
his or her own price – by fixing a_{i2}.

Needless to say, IBM's policy was very analogous – as already noted in
earlier chapters – to the device of presenting a block tariff and letting the
customer decide which block he or she wants to be in. Notice also that p_B^i
is a two-part tariff, with p_1 the entrance fee and $a_{i2} p_2$ the variable part.
Here price differences result only from $a_{i2} p_2$, the entrance fee being the
same for all customers. Conversely, it should be clear that Xerox's policy
of making its machines available only for lease (not for sale) and pricing
these machines on a per copy basis – charging p_1 (= \$25) per unit of time
plus p_2 (= \$0.035) *per copy* per unit of time – is equivalent to a tie-in sale
of a copying machine and the paper required to use it.

We should not conclude, though, that the use of a two-part leasing
arrangement (or a variable rental rate contract) is per se evidence that
price discrimination is being practiced. When the amount of services (of
a durable) used by a particular user is the same as the user's durable good
possession time, a simple time fee will do: This is the case for taxicabs.
But when there is a lack of correspondence between possession time and
economic use, then the pricing of a unit of the former cannot serve as a
proxy metering price for the latter, and a two-part leasing arrangement is
in order. This is the argument developed by Hansen and Roberts (1980),
who insist on the fact that durability is not taken into account in the

two-part tariff literature. To conclude that price discrimination is present, it does not suffice, therefore, to show that different customers pay different (per period) prices for the durable. We must also show that these differences do not correspond to differences in the costs of serving each particular use (remember our definition of price discrimination!) In the case of a copying or tabulating machine, where the costs of usage are negligible, the discriminatory nature of two-part leasing arrangements should be easy to establish.

Tying and vertical integration

The advantages of commodity bundling as a surplus extracting device could induce firms that happen to produce components of a bundle independently to merge. This is the point made recently by Paroush and Peles (1981). It parallels analogous remarks made above about vertical integration into the transportation sector or the distribution sector, to reap the benefits of freight absorption or of sticky prices.

What about tying arrangements? Here the situation is different and quite opposite. Rather than providing a motivation for merging the producers or transformers of the tied commodities, tying appears as an alternative to vertical integration when the commodities are inputs to a downstream industry. Imagine – with Blair and Kaserman (1978) – that $p(q)$ is the final-product inverse demand, and $q(x_1, x_2)$ is the final-product production function, assumed linearly homogeneous in inputs x_1 and x_2, and c_i is the constant marginal cost of input x_i, $i = 1, 2$. The production of x_1 is monopolized, whereas the markets for x_2 *and q* are competitive.

If $q(x_1, x_2)$ admits variable proportions, the monopolist producing x_1 cannot reap the full monopoly rents available in the final-product market. Indeed, the derived demand for x_1 will reflect both final consumer and downstream producer substitution. The production substitution can be circumvented through forward integration.[8] If such integration results in successful monopolization of the market for q, then the profit function for the integrated monopolist is

$$\Pi_I = p(q) \cdot q - c_1 x_1 - c_2 x_2 \tag{11.3}$$

with x_1 priced internally at marginal cost.

Alternatively, the producer of x_1 can purchase x_2 at the competitive price c_2 and can tie its purchase by competitive downstream producers to the purchase of x_1. Then the producer's profit function is

$$\Pi_T = p_1(x_1, x_2) \cdot x_1 + p_2(x_1, x_2) \cdot x_2 - c_1 x_1 - c_2 x_2 \tag{11.4}$$

where p_i is the price for the ith input to the downstream producers.

Blair and Kaserman show that vertical integration and tying are economically equivalent under these conditions, first, because they yield identical profits (to the input monopolist), and second, because inputs x_1 and x_2 will be employed in efficient proportions in both cases.

The first proposition results from the fact that, comparing Equations (11.3) and (11.4) and canceling input costs,

$$p(q)q = p_1(x_1,x_2) \cdot x_1 + p_2(x_1,x_2) \cdot x_2 \qquad (11.5)$$

Indeed, the competitive downstream producers accept p_1, p_2, and p as given, so that they equalize the value of the marginal product of each input to its price, or

$$p(q) \cdot \frac{\partial q}{\partial x_i} = p_i(x_1,x_2) \qquad (11.6)$$

As a result,

$$p(q) \cdot q = p(q) \cdot \left(\frac{\partial q}{\partial x_1} x_1 + \frac{\partial q}{\partial x_2} x_2 \right) \qquad (11.7)$$

However, Euler's theorem for linear homogeneous functions implies that $q = x_1(\partial q/\partial x_1) + x_2(\partial q/\partial x_2)$. The proof of the second proposition uses Euler's theorem to show that the marginal rate of transformation of the two inputs is equal to the ratio of their marginal costs, both under a tying arrangement and with vertical integration.

The private effects (profits) and the social effects (efficient use of inputs) being the same, a firm holding monopoly power over an input (for which substitutes exist) must choose between tying and vertical integration on the basis of factors that lie outside the simple model outlined above. Those factors include characteristics of the intermediate products (how many inputs have to be tied to ensure efficient downstream production?), potential cost savings due to vertical integration,[9] and antitrust policy.

The *Northern Pacific, International Salt,* and *Loew's, Inc.* cases mentioned in Chapter 9 indicate that a tying arrangement has a good chance of being found illegal per se under section 1 of the Sherman Act. Quite to the contrary, vertical integration will be challenged only if concentration at the downstream stage approaches the monopoly level, and then the case would be subject only to a rule-of-reason treatment. This asymmetric treatment of basically symmetric cases is hard to defend on theoretical grounds.

CHAPTER 12

Imperfect information

In a sense, all discriminatory devices discussed in this essay result from the circumstance that sellers are imperfectly informed about the different demands they are facing. When space or time separated their markets, they could use third-degree discrimination. Here, segmentation is based on income differences. But incomes differ from person to person and are in general difficult to ascertain.

Hence the use of two-part tariffs, where different entrance fees roughly separate income classes; or the more refined use of block tariffs, quantity discounts, or commodity bundling as self-selection devices, to lead the buyer to *reveal* his or her reservation prices; or again, the clever use of tie-ins, to make the buyer reveal his or her demand for durable equipment through the intensity of its use.

In this chapter, I shall explore the economics of imperfect information in more detail and shall try to show how specific properties, due to lack of information, can lead to price discrimination (or, inversely, how price discrimination might be used to obtain better information).

Consumer search

Until now, problems of information arose on the supply side only. It is high time to consider the demand side and to see how buyers react to lack of information about prices (leaving their reactions to quality uncertainty for a later chapter).

The seminal paper on consumer search is Stigler's (1961) "The Economics of Information." Stigler starts by emphasizing the fact that price dispersion is ubiquitous even for homogeneous goods,[1] and comments on it as follows:

> Price dispersion is a manifestation – and, indeed, it is the measure – of ignorance in the market. Dispersion is a biased measure of ignorance because there is never absolute homogeneity in the commodity if we include the terms of sale within the concept of the commodity. Thus, some automobile dealers might perform more service, or carry a larger range of varieties in stock, and a portion of the observed dispersion is presumably attributable to such differences. But it would be metaphysical, and fruitless, to assert that all dispersion is due to heterogeneity. [1961, p. 214]

Suppose then, for the sake of clarity, that the consumer faces a distribution of prices for the same good on a local market and tries to find the retail outlet that charges the lowest price. Suppose, further, that the consumer knows the distribution of prices but has no means of knowing, without searching, which outlet charges the lowest price. The problem then is to determine how long he or she will search before buying, that is, how many sellers he or she will canvass, given that search has a cost in time and forgone earnings and that, after some point, a continued search may be more costly than the gain that is to be expected from it.

Stigler models this search (visit to another retail outlet) as a drawing from a particular random distribution (a normal and a uniform distribution, in fact) and argues that consumers will visit a fixed number, n, of stores and will then buy from the store with the lowest price. To determine this number of searches, n, one does not have to specify a particular distribution. All one has to do is to suppose that there is a known (continuous) distribution function, $F(m)$, giving the probability that the price observed at the ith search is below some minimum, m, or

$$\text{prob}(p_i \leqslant m) = F(m) \tag{12.1}$$

After n searches, we have[2]

$$\text{prob}[\min(p_1, p_2, \ldots, p_n) \leqslant m] = 1 - \text{prob}(p_i \geqslant m, \text{ all } i)$$

or, since we suppose independent random drawings,

$$\text{prob}[\min(p_1, p_2, \ldots, p_n) \leqslant m] = 1 - \prod_i \text{prob}(p_i \geqslant m)$$

However, $\text{prob}(p_i \geqslant m) = 1 - F(m)$, so that, finally,

$$\text{prob}[\min(p_1, p_2, \ldots, p_n) \leqslant m] = 1 - [1 - F(m)]^n \tag{12.2}$$

This is the distribution function of the minimum price after n searches. We can then find the expected price the consumer pays by taking the expected value[3] of that minimum price, after n searches, that is,

$$E(m) = \int_0^\infty [1 - F(x)]^n \, dx \tag{12.3}$$

Clearly the expected minimum price decreases as n increases, since $[1 - F(x)]$ is always between zero and one.

What is the expected gain, g_n, say, of searching one more time (given that n searches have been completed)? We have

$$g_n = \int_0^\infty [1 - F(x)]^n \, dx - \int_0^\infty [1 - F(x)]^{n+1} \, dx$$

that is, the difference between two successive expected minimum prices, or

$$g_n = \int_0^\infty \left\{ [1 - F(x)]^n - [1 - F(x)]^{n+1} \right\} dx$$

$$= \int_0^\infty [1 - F(x)]^n \{1 - [1 - F(x)]\} dx$$

$$= \int_0^\infty [1 - F(x)]^n F(x) \, dx \qquad (12.4)$$

which is again a decreasing function of n. Searching longer is less and less productive. With a positive (and possibly increasing) cost of search, the consumer will have an equilibrium point at some positive value of n, possibly zero. This point is such that the expected gain is equal to the cost of search. Note that, in this formulation, the gain is simply the expected reduction in price. This situation could be made more realistic by making g_n the expected rise in utility as a consequence of the reduction in price, which would allow for the fact that consumers search longer when contemplating the purchase of a durable than when buying matches.

Evidently, the cost of search differs from person to person, not only as a result of differences in taste, but also because time is more valuable to a person with a larger income: Rich people have a high cost of search, poor people have a low cost of search. Since this essay is devoted to income differences, this is the feature I want to emphasize. Search costs plainly also differ according to the type of good being looked for: The efficiency of personal search is much lower for a used Steinway grand piano (a quite unique good, very hard to find) than for a new Steinway grand piano. Hence institutions such as classified ads or flea markets (Portobello Road in London or the Marché aux Puces in Paris).

Sequential search

Stigler notes that equalizing the expected gain and the cost of search is an unambiguous rule when a unique purchase is being made – a used grand piano. If purchases are repetitive, one has to take the evolution of prices over time into account. The initial number of searches is the only one that need be undertaken if the correlation of asking prices of dealers over successive time periods is perfect. If the correlation were zero, search in each period would be independent of previous experience. When it is positive but not perfect, consumer search is larger in the initial period than in subsequent periods.

Yet these remarks should not hide the fact that Stigler's search rule determines the number of searches *prior to searching*. After searching, the consumer simply chooses the best of the alternatives examined. What he or she actually finds does not affect the number of searches, which was determined before the visits to different outlets. This supposition is unrealistic and sometimes quite silly. For example, a person who follows Stigler's rule will, even after being quoted a price less than the cost of search, keep on sampling until his predetermined quota of price quotations is fulfilled. Several authors (e.g., Nelson 1970 and Rothschild 1973, 1974) have argued that Stigler's decision rule is not optimal, since it ignores the fact that the consumer can learn during a search and that a better strategy is to use the information of the search as it comes to hand.[4] The optimal rule is *sequential:* After receiving each price quotation, the consumer decides whether to continue searching or to accept the quoted price.

Indeed, a consumer who knows the distribution function can recognize a good price when one presents itself. Let m therefore be redefined as the minimum price *so far observed.* Then the expected gain from another search is to be redefined as

$$E[m - x] = \int_0^m (m - x)f(x)\,dx = \int_0^m F(x)\,dx = g(m) \qquad (12.5)$$

where the second integral is derived by integrating by parts. Now, it pays to search again as long as $g(m)$ is larger than the cost of search and to stop searching as soon as a price is found that is below R, where R is the solution to

$$g(R) = \text{cost of search} \qquad (12.6)$$

(at least when the search cost is constant). R is called the reservation price and is a function of both search costs and the shape of the distribution of prices. This reservation price is such that the searcher will accept any price less than or equal to R but will reject a price higher than R.

Rothschild (1974) notes that this sequential rule has the same properties as Stigler's (fixed-sample-size) rule:

1. If all its potential customers follow one of these rules, then a firm faces a well-behaved (downward-sloping) demand function.
2. Customers' search behavior is a function of the cost of search and the distribution of prices.
3. In particular, if the cost of search increases, the amount of search decreases. (With the sequential rule, R increases with search costs so that the intensity of search is lower.)
4. If prices become more dispersed, expected total costs decrease, because the expected minimum price as well as the reservation price decreases. Other things equal, customers prefer to draw from riskier distributions!

The sequential rule implies in addition that increased price dispersion increases the intensity of search.

Rothschild (1974) emphasizes that these results depend on the assumption that the consumer behaves as if he or she knew the distribution of prices. From an economic point of view, this assumption is hard to accept. How could a consumer know this distribution, when most professional economists have no idea about the actual dispersion of prices, and studies on this problem are in their infancy? On the other hand, since the sequential search rule *is* optimal, it is important to know whether it could be followed,[5] even by a person who (explicitly or implicitly) uses the wrong distribution, or more generally what a person should do when the price distribution is not known.

Rothschild (1974) managed to derive and characterize optimal-search rules from unknown distributions. He concludes that, under special but not unreasonable assumptions, these rules have the same qualitative properties as those listed above for rules from known distributions. Without great loss, we can thus assume that rich people have a high cost of search and a high reservation price and therefore search less than poor people who have a low cost of search and a low reservation price.

The noisy monopolist

A natural question is whether a seller might not deliberately use this knowledge and introduce price dispersion in order to split up the market and make price discrimination possible. Why not charge high prices to individuals who have high search costs and thus do *not* seek out the low-price outlets, at the same time charging low prices to consumers who have low search costs and thus do seek out the low-price outlets? This arrangement would increase profits, if the submarket with high-cost consumers is more price inelastic. And the fact of charging different prices would separate the buyers and thus make price discrimination feasible, since those who search less will stop searching at the higher price, whereas the others will continue their search until the lower price is found. In his interesting analysis of what he calls the "noisy monopolist," Salop (1977) analyzes the conditions under which this type of dispersion is profitable. Before delving into his formal analysis, it is worth noticing – to establish links with previous chapters – that this use of dispersion as a sorting device is analogous to a two-part tariff arrangement or a tie-in. Here the commodity offered is tied in with a search, whose cost is the entrance fee. In Salop's words:

> The only difference between dispersion and more traditional tie-ins and other non-linear pricing schemes such as quantity discounts, spatial discrimination and entrance fees is that it uses resources.

The static price dispersion analysed here is seldom directly observed in the economy. However, noisy monopolists exist in subtler forms through unadvertised specials, random sales, changes in product specifications and packaging, product lines with some contrived heterogeneity, vague guarantees, and other forms of "noise" in price and quality. [1977, p. 403]

Suppose the consumer has constant unit search cost, c. The total expected cost of buying one unit of a commodity is

$$\pi = p(R) + \sigma(R) \cdot c \tag{12.7}$$

where $p(R)$ is the expected purchase price, R is his reservation price and $\sigma(R)$ is the expected number of searches. This consumer will choose an optimal $\hat{R}$ by minimizing π with respect to R, that is, such that

$$p'(\hat{R}) + \sigma'(\hat{R}) \cdot c = 0 \tag{12.8}$$

or

$$-p'(\hat{R}) = \sigma'(\hat{R}) \cdot c$$

The marginal decrease in reservation price decreases expected purchase price and increases search costs by equal amounts. (This statement implies, in turn, that the expected gain of search equals its cost, as I just explained.)

Given this result, we ask what the effect is of a rise in unit search cost c. Remembering that $\hat{R}$ is a function of c, and using Equation (12.8), we find

$$\frac{d\pi(c)}{dc} \equiv \pi'(c) = s(c) \geqslant 0 \tag{12.9}$$

$$\frac{d^2\pi(c)}{dc^2} = s'(c) \leqslant 0 \tag{12.10}$$

where $s(c) \equiv \sigma(\hat{R}(c))$, that is, the number of searches as a function of the cost of search, or the search time for individuals with search cost c.

Salop's idea is to use these two properties of consumer search as constraints on the seller's pricing policy. Equation (12.9) says that the increase in total cost, as a result of an increase in search cost, just equals the number of searches, whereas Equation (12.10) says that total cost rises with search costs at a decreasing rate.

Of course, the seller receives only $p(c) = \pi(c) - s(c)c$. (Indeed, $\pi(c)$ is analogous to a delivered price in spatial economics, whereas the total search cost $s(c)c$ implied in the purchase of one unit of the good, is analogous to a transport cost paid by the buyer; $p(c)$ is thus the net price received by the seller, equal to the asking price.)

The seller will want to choose the price $p(c)$, the number of searches $s(c)$, and the total cost $\pi(c)$ that maximize *his or her* profits. To do so, the seller must act in accordance with the conditions of consumer equilibrium, that is, Equations (12.8) to (12.10). On the other hand, these conditions facilitate the task, since the seller has to maximize only with respect to the number of searches $s(c)$ – the "noise" to be created. This number is determined by $d\pi(c)/dc$, and the equilibrium conditions give the profit-maximizing $\pi(c)$. The difference between the two finally gives $p(c)$. More formally, $s(c)$ thus appears as the only control variable in the following optimal control problem:

$$\max \int_0^z [\pi(c) - s(c)c]X[\pi(c), c]\, dc \qquad \text{subject to:} \quad \begin{aligned} \pi'(c) &= s(c) \\ s'(c) &\leqslant 0 \\ \pi(c), s(c) &\geqslant 0 \end{aligned}$$

$$(12.11)$$

In this formulation, c is supposed to vary between zero and some maximum z. Consumers with search cost c are supposed to have a gross demand function $X[\pi(c), c]$, which has both $\pi(c)$ and c as arguments.

The solution[6] implies, inter alia, that if the seller forces type c consumers to search, the marginal value of an increase in their data-gathering time $\lambda(c)$ equals the marginal dead-weight loss of that search time (cX), that is,

$$\lambda(c) = cX \qquad (12.12)$$

and that

$$\lambda'(c) = -[X + (\pi - sc)X_\pi] \qquad (12.13)$$

where $X_\pi = \partial X/\partial \pi$. The right side of (12.13) is the marginal revenue, for the seller, of increasing p.

To find the profit-maximizing $\pi(c)$, it suffices to combine Equations (12.12) and (12.13) in the following way. Differentiate (12.12) to get

$$\lambda'(c) = X + cX_c + cX_\pi \pi'(c) \qquad (12.14)$$

and set this equation equal to Equation (12.13), recalling that $\pi'(c) = s$. We then have

$$2X + \pi X_\pi + cX_c = 0 \qquad (12.15)$$

which describes the profit-maximizing $\pi(c)$.

To illustrate, Salop specifies the demand function as

$$X(\pi, c) = \alpha - \beta\pi + \gamma c$$

where $\alpha > 0$, $-\beta = X_\pi$, and $\gamma = X_c$. Substituting into Equation (12.15),

$$2[\alpha - \beta\pi + \gamma c] - \beta\pi + \gamma c = 0$$

and

$$\pi(c) = \frac{2}{3}\frac{\alpha}{\beta} + \frac{\gamma}{\beta}c$$

Differentiating with respect to c, we have

$$s(c) \equiv \pi'(c) = \frac{\gamma}{\beta}, \text{ a constant}$$

Since $s(c)$ must be nonnegative, it is clear that a necessary condition for this sort of price dispersion, based on "noise," is that $\gamma > 0$, that demand rises with unit search costs. This implies that at any price π, there are more high-cost (rich) customers than low-cost (poor) customers, with the result that price elasticity declines with increases in unit search costs.[7] The seller then wishes to charge a higher price to buyers with more inelastic demand.

Imperfectly informed sellers: The insurance market

In the preceding discussion, the buyers were badly informed about prices, so that they had to search. The result was that high-cost customers had high reservation prices and searched less, whereas low-cost customers had low reservation prices and therefore spent more time searching. The sellers could use this circumstance to their advantage, with the help of devices that make the poor customers search longer: The sellers could offer unadvertised specials, could organize sales at times that are not known in advance, could offer different specifications that make comparisons difficult or different packages to the same effect, and so on. Those who search longer then get a better price.

I now return to the opposite situation, where it is the *seller* who is imperfectly informed about some characteristics of the customers other than their incomes. (We know from previous chapters how nonlinear price schedules act as a self-selection device whereby customers reveal their reservation prices and thus their incomes.) The insurance market is particularly interesting in this respect, since insurance companies have no way of observing the accident probability of a particular customer at the time the insurance contract is signed. On the other hand, they must define with precision both the price and the extent of the risk to be covered, that is, the premium and the amount of insurance that the customer can buy at that price.[8] Will they offer one type of contract to all customers? Or will they try to insure all types of risk, high as well as low, at different premiums? Will they possibly refuse to cover high risks? Or will they do the reverse? The answer is not what you might expect: The high-risk

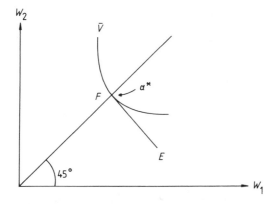

Figure 12.1. A competitive insurance market with identical customers.

customer will receive full coverage, whereas the low-risk customer will get only partial coverage or no coverage at all. Homeowners in the United States are offered contracts with full coverage (fire, theft, flooding, family insurance, and whatnot, all in one contract) but cannot buy fire insurance separately!

Consider the simple case described by Rothschild and Stiglitz (1976). An individual has an income of W if he (or she) is lucky enough to avoid accident. In the event an accident occurs, causing damage d, the income is only $(W-d)$. The individual can become insured by paying to an insurance company a premium α_1, in return for which a sum $\hat{\alpha}_2$ will be paid if an accident occurs. If insurance is purchased, income becomes $(W_1 = W - \alpha_1)$ if no accident occurs. If the person is unlucky, income is further reduced: $W_2 = W - d + \alpha_2$, where $\alpha_2 = \hat{\alpha}_2 - \alpha_1$.

In a competitive insurance market with identical customers, equilibrium would occur, in Figure 12.1, at point α^*, which represents the equilibrium insurance policy $\alpha^* = (\alpha_1^*, \alpha_2^*)$, that is, a policy with premium α_1^* and payment $\hat{\alpha}_2^*$. Indeed, start from point E, which represents the typical customer's uninsured state $(\alpha_1 = 0, \alpha_2 = 0)$. The curve $\bar{V}$ is the indifference curve in terms of expected utility[9] of W_1 and W_2, the same for all customers. Purchasing an insurance policy moves the customers away from E to the northwest: W_1 is decreased by α_1 and W_2 is increased by α_2. In perfect competition with free entry, expected profits are zero, so that $\alpha_1(1-p) + \alpha_2 p = 0$, where p is the probability of incurring an accident. The set of all insurance policies that break even is given by the "fair odds" line EF, with a slope $(1-p)/p$. The policy α^* is the one that will be chosen in equilibrium, since it is on the EF line (zero profit) and locates the customers at the tangency of their indifference curve with EF

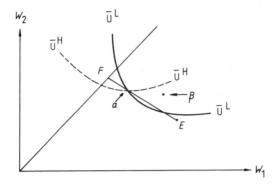

Figure 12.2. A competitive insurance market with different customers.

and thus provides the highest expected utility. Notice that along the 45°
line, $W_2 = W_1$, or $W - d + \alpha_2 = W - \alpha_1$, or $d = \hat{\alpha}_2$, so that the payment
just covers the damage in the event an accident occurs. That is why the
line EF cannot cross the 45° line. The equilibrium policy α^* lies on the
45° line, since the marginal rate of substitution[10] between W_1 and W_2 is
$(1-p)/p$ when $W_2 = W_1$.

We are interested in the case where customers *are* different and the
insurance companies do not know their characteristics (accident probabilities). These companies will try to find ways to force customers to
make choices in such a way that they both reveal their characteristics and
make the choices the companies would have wanted them to make had
their characteristics been known. Suppose, then, that there are only two
kinds of customers: low-risk individuals with accident probability p^L and
high-risk individuals with accident probability $p^H > p^L$. Could it be that
both groups will be offered the same contract, as was the case in Figure
12.1 above? No. Competitive equilibrium now implies that different
types purchase different contracts.

If they were offered the same contract, it would have an average acci-
dent probability $\bar{p} = \lambda p^H + (1-\lambda)p^L$, where λ is the fraction of high-risk
customers. Such a contract could be represented by point α in Figure
12.2. It is located on the zero-profit line EF, which now has a slope of
$(1-\bar{p})\bar{p}$. This line EF is called the "market odds" line. At that point the
indifference curve for high-risk customers $\bar{U}^H$ crosses the low-risk indifference curve from below.[11] However, there is a contract, β, near α,
which low-risk types prefer to α. (The high-risk customers prefer α to β.)
It is also profitable for the insurance companies to have the less risky buy
β. Indeed, these β contracts would give almost the same profit as if the α
contracts were offered to the less risky only. And the latter contracts

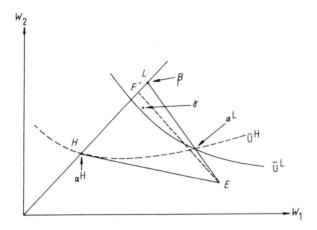

Figure 12.3. Equilibrium contracts for high-risk and low-risk customers.

would, by definition, be more profitable than if they were offered to all customers. The policy α cannot be an equilibrium: If there is an equilibrium, each type of customer must purchase a separate contract.

The nature of these two contracts is illustrated in Figure 12.3. First of all, we need two "fair odds" lines, say EH and EL. The contract on EH most preferred by high-risk customers is α^H and gives complete insurance. Of all contracts on EL, low-risk types would prefer β. However, β cannot be part of the equilibrium! It gives complete insurance but also gives more income than α^H, so that high-risk types will prefer it to α^H. If both β and α^H are offered – and since insurance companies cannot distinguish between the two sets of customers, although it would be profitable to do so – all will demand β and must be sold β. Profits will be negative, since β gives zero profits for *low*-risk customers only. In other words, the set (α^H, β) is not an equilibrium.

The fact that high-risk individuals will switch to β implies that low-risk types must be offered a less attractive contract such that the high-risk customers are indifferent to it. The contract α^L, on the intersection of the two indifference curves, has this property and is also the one that low-risk types most prefer. We conclude that the set (α^H, α^L) is the only possible equilibrium for a market with low- and high-risk customers, if it *is* an equilibrium.

Indeed, (α^H, α^L) may not be a competitive equilibrium. If a common contract γ were offered by a new firm, all customers would prefer it. And it may be a profitable one, if there are relatively few high-risk insurance customers, so that the "market-odds" line – with slope $(1 - \bar{p})\bar{p}$ – is EF', say. As a result, the original contracts make a loss.

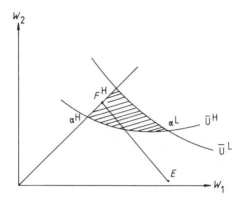

Figure 12.4. Discriminating monopolistic insurance companies, α^L given.

It is, of course, unrealistic to suppose that the insurance market is perfectly competitive and that the insurance companies make zero profit. The preceding discussion shows that these assumptions also lead to the conclusion that a competitive market may have no equilibrium, since (α^H, α^L) was the only possible equilibrium. However, the discussion was interesting, because it showed that the presence of high-risk individuals exerts a negative externality on the low-risk individuals: Even under competition, low-risk types will have incomplete coverage.

Consider, then, a market with profit-maximizing insurance companies that are able to discriminate. Under the assumptions made, they will offer a menu of contracts: With two types of customers, they will offer a full-coverage contract to the high-risk type and partial insurance or no insurance at all to low-risk types. This Stiglitz (1977) established in the following way.

The negative externality implies that a monopolistic seller must sell high-risk individuals a contract that they prefer to the contract purchased by the low-risk group, say α^L. It should thus be located in the shaded area in Figure 12.4, given α^L. The line EF^H is not a zero-profit line but corresponds to a given positive profit on contracts offered to the high-risk group. A higher profit leads to another parallel isoprofit line, located to the left of EF^H, since moving to the left implies a higher premium (or smaller W_1) and a lower payment (smaller W_2). The profit-maximizing contract for the high-risk group must be located at the point where the slope of $\bar{U}^H$ is equal to the slope of an isoprofit line and is therefore on the 45° line. It must be α^H, at the intersection of the 45° line and the high-risk individuals' indifference curve through α^L. Each type of individual prefers his or her contract to the other contract, and profit is maximized.

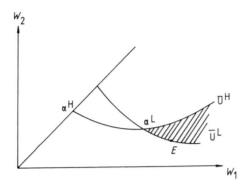

Figure 12.5. Discriminating monopolistic insurance companies, α^H given.

Now assume the contract α^H is given (Figure 12.5). It must lie along the 45° line. Draw the high-risk indifference curve through it. Also draw the low-risk indifference curve through E (the no-insurance point). The set of contracts that a monopolistic seller can choose and that separate the groups are the points *below* the indifference curve (through α^H) and *above* the curve through E. The fact that the indifference curves are flatter than the isoprofit lines implies that profits are maximized at the point located most to the left, that is, at α^L. This establishes that the low-risk individual's utility is very close to what it would have been with the purchase of no insurance. Such a person might as well decide to stay at E – to remain uninsured.

All this implies that high-risk and low-risk individuals will never be offered the same contract. If they were, and the common contract involved incomplete insurance, then it would always be profitable to introduce an additional policy offering complete insurance (moving to the left in Figures 12.2–12.5). If the common contract involved complete insurance, it would always be profitable to introduce an additional policy involving incomplete insurance.

The time has come to note the nice analogy between the discoveries just made and results established in earlier and later chapters. Only high-risk people – the rich – are offered the full insurance they would obtain under competitive conditions, because they can always switch to partial insurance, and insurers seek to prevent this switching. In a similar way, only the rich were seen, in Essay II, to benefit fully from technical progress at the right moment when buying new products, because they could always choose to wait, and sellers try to prevent this waiting. In an earlier chapter in this essay, only the big consumers – the rich again – were offered marginal prices equal to marginal costs, because they could always choose to buy less, and sellers want to prevent this reduction in the quantities purchased. Similarly, we will discover in the next essay that only the rich are offered the optimal price–quality combination, because they can always switch to products of lesser quality, and sellers seek to prevent them from doing so. The presence of the rich indeed exerts a negative externality on the poor in many ways.

Quality differences

CHAPTER 13

Business practices

We note that income differences are often associated with quality differences. On the one hand, richer customers might insist on receiving a better service or buying higher-quality goods. On the other hand, sellers might find it profitable to offer better quality to richer customers and to make sure that they actually do buy *only* this better quality, leaving the lower-quality goods for lower-income segments. Products of a given quality are also often offered in different varieties, with small differences in specification, presentation, or wrapping. This is the so-called product differentiation policy discussed in the literature on "monopolistic competition."

In this fourth essay, I want to investigate the extent to which both policies – those of quality differentiation and of product differentiation – create opportunities for or are linked with price discrimination. This chapter presents a description of what actually happens in a number of typical cases – the emphasis being on the relationship between product selection and pricing. The next chapters will try to develop some theoretical insights.

Product selection: Automobiles

The automobile market is, no doubt, one of the richest examples to use to study product selection.[1] A first possible strategy is deliberately to ignore income and taste differences among consumers and to develop a single product aimed at reaching the largest number of "average" buyers. It is a policy of standardization and mass production, based on minimization of production, storage, and advertising costs. Volkswagen's initial policy (with the famous "Beetle") is an example that comes to mind. Ford's initial policy, selling only one model with one color, the black Ford Model T, is another.

But consider what happened to the Model T. Before its appearance in 1908, the automobile was considered a luxury good, a leisure good for upper-class people. Its introduction revealed a large market segment that had previously been unknown to producers. However, during its entire lifetime – until 1927 – the Model T remained attached to this segment, without adapting to the segment's evolution. At the beginning, its market included middle-class people and farmers. In the 1920s incomes went up, and customers wanted better quality and began to look elsewhere. (Admittedly, the car's market segment filled up from below, but at a slower rate, so that decline was inevitable.)

In the long run, it is probably more profitable to follow another strategy, which is to attack several market segments simultaneously with a series of models. From a technical point of view, such a policy is not necessarily incompatible with large-scale economies. Quite to the contrary, part of the production process of each or several models may be common and may use the same equipment, so that mass production and product or quality differentiation may go together. We are of course more interested in the commercial point of view, in which surplus extraction is the main preoccupation.

This second type of policy takes different forms. Two basic possibilities emerge: A firm can engage in what I will call *vertical* differentiation, or quality changes, following Lancaster (1979); it can also develop *horizontal* differentiation. Vertical product differentiation of a commodity with several characteristics is said to be present when the absolute amount of all (or most) characteristics per unit of a good is increased or decreased. There is a "quality change." The classic example is the distinction between a Volkswagen Rabbit and a Mercedes for the case where different producers are involved. In the case of a single producer, a good example is the difference between a Renault 5 and a Renault 20.

Upward vertical differentiation was involved when Peugeot launched its Peugeot 604 in 1975, after concentrating on models of more average quality. In such a case, the car maker is interested in reaching a limited, very specific market segment, on the assumption that it will expand with the increase in the standard of living. Downward vertical differentiation often aims at people who buy a car for the first time, as with the Peugeot 104, the Ford Fiesta, the Toyota Starlet, and the Citroën Visa.

Alternatively, vertical differentiation may increase through an enlargement of the number of models of intermediate quality, within an existing series of models. In 1976, Renault launched the R14. This car was located, so to speak, between the R4, R6, and R12, on the one hand, and between the R15, R17, R16, R20, and R30 on the other hand. Apparently Renault wanted to fill a gap (see Figure 13.1 below) and sought to cover the entire range of the market for cars. Citroën was satisfied for a long time with selling at the two extremes of the market (the DS and the 2CV) but then introduced a series of intermediate models (the Dyane 4, Dyane 6, Ami 8, and GS).

Horizontal differentiation can also take a number of forms. One way is to derive varieties that correspond to different usages: A berline is

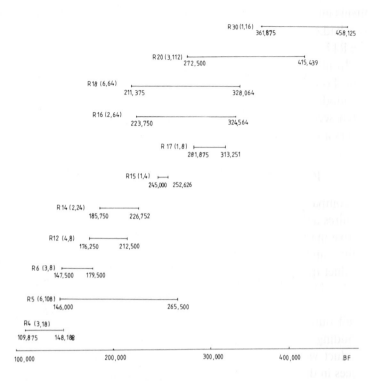

Figure 13.1. Renault's product selection, showing price range. Figures in parentheses indicate the available number of varieties and the total possible number of combinations, respectively, (*Source:* Pilati 1979, p. 66.)

transformed into a break or a coupe. Another sort is of greater interest to us. A model with a series of options is offered, and the customer is asked to determine the combination of options he or she prefers. Different varieties use the same body but different motors, have a different number of doors, and so forth. The idea obviously is to approach first-degree discrimination as closely as possible, each customer being asked "to construct his (or her) own Golf": "Everyone his own Golf: 5 models, 22 varieties, 15 colors."[2] One has the impression that extra options are overpriced, to extract the highest possible price from those who want fancy tires or extra horsepower.

Figure 13.1 reproduces Renault's series of models, as offered on October 9, 1978, to the Belgian public. This figure displays several interesting features. First of all, it is rather striking to see how no segment of the market, between a reservation price of 100,000 and 458,125 BF, is neglected. Second, a clear-cut case of price discrimination occurs where different models are offered at the same price to different market segments and therefore to different consumers. For example, for 281,875 BF, one had the choice, on October 9, 1978, between a particular variety of the R17, the R16, the R18, and the R20. Third, the length of the different horizontal lines corresponds to varying degrees of horizontal differentiation. Fourth, vertical differentiation corresponds to differences between the models. However, the quality differences between successive models often seem to be blurred. It is not clear which variety of, say, an R18 offers a better quality than the more highly priced R16 varieties.

Price–quality frontiers

To compare qualities and the corresponding prices is a difficult task and requires a lot of information. Some people think quality is a purely subjective matter, so that the task is hopeless. Maynes (1976) argues forcefully – and convincingly, in my opinion – that it is feasible to measure product quality, so that prices and quality are commensurable. Using a quality index normalized between zero and one, he is able to construct charts in which (retail) prices of consumer durables (charged in different retail outlets located in the same town) are plotted against the corresponding quality index. These plots typically reveal price dispersion, product varieties with the same quality content being sold at different prices in different stores. This dispersion reflects to some extent the differences in services provided but can also be interpreted as a measure of the informational effectiveness of the market.

Maynes then defines the (objective) price–quality frontier as the set of points and the line segment connecting them, for which the different qualities of a commodity may be purchased at the lowest prices. This frontier is of particular interest, as the rational consumer would proceed along it. (It is the analog, in a world of imperfect competition, of Rosen's 1974 hedonic price function for a purely competitive market.) The slope of the frontier is one of the pieces of information consumers would like to have. (They would like to compare it with the slopes of their subjective price-quality curves.)

The price–quality frontier is relevant to the price discrimination problem to the extent that points on it represent different qualities or varieties of the same quality put on the market by the same producer and reflect that producer's (wholeslale) prices. There is discrimination when price differences between qualities do not reflect costs of quality changes or when the same quality is sold at different prices to different customers by

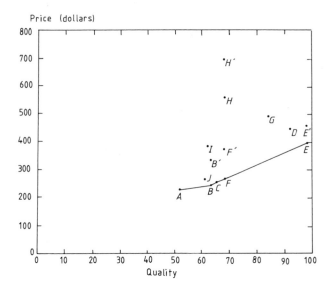

Figure 13.2. Price–quality frontier for sofa beds, Minneapolis. Letters represent various specimens. Where an identical letter appears twice, the primed designation represents a "regular" price, whereas the unprimed designation represents a sale price. The efficiency frontier is *ABCFE*. (*Source:* made available by Prof. S. Maynes.)

the same seller. Figures 13.2–13.4 reproduce typical price–quality frontiers for durables as diverse as sofa beds and pocket cameras, based on retail prices collected in several local American markets.[3]

Physicians and quacks

Nowhere is quality more important than in the market for physicians' services. And nowhere, perhaps, is the uncertainty about the quality of the service being offered higher. This market may therefore be particularly well suited for use as a case study to introduce the problem of quality uncertainty and its relationship to prices, the more so as physicians are known to charge rich patients more than poor patients. In a pioneering study, Kessel (1958) suggested that the pricing behavior of physicians is based on collusive profit maximization, facilitated by medical societies such as the American Medical Association (AMA). However, this thesis does not seem to be entirely compatible with empirical evidence.

Historically,[4] medical doctors practiced price discrimination in the United States long before the AMA achieved its monopoly power (in

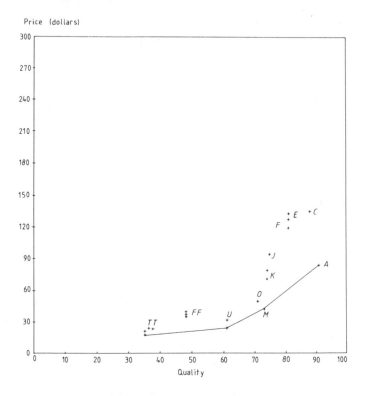

Figure 13.3. Price–quality frontier for pocket cameras, Ann Arbor, November 1976. Letters denote varieties of pocket cameras. Each + represents an actual price quotation. (*Sources:* Quality scores are from *Consumer Reports,* June 1976, and prices were collected by Anthony Sciano on July 29, 1976.)

1910). On the other hand, price discrimination based upon the AMA's monopoly power cannot explain the prevalence of free medical services provided by private physicians. Kessel attributed these services to doctors' desire to develop new skills or to practice existing ones, whereas it is evident that charitable considerations have played a role. It would be nice to be able to show that monopoly power and charity are not inconsistent. In addition, there is a clear trend – since the 1950s – toward a decrease in the amount of charity performed and toward a less pronounced prevalence of price discrimination among mid- and low-income classes. And finally, the number of quacks has been considerably reduced in the course of the century.

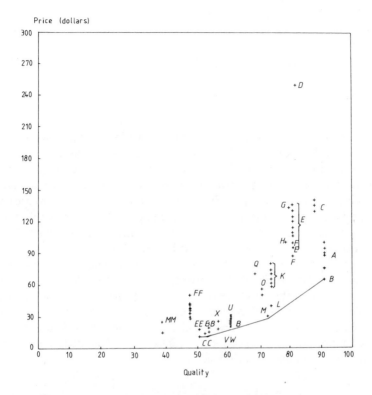

Figure 13.4. Price–quality frontier for pocket cameras, Ithaca, November 1976. Letters denote varieties of pocket cameras. Each + represents an actual price quotation. (*Sources:* Quality scores are from *Consumer Reports,* June 1976, and prices were collected by Patience Nelson from July 22 to August 2, 1976.)

It will turn out that a coherent explanation of these different phenomena can be given when due account is taken of the fundamental asymmetry in the information available to buyers and sellers (buyers have relatively much less information than sellers) and of the resulting search costs incurred by the buyers.

Product selection

Chapter 11, on multiproduct pricing, has made us familiar with the idea that several products, and bundles of them, can be used to partition a market into segments and to extract consumer surplus from each segment. The same idea is obviously applicable when product differentiation is possible, either through the production of different varieties of the same basic commodity (horizontal product differentiation) or through the production of commodities of different quality (vertical product differentiation). In both cases, the seller must simply ascertain that each market segment is actually buying the particular variety or the particular quality assigned to it. To this effect, the seller has only to fix prices in such a way that the purchase of the assigned variety or quality provides a higher surplus than the purchase of any other variety or quality. This is the basic message of the present chapter. I shall discuss horizontal differentiation first and shall then consider vertical differentiation and problems of imperfect information.

Hotelling and the analogy between space and quality

Before considering multiproduct pricing again, it is of interest to discuss the so-called Hotelling approach, as horizontal product differentiation is usually discussed in the framework set up by Hotelling (1929) in his famous article "Stability in Competition." Hotelling wanted to show that horizontal product differentiation can lead to a stable solution in the competitive struggle between a small number of competitors, and he also wanted to characterize this solution. His basic idea is that product differentiation implies that customers prefer certain varieties over others, so that a price reduction for one variety by its producer will not necessarily induce all customers to switch[1] to this variety. The purpose of his analysis is obviously to escape from the assumption of homogeneous products that underlies the perfect competition and the Cournot–Bertrand models. It will become clear, in a moment, that Hotelling did not depart far enough from the other assumptions that underpin these models for him to come to grips with the phenomenon of price discrimination.

To make the presentation simple, Hotelling exploits the analogy between the space domain and the quality domain and treats differences among varieties as if they were differences in the location of sellers along a straight line. Differences in the preferences of the buyers for particular varieties are then treated as transport costs from the buyer's place to the seller's location. A particular distance thus represents the extent to which a variety is different from what the buyer would like it to be. More specifically,[2] Hotelling uses the following assumptions:

1. Each consumer buys at most one unit of the commodity per unit of time.[3] In other words, each consumer has only one reservation price, valid for one unit only (so that he or she will never buy a second unit). In technical terms, the demand function of the consumer is completely price inelastic and finite: It reduces to one single demand price. I have used this assumption in earlier chapters and will continue to use it all along.
2. Each reservation price is independent of the reservation prices of other varieties, so that the reservation price for a bundle is the sum of the reservation prices of its components. Again, this assumption is familiar by now.
3. Other familiar assumptions are that marginal costs of production are constant (possibly zero) and that there are no fixed costs.
4. Changes in specifications of the varieties (or changes in quality) are costless. This is a curious assumption indeed. It is one thing to assume, as we did before, that the bundling of two products does not involve any extra cost. But how could one imagine that adding luxury to a basic car is a costless operation? However, since I am interested in price discrimination, and since the possibility of discriminating depends upon differences in *demand,* I am not going to dwell on this assumption.
5. New is the assumption that the N customers are uniformly placed along a straight line (or a circle). To each unit of distance corresponds a one-unit element of differentiation.
6. The cost of transporting one unit of the commodity over one unit of distance is constant. This transport costs represents the degree of disutility resulting from the fact that a consumer does not obtain, given the varieties offered (the locations of the producers), the variety he or she prefers. In other words, consumers are supposed to move from their locations to that of the nearest seller (to take a less preferred variety) if the two locations do not coincide (if the consumer's preferred variety is not on the market).
7. Assumption 6 is crucial and implies that producers adopt fob-mill prices: The buyer takes care of the transportation problem. Producers somehow ignore the fact that they could sell at delivered prices and absorb freight or could charge phantom freight (could sell different varieties at discriminatory prices).
8. Assumptions 6 and 7 in turn are quite naturally accompanied by the assumption that each producer has only one location (sells one variety or quality).

The reader who has read the preceding essays will no doubt object to Assumptions 6 to 8. They allow escape from perfect competition or homogeneous duopoly into a very simple form of monopolistic competition, in which consumers move around, whereas producers care only about finding *the* optimal location (variety, quality) but never consider more refined forms of pricing and locating, involving multiple-product profit maximization. Nevertheless, these assumptions do not seem to have been questioned in the voluminous standard literature on product selection and monopolistic competition.[4]

Anyway, Hotelling's Assumptions 6-8, although most helpful in other ways, do not provide a natural framework in which to study price discrimination. In fact, by assumption, price discrimination is eliminated! It should be no surprise to discover that Lancaster (1979, p. 283, n. 1) – who generalizes Assumption 6 to preferences for combinations of characteristics of a commodity – asserts that price discrimination would be impossible or difficult to exercise under horizontal differentiation because of the difficulty of identifying the distance between the most preferred and the available varieties for each customer. In addition, he says, the possibility of trade between customers would have to be ruled out.

These assertions are of course contradicted by the literature on self-selecting devices such as commodity bundling. By offering a choice among basic models and varieties around it, customers are put in a position in which they will *reveal* their reservation prices, by selecting the market segments they want to be in. The difficulty of measuring subjective disutilities is thus easily circumvented. Furthermore, the possibility of trade might simply not exist: Dishes in a restaurant are hard to trade among patrons; I shall emphasize in the next section that the luxury aspect of a car does not have a separate price. Or trade may be difficult and costly in terms of time and effort, as with a theater ticket. In addition, asymmetric information about the quality or the characteristics of a commodity may preclude resale at a profit, as in the market for lemons, to which I shall turn later on. For the time being, I simply want to recall the features and properties of commodity bundling in cases where luxury is combined with a basic service, such as transportation.

Commodity bundling again

Consider an automobile producer who puts different varieties of a given model (e.g., the L, TL, GTL, TS, Alpine, Gordini, and Turbo varieties of the Renault 5) on the market. For each variety, a number of options (automatic transmission, power steering, etc.) are also made available. This arrangement can be rationalized in the framework of the commodity bundling model as offering a choice between a type of car (the R5 TL) providing certain transportation services on the one hand, some luxury items complementary to it on the other hand, and a bundle (a R5 TS, combining the features of the R5 TL and a number of luxury items).

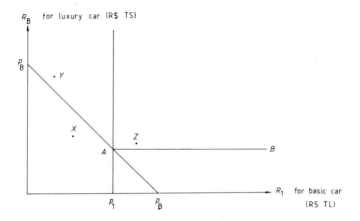

Figure 14.1. Choice between a basic car and a luxury variety.

Figure 11.3 is directly applicable, with the reservation prices for the R5 TL (product 1) measured on the horizontal axis and the reservation prices for the luxury options (product 2) measured on the vertical axis.

We know from Chapter 11 that mixed bundling (offering the R5 TL, the options *and* the luxurious R5 TS simultaneously) is more profitable than simple bundling (offering only the R5 TS) whenever some customers have reservation prices for particular luxury items that are below marginal cost (some do not care for power steering but are ready to pay a high price for metallic paint, whereas others have the reverse attitude). Prices for the options will be very high and will exclude those who have low reservation prices for particular options. But the same options will be available at a lower price for customers who are ready to buy the bundle R5 TS in which they are incorporated, because these (more "bourgeois") types evaluate transportation and luxury in a more balanced way. Discrimination is against people with "fancy" tastes (the young and individuals who want to show off) and favors the richer people, on the condition that they value transportation as highly as luxury (remember the example in Figure 11.4).

What are the welfare implications? To examine Pareto optimality, Adams and Yellen (1976) consider the choice between a basic car (the R5 TL) and a more luxurious version of it (the R5 TS) and draw Figure 14.1, where p_1 is the price for the basic car and p_B is the price of the bundle (the TS version). Customers with reservation prices southeast of p_1AB consume the basic car and customers northeast of p_BAB consume the luxury version, since the surplus $R_B - p_B > R_1 - p_1$ in the latter area.

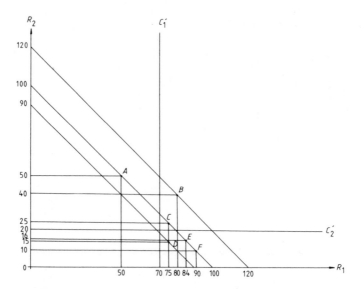

Figure 14.2. Luxury cars and welfare. (*Source:* Adams and Yellen 1976, p. 494.)

To the extent that luxury cannot be disembodied from transport services, so that it has no value independently of the latter, no mutually beneficial trades among potential customers are possible. Although Mr. X values transport more highly than Mr. Y, the latter (who buys the R5 TS) cannot sell the transport services of his car to Mr. X and keep the luxury. Similarly, Mr. Z (who also buys the R5 TS) will not sell its chrome to Mr. X, although the latter values luxury more highly than he does. (The situation is thus different from that discussed in Chapter 11, where beneficial trades were possible because the courses in a complete dinner could be evaluated independently of each other.)

To what extent is the output of the basic car and of its luxury version just sufficient to supply all customers with reservation prices equal to or above their marginal cost? In Figure 14.2, only customers A, B, and C should purchase luxury, since the other customers have reservation prices for product 2 (the luxury options) below its marginal cost of twenty. The seller's profit-maximizing strategy, however, results in selling a bundle (the luxury car) at a price $p_B = 100$ to A, B, C, *and* E, in selling the basic car (product 1) to F at $p_1 = 90$ and selling nothing to D. Such a sale gives a profit of $[100 - (70 + 20) + (90 - 70) = 40 + 20 =] 60$. Selling the luxury car only (pure bundling) at $p_B = 100$ (to A, B, C, E, and F) would yield a smaller profit of $[(100 - 90) \cdot 5 = 50]$. Mixed bundling leads to luxury being oversupplied: E is the typical customer (you and me) whom a clever salesman talked into buying a more expensive variety than we intended. Basic transportation is undersupplied, since D was ready to pay more than the marginal cost of a basic car and is excluded from the market. It can be shown that, when luxury can be embedded in a basic commodity, the basic commodity is never oversupplied, although the production of luxury can either exceed or fall short of ideal output. Indeed, it is never profitable to talk a customer into buying a cheaper type of car! Notice also that, in the example of Figure 14.2, pure bundling implies that luxury is even more oversupplied, since *E and F* are talked into buying the luxury car, so that mixed bundling again Pareto-dominates pure bundling.

Vertical product differentiation and price discrimination

It is my contention that there is also room for price discrimination when products are vertically differentiated.[5] When a firm sells both high- and low-quality products, the firm may find it profitable to ask prices which discriminate against the rich or the poor or at least the class-conscious, as the case may be. Segmentation of the markets is achieved through well-identified trademarks or models, possibly used as self-selection devices. For price discrimination to be possible, though, the seller must find ways to limit or to eliminate transfers of units of demand from high-price segments to low-price segments of the market. One condition is to make sure that *price* differences between qualities stay within certain limits. However, the seller may also find it profitable to enlarge the differences between the *qualities* put on the market, so as to be able to enlarge the price differences without inducing transfers of demand. When the seller does so, a larger surplus may be taken away from the consumers as a whole. Price discrimination and product selection may thus be linked, the qualities put on the market being endogenous to the extent that they have to be determined together with the prices of the different models. The purpose of the following section is to identify and to analyze the mechanisms described in this paragraph and, by the same token, to put the available literature into a better perspective. This literature is, indeed, rather scarce and disorganized.[6]

It is often said that product differentiation and price discrimination are closely linked. In particular, the frequent occurrence of vertical market segmentation is noticed by Pigou (1920, part 2, chap. 17, p. 277), whereas Maroni (1947) stresses that vertical product differentiation and price discrimination go hand in hand. An analytical treatment of the appropriate pricing policy does not seem to be available, however.[7]

As for the relationship between quality choices and price discrimination, I know of only three references. The first one is a fascinating remark made by Dupuit in his discussion of railroad tariffs for passenger traffic. The following excerpt, taken from Ekelund, introduces the idea of a *reduction* in quality (of the *lower*-quality goods) as a market segmentation technique:

> It is not because of the few thousand francs which would have to be spent to put a roof over the third-class carriages or to upholster the third-class seats that some company or other has open carriages with wooden benches... What the company is trying to do is to prevent the passengers who can pay the second-class fare from traveling third-class; it hits the poor, not because it wants to hurt them, but to frighten the rich... And it is again for the same reason that the companies, having proved almost cruel to third-class passengers and mean to second-class ones, become lavish in dealing with first-class passengers. Having refused the poor what is necessary, they give the rich what is superfluous. [1970, p. 275]

Dupuit did not work out an analytical solution to the problem, nor did Ekelund.

Walras echoes Dupuit's remark in his recently published essay "The State and the Railways":

> French companies charge 10c. for the first class, 7.5c for the second, and 5.5c. for the third; but they put 24 passengers in a first class coach, 30 in a second class and 40 in a third class. They also vary the comfort of the seats, etc. Neither in terms of space nor comfort provided is the service identical, and the prices seem to be related to the differences. They would in fact be so if they were roughly equal to the costs: 1.12c., 0.56c., and 0.24c.; but as they are far higher, and so completely independent of the nature of the service, we must reason otherwise. In reality, the companies consider, rightly or wrongly, the average price of 7.66c., which is quite close to the second class price of 7.5c., to be the profit-maximising price; but they do not want to miss the chance of taking more from passengers willing to pay more, nor to turn away passengers not willing to pay as much. This is why there are three separate classes, and great efforts made to accentuate on the one hand the advantages of the first class and on the other hand the disadvantages of the third class. When some time ago there was an outcry that third class coaches should have windows fitted as laid down in the regulations for 1857–8, and now when heating is demanded for them in the winter, people complain about the meanness of the companies without understanding its true cause. If the third class coaches were comfortable enough for many first and second class passengers to go in them, total net product would fall. That is all there is to it. [1875/1980, p. 94]

We had to wait[8] until publication of the paper by Mussa and Rosen (1978) to understand why the implementation of price discrimination may imply a quality reduction at the lower end of the quality scale only. Unfortunately, given the complexity of the problem, Mussa and Rosen had to be satisfied with the analysis of a very special preference ordering, implying inter alia that each consumer chooses one quality, buys at most one unit of that quality, and has fixed reservation prices that are proportional to the qualities.

Admittedly, the discriminating monopolist has shown up in the literature on socially optimal product selection. Guasch and Sobel (1979) have shown that the *perfectly* discriminating monopolist will provide the same range of products that the social optimum would, but at a higher price. (Using the characteristics approach, White [1977] and Stewart [1979b] arrive at the same conclusion for the case of horizontal product differentiation.)

Real life product selection problems refer to cases of second- or third-degree discrimination, in which the market is partitioned into segments. In third-degree discrimination (in which consumers have demand *curves,* because more quantity can be traded for less quality), no results whatsoever are available. Second-degree discrimination fortunately creeps in (but through the back door, so to speak) in discussions of the impact of market structure on product differentiation. In their discussion of a theorem[9] by Lancaster (1975), Guasch and Sobel (1980) present a case of second-degree price discrimination, in which the monopolist provides a strictly larger set of products than is socially optimal, although fixed costs are involved (with the result that returns to scale are increasing). In his discussion of a 1974 paper by Meade, Gabszewicz (1980) shows that a smaller set of products than is socially optimal may be associated with monopoly power or duopoly, even in the absence of fixed costs. Again, strong simplifying assumptions about the preference orderings are used, and no substitution between quantity and quality is allowed for.

The next section disentangles at some length the relations between product selection and surplus extraction through second-degree price discrimination. While still employing the simple demand assumptions used by Mussa and Rosen (1978) and by Guasch and Sobel (1979) – that at most one unit of the good is consumed and that each consumer has a fixed reservation price for each different level of quality – I generalize the analysis to consider all possible combinations of consumers with differing reservation prices. For each combination of reservation prices by two types of individuals with different incomes and for two quality levels of a commodity, I identify the profit-maximizing product selection for a monopolistic producer and analyze the extent and direction of price discrimination. I then set up a parametrization and use it to derive conclusions about the relationships between socially optimal product selection and the selection that firms will find most profitable (for three quality levels). The analysis highlights the counteracting influences of additional fixed costs to market a wide product variety and surplus extraction through increased quality dispersion. A final section considers n given qualities and n corresponding income classes. I maintain throughout the assumption that one unit of the commodity – at most – can be bought.

Two qualities

Consider two types of consumers with different reservation prices for two different quality types of the same commodity (e.g., A- and B-type consumers' preferences for red or blue cars). In this partial equilibrium analysis, each consumer can purchase either one or no car (never two), and each customer will be presumed to have consistent, utility-maximizing objectives in the following sense: (a) No car will be purchased unless the consumer's reservation price exceeds or just equals the producer's price; (b) if a red car is preferred to a blue car and the consumer is able to purchase a blue car, then the choice will be shifted to the red car only if the change in benefit, indicated by the difference in reservation prices, exceeds the increase in cost.

Mathematically, let $R_{r,b}^{A,B}$ be the reservation price of consumer type A or B for a red (r) or blue (b) car, and $p_{r,b}$ is the producer's price for a red or blue car. Then if $R_r^A > R_b^A$, and if

$$R_b^A < p_b \qquad \text{and} \qquad R_r^A < p_r \tag{14.1}$$

A will not buy any car. If

$$R_b^A \geqslant p_b \qquad \text{but} \qquad R_r^A - R_b^A < p_r - p_b \tag{14.2}$$

A will buy a blue car. If

$$R_b^A \geqslant p_b \qquad \text{and} \qquad R_r^A - R_b^A \geqslant p_r - p_b \tag{14.3}$$

or if

$$R_r^A \geqslant p_r \qquad \text{and} \qquad R_b^A < p_b$$

A will buy a red car. Notice that (14.3) also guarantess that $R_r^A \geqslant p_r$. These conditions are summarized in Figure 14.3, where the axes represent the consumer's surplus, $R_r^A - p_r$ and $R_b^A - p_b$, derived from having a red or blue car at the quoted price. Notice that the second inequality in (14.2) and (14.3) can be transformed into

$$R_r^A - p_r \gtreqless R_b^A - p_b \tag{14.4}$$

so that the choice of a red or a blue car hinges on which yields the larger consumer surplus. So, given the producer's prices, any consumer with arbitrary reservation prices can be located in Figure 14.3. If the consumer is located above the 45° line in the first quadrant or anywhere in the

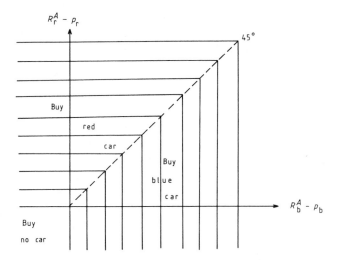

Figure 14.3. Consumption map for A-type consumer.

second, a red car will be purchased. If he or she is located below the 45°
line in the first quadrant or anywhere in the fourth, a blue car will be
bought. Only if the consumer's surplus is negative everywhere (located in
the third quadrant) will no purchase be made.

In order to consider all possible combinations of the two consumer
types, the following five cases must be considered (see Figure 14.4a–e):

Case 1: Both consumers prefer the same type of car; one consumer's reservation
prices dominate the other's for both types of cars; this dominating consumer has the *strongest* relative preference for the commonly preferred
car.

Case 2: Both consumers prefer the same type of car; one consumer's reservation
prices dominate the other's for both types of cars; the dominating consumer has the *weakest* relative preference for the commonly preferred
car.

Case 3: Both consumers prefer the same type of car; each has a dominant reservation price for one of the two types of cars.

Case 4: Each consumer prefers a different type of car; one consumer's reservation prices dominate the other's for both types of cars.

Case 5: Each consumer prefers a different type of car; each has a dominant
reservation price for one of the two types of cars.

Since the profit-maximizing price strategy of a producer capable of
supplying both types of cars will be explored, it is convenient to transfer
the origin in Figure 14.3 so that the axes measure reservation prices and
consumer prices directly. Thus the origin of Figure 14.3 becomes the pro-

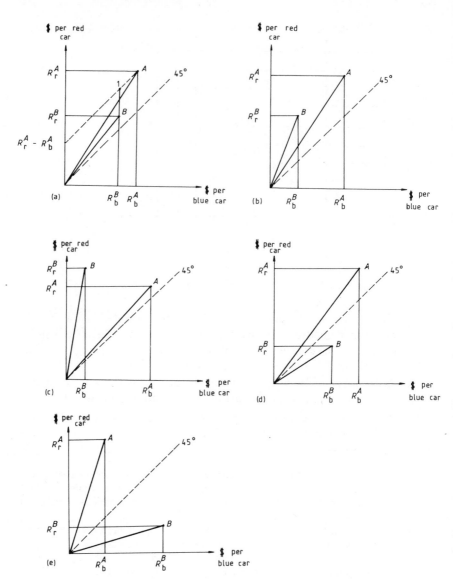

Figure 14.4. Combinations of consumer types.

ducer's price point throughout Figure 14.4 and consumer's surplus is measured as the distance between the reservation price and producer's price points. It is assumed that the producer has to charge both types of consumers the same price for the same color car.

Case 1

In Figure 14.4a, points A and B indicate the locus of reservation prices for the respective consumer types. In this section, for simplicity we suppose zero costs of production, design, and marketing (some positive production cost would be represented by yet another transposition of axes). What is the product (price) selection that will yield maximum profits?

In this case, three possibilities exist: Sell a red car only to A, sell red cars to A and B, or sell a red car to A and a blue car to B. (It never makes sense to sell A a blue car in this case when $R_r^A \geqslant R_b^A$.) Let N_A be the number of A-type consumers and N_B the number of B-type consumers.

Selling a red car to A alone is the most profitable policy if

$$N_A R_r^A > (N_A + N_B) R_r^B \qquad (14.5)$$

and

$$N_A R_r^A > N_B R_b^B + N_A p_r = N_B R_b^B + N_A (R_b^B + R_r^A - R_b^A) \qquad (14.6)$$

Inequality (14.5) states the conditions under which it will be most profitable to sell only one red car to each A-type consumer as compared with selling a red car to both A and B types. The price p_r will then be set right at R_r^A, but $p_b > R_b^A$ to ensure that A does not want a blue car. The price point is in the neighborhood of A (so that, in terms of Figure 14.3, B is in the third quadrant and does not buy any car).

If it is most profitable to sell *each* consumer type a red car, then the price p_r cannot exceed the reservation price of type B consumers, R_r^B. The price of a blue car, p_b, must be set slightly in excess of R_b^B to ensure that B-type consumers will not choose a blue car, so that the relevant price point is in the neighborhood of B in Figure 14.4a. Here A will not choose a blue car, even though $R_b^A > p_b$, since the slope of the line connecting A and B is greater than one. Thus A will reap greater consumer surplus buying a red car, even though he or she can afford either. (Again, the placement of prices at point B can be considered in terms of Figure 14.3, where B is the origin and A lies above the 45° line. Thus, from Figure 14.3, A chooses the red car.)

Equation (14.6) is the condition that guarantees that selling a single red car to A's is also more profitable than selling a red to A's and a blue to B's. In the case where A's are actually sold red cars and B's are sold blue cars, $p_b \leqslant R_b^B$, so the price pair is restricted to the vertical line through R_b^B in Figure 14.4a. The price for a red car is restricted by the second inequality in (14.3), and the highest level for p_r is at price point 1 in Figure 14.4a. Notice that the slope of the line between point 1 and point A is one, so that in terms of Figure 14.3, the origin is at point 1 in

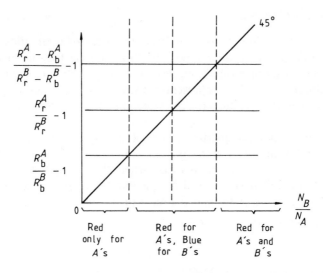

Figure 14.5. Product selection by a monopolist under Case 1 conditions.

Figure 14.4a, and point A lies right on the 45° border between buying a red or a blue car, whereas B is on the border between buying a blue car or no car. In this case, $p_b = R_b^B$ and $p_r = R_b^B + (R_r^A - R_b^A)$. The inequality guaranteeing that the policy just described is more profitable than selling red cars to both A's and B's is summarized in (14.7):

$$N_B R_b^B + N_A (R_b^B + R_r^A - R_b^A) > R_r^B (N_A + N_B) \qquad (14.7)$$

The inequalities in (14.5), (14.6), and (14.7) can be rearranged and summarized as a function of the ratio of N_B to N_A, as shown in Figure 14.5. It establishes the conditions under which the manufacturer decides to produce the various combinations of cars in Case 1. (A similar figure can be drawn in Cases 2 to 5. The various bounds shown as horizontal lines then change in order and magnitude.)

Under Case 1 consumer demand conditions, only red cars are produced, and they are priced so that only A-type consumers will buy them if $N_B/N_A < (R_b^A/R_b^B - 1)$. The manufacturer will produce both blue and red cars, pricing them so A's buy red cars and B's buy blue cars, if

$$\frac{R_b^A}{R_b^B} - 1 \leqslant \frac{N_B}{N_A} < \frac{R_r^A - R_b^A}{R_r^B - R_b^B} - 1$$

The producer once again finds it profitable to produce only red cars when

$$\frac{R_r^A - R_b^A}{R_r^B - R_b^B} - 1 \leqslant \frac{N_B}{N_A}$$

but here the price of red cars is lowered so both A- and B-type consumers will buy them.

Thus, starting with very few B-type customers, only red cars are produced, and B-type customers are priced out of the market. This situation enables the manufacturer to extract all of the consumer surplus from A's. As N_B increases, both red and blue cars are produced. The blue cars are priced to extract all of B's consumer surplus, but only a part of A's surplus is extracted. (If p_r were larger, the A-type consumer would shift to blue cars!) As N_B becomes very large, once again only red cars are produced and are priced to extract all of B's surplus. Here the surplus extraction from A-type customers is even lower than when red and blue cars were both produced. As the proportion of B-type consumers increases, the amount of surplus extraction from B-type consumers increases (as $R_r^B > R_b^B$) and from A-type consumers decreases.

One obvious reason why the B-type consumer may have lower reservation prices might be that the B's have smaller incomes than the A's.

Case 2

Suppose that A's reservation price for both red and blue cars dominates B's as before but that B's relative preference for red cars is greater, as indicated by the steeper slope of B's ray through the origin in Figure 14.4b.

The three inequalities in (14.5), (14.6), and (14.7) still apply. However, their magnitudes and relationships to one another are altered, because of B's greater relative preference for red cars. Through an analysis similar to the one outlined in Figure 14.5 for Case 1, it can be shown that, in Case 2, only red cars will be produced. Indeed, the red cars will be priced out of the range of a small number of B-type consumers. As the number of B-type consumers increases, the price of red cars will be lowered so that both types of consumers can buy a red car. The interested reader is referred to Table 14.1, which summarizes the production, pricing, and consumption decisions for this case as well as for the preceding and the following cases.

Case 3

Suppose that the relative preferences for red and blue cars of Case 2 are maintained but that the intensity of B's desire for red is such that $R_r^B > R_r^A$, whereas A's reservation price for blue cars still exceeds B's, as illustrated in Figure 14.4c. (The length of B's ray through the origin can be longer than A's, but it is restricted by the requirement $R_b^A > R_b^B$. Otherwise, the analysis would be the same as in Case 1, with the letters reversed.)

Table 14.1. *Summary of production and consumption choices with two product qualities and two consumer types*

Case	Consumers' Characteristics	Range of N_B/N_A	Car colors produced	Optimal prices p_r	Optimal prices p_b	Cars purchased A consumers	Cars purchased B consumers	Consumer surplus A consumers	Consumer surplus B consumers	Socially optimal purchases A consumers	Socially optimal purchases B consumers	Maximum consumer surplus/consumer A consumers	Maximum consumer surplus/consumer B consumers	Welfare loss/consumer due to product selection A consumers	Welfare loss/consumer due to product selection B consumers
I	$R_r^A > R_r^B$ $R_b^A > R_r^B$ $\frac{R_r^A}{R_b^A} > \frac{R_r^B}{R_b^B} > 1$	$< \frac{R_b^A}{R_b^B} - 1$	red	R_r^A	$R_b^A + \epsilon$	1 red	0	0	0				R_r^B	R_r^A	R_r^B
		$\left[\frac{R_b^A}{R_b^B} - 1,\; \frac{R_r^A - R_b^A}{R_r^B - R_b^B} - 1\right)$	red & blue	$(R_r^A - R_b^A + R_b^B)$	R_b^B	1 red	1 blue	$R_b^A - R_b^B$	0	1 red	1 red	R_r^A	R_r^B	$(R_r^A + R_r^B - R_b^A) < R_r^A$	R_r^B
		$> \frac{R_r^A - R_b^A}{R_r^B - R_b^B} - 1$	red	R_r^B	$R_b^B + \epsilon$	1 red	1 red	$R_r^A - R_r^B$	0					R_b^B	R_r^B
II	$R_r^A > R_r^B$ $R_b^A > R_b^B$ $1 < \frac{R_r^A}{R_b^A} < \frac{R_r^B}{R_b^B}$	$< \frac{R_r^A}{R_b^B} - 1$	red	R_r^A	$R_b^A + \epsilon$	1 red	0	0	0	1 red	1 red	R_r^A	R_r^B	R_r^A	R_r^B
		$> \frac{R_r^A}{R_b^B} - 1$	red	R_r^B	$R_b^A + \epsilon$	1 red	1 red	$R_r^A - R_r^B$	0					R_r^B	R_r^B
III	$R_b^A < R_r^B$ $R_b^A > R_b^B$ $1 < \frac{R_r^A}{R_b^A} < \frac{R_r^B}{R_b^B}$	$< \frac{R_r^A - R_b^A}{R_r^B - R_r^A}$	red	R_r^A	$R_b^A + \epsilon$	1 red	1 red	0	$R_r^B - R_r^A$	1 red	1 red	R_r^A	R_r^B	R_r^A	R_r^A
		$> \frac{R_b^A - R_b^B}{R_b^B - R_r^A}$	red & blue	R_r^B	R_b^A	1 blue	1 red	0	0					R_r^A	R_r^B
IV	$R_r^A > R_r^B$ $R_b^A > R_b^B$ $\frac{R_r^A}{R_b^A} > 1 > \frac{R_r^B}{R_b^B}$	$< \frac{R_b^A}{R_b^B} - 1$	red	R_r^A	$R_b^A + \epsilon$	1 red	0	0	0	1 red	1 blue	R_r^A	R_b^B	R_r^A	R_r^B
		$> \frac{R_b^A}{R_b^B} - 1$	red & blue	$(R_r^A - R_b^A + R_b^B)$	R_b^B	1 red	1 blue	$R_b^A - R_b^B$	0					$(R_r^A + R_r^B - R_b^A) < R_r^A$	R_r^B
V	$R_r^A > R_r^B$ $R_b^A < R_r^B$ $\frac{R_r^A}{R_b^A} > 1 > \frac{R_r^B}{R_b^B}$	$[0, \infty)$	red & blue	R_r^A	R_b^B	1 red	1 blue	0	0	1 red	1 blue	R_r^A	R_b^B	R_r^A	R_b^B

The inequalities in (14.5), (14.6), and (14.7) must now be altered, since B-type consumers have the largest reservation prices for red cars and A-type consumers have the dominant reservation price for blue cars. Since the preference points for both consumers still favor red cars at a zero price, the profit-maximizing options to be considered are selling a red car to B's only, selling red cars to A- and B-type consumers, or selling red cars to B's and blue cars to A's. The condition

$$N_B R_r^B > (N_A + N_B) R_r^A \qquad (14.8)$$

guarantees that selling one red car to B's only is more profitable than selling red cars to both A and B types. Inequality

$$N_B R_r^B > N_A R_b^A + N_B R_r^B \qquad (14.9)$$

indicates that selling red cars only to B's is never preferable to selling red cars to B's and blue cars to A's, since this inequality can never be satisfied. Inequality

$$(N_A + N_B) R_r^A > N_A R_b^A + N_B R_b^B \qquad (14.10)$$

gives the conditions under which it is more profitable to sell both A's and B's red cars than to sell B's red and A's blue. In this case, the profit-maximizing price of the combination of red and blue cars is easily computed, since each consumer has a dominant reservation price for a different quality car. Under this situation, the producer can always price each color at the reservation price of the dominant consumer and will not have to worry about violating (14.3): For either consumer type, the purchase of one quality is unfeasible because the quoted price exceeds the reservation price for it.

After rearranging the inequalities in (14.8), (14.9), and (14.10), the conditions for profit-maximizing supply can be summarized as shown in Table 14.1. With small numbers of B-type consumers, red cars will be sold to both A's and B's, but as the proportion of B types increases, it pays to segment the market, selling red cars to B's and blue cars to A's. It then becomes worthwhile to extract the maximum possible profit from B types, even though doing so means giving up some profit from A's as they are forced to consume the less-preferred blue cars.

Case 4

Suppose that A-type consumers once again have the dominant reservation prices for both colors but that B's have a relative preference for blue, so that $R_r^B / R_b^B < 1$, as shown in Figure 14.4d. The inequalities in (14.5), (14.6), and (14.7) once again are relevant. However, because of the position of B below the 45° line, it is never profitable to sell red cars to both consumer types.

As Table 14.1 shows, only red cars are produced at low N_B/N_A, and they are sold only to A-type consumers at their reservation price. As the proportion of B-type consumers increases, the market is segmented and blue cars are sold to B's at their reservation price R_b^B, but the price of red cars sold to A's must be reduced to $(R_r^A - R_b^A + R_b^B)$ so that (14.3) is not violated.

Case 5

Suppose that each consumer type has a dominant and clear preference for a different color, as illustrated in Figure 14.4e. Then it always pays to supply both red and blue cars and to sell each to the relevant consumer group at their respective reservation prices, as can be confirmed by manipulating Inequalities (14.8), (14.9), and (14.10) – see Table 14.1.

These five cases cover all possible combinations of reservation prices for two consumer types faced with the choice of two product qualities. All other possibilities are merely symmetric cases, and the consequences can be inferred by switching the labels on the reservation price points in one of the five cases presented.

Because of the assumption of zero production costs, some welfare implications can be readily inferred. First of all, *the monopolist will not always produce the socially optimal quality mix. Sometimes too much product variety is present; other times there is less product variety than would be socially optimal.* Second, *in several cases* where B-type consumers are willing to buy cars at prices in excess of costs, *only one type of car is produced,* and it is priced beyond their reach. This situation occurs only when A-type consumers have dominant reservation prices for all types of cars. In all cases, the policy of exclusive sales to A's is dropped at some point, as the proportion of B-type consumers increases.

The last column in Table 14.1 summarizes the surplus taken away (i.e., the "welfare loss per consumer"). Except in Cases 3 and 5, *the welfare loss of B-type consumers remains constant* as their proportion is increased, *whereas the loss to A-type consumers goes down.* This phenomenon happens whenever the A-type consumers have dominant reservation prices. Since it could be the result of higher income levels, the extent of welfare loss borne by A-type consumers declines as the fraction of poorer consumers increases. Thus my analysis suggests that the shape of the income distribution can influence product selection decisions. In particular, a decline in the proportion of rich people can have favorable effects for the rich, to the extent that the decline enables them to keep a larger consumer surplus.

Three qualities

In this section I want to consider when and why it might be profitable to reduce quality at the lower end of the quality scale, as suggested by Dupuit in his railway illustration. Does it always pay to offer wooden benches and no roof to third-class passengers? The answer is that it sometimes pays to reduce the quality offered to consumers with low reservation prices.

Suppose our manufacturer is capable of producing three qualities (red, blue, and gray, in that order) to be sold to two types of consumers. There are five different combinations of reservation prices for blue and gray cars, and five cases for red and blue cars as noted in the preceding analysis: Thus in total there are twenty-five combinations of reservation prices for red, blue, *and* gray cars to be considered. It would be a tedious task to analyze all possible combinations. Instead, I will present several numerical illustrations that make my point.

Assume that the A group has two members and that $N_B = 1$. All costs are still assumed to be zero.

Case 1-1

Suppose A's reservation prices dominate B's for all three colors and that the dominating consumer group has the strongest relative preference for red over blue and for blue over gray. The reservation prices are as follows:

	red	blue	gray
A-type consumer	150	120	105
B-type consumer	120	110	100

Pareto optimality requires that only red cars be produced, as the social surplus is dominated by the reservation prices for red cars in both groups. A monopolist, however, will find it profitable to sell red cars to A-type consumers at the price of ($p_r = 140$) and blue cars to B-type consumers at the price of ($p_b = 110$): The monopolist's profit is then [$2(140) + 110 = 390$]. Selling red cars only would give a revenue of [$3(120) = 360$]. A-type consumers transfer their demands from red to blue cars when $R_r^A - R_b^A = 150 - 120 < p_r - p_b$; that is why, given that $p_b = 110$, p_r cannot be higher than ($p_b + 30 = 140$).

Instead of producing blue cars, the seller might have produced gray cars: It is as profitable to sell blue as to sell gray. Indeed, transfers of demand from red to gray to A-type consumers are avoided as long as $p_r - p_g \leqslant 150 - 105 = 45$, so that a red-gray product line would give a revenue of $[2(145) + 100 = 390]$. Although profitability is the same, A-type consumers would have seen their surplus reduced from 10 to 5.

Case 1–3

Suppose, however, that whereas the reservation prices for red and blue cars are as in Case 1, those for blue and gray cars are as in Case 3:

	red	blue	gray
A-type consumer	150	120	90
B-type consumer	120	110	100

Although it is still Pareto-optimal that only red cars be produced, the monopolist will now find the red–gray product line most profitable: $2(150) + 100 = 400$. Red cars can now be sold at $p_r = R_r^A = 150$. No surplus is left for anybody, because the constraint $(p_r - p_g \leqslant 150 - 90 = 60)$ is not binding any longer, and $p_g = 100$.

Case 2–2

If both the red–blue and the blue–gray combinations of reservation prices are as in Case 2, "red only" would be the socially optimal product selection. And it would be the most profitable, too, as can be checked using the following numbers:

	red	blue	gray
A-type consumer	150	120	110
B-type consumer	145	110	90

Profit maximization requires that $p_r = 145$, with a revenue of $[3(145) =]$ 435.

Case 2–3

What if Case 2 applies to red and blue, but the reservation prices for blue and gray are as in Case 3?

	red	blue	gray
A-type consumer	150	120	90
B-type consumer	145	110	100

"Red only" is still the most profitable policy: Under the assumptions made, there is no greater profit to be expected from introducing gray cars in the market.

Case 4-4

In the previous examples, everybody has a relative preference for red over blue over gray. We now consider what happens if B-type consumers prefer gray and blue over red (while maintaining the dominance of A's reservation prices for all colors). Imagine the following reservation prices:

	red	*blue*	*gray*
A-type consumer	150	100	80
B-type consumer	50	60	60

If only red and blue cars were considered, it would be socially optimal to sell red cars to A-type consumers and blue cars to B-type consumers. But it would be profitable to sell only red cars to A-type consumers at $p_r = 150$, given that $N_B/N_A = \frac{1}{2}$. No surplus would be left to the A group, and the B group would not be served.

A clever monopolist would, of course, not be so myopic: He or she would consider reducing the quality of the blue car so that it becomes "gray." A monopolist would take this step after determining that the B group is consistently misinformed about the objective quality differences. Alternatively, there may be no objective quality differences involved, so that everything is a matter of taste (*De gustibus et coloribus*), and the B group might be composed of dull people who prefer gray and blue to red, whereas the A group is young and gay. Whatever the reason, suppose the A group reduces its reservation price to eighty, whereas the B group holds its reservation price at sixty, when gray is added to the choice spectrum.

In this situation, it is socially optimal to sell red cars to A-type consumers and gray cars to B-type consumers. And the red–gray product line is also the most profitable policy for a monopolist to follow [revenue would be $2(130) + 60 = 320$]. The A-type customers keep a surplus of $(150 - 130 =)20$, and the B-type consumers can now drive a car, though a gray one, with no surplus left.

Case 4-5

What if the producer could find a third color, like gray, such that B's reservation price for gray dominates A's?

	red	*blue*	*gray*
A-type consumer	150	100	50
B-type consumer	50	60	70

Optimality still requires that red cars be sold to A-type consumers and gray cars be sold to B-type consumers. The red–gray product mix is also still the most profitable, but the price of red cars can be raised from 130 to 150 in this case, since the constraint ($p_r - p_g \leqslant 150 - 50 = 100$) is not binding with $p_g = 70$. No surplus is left to anybody and all consumers are served, but the B's get low quality.

To sum up, the red–gray product mix may be more profitable than the red only or the red–blue mix, depending upon the numerical values of N_B/N_A and the reservation prices. However, for given N_B/N_A, quality reduction can be described as a surplus extracting device (on the assumption, obviously, that it is profitable to put two colors on the market). It appears as such when each consumer group prefers a different type of color, even though one group's reservation prices dominate the other's for both types of car (see Case 4–4).

If, on the other hand, one group ceases to dominate the other, so that each group has a dominant reservation price for one of the two colors, then there may be a possibility of extracting the *entire* surplus by reducing quality: This happens in Cases 1–3 and 4–5. Quality reduction is seen to achieve perfect price discrimination. Indeed, when each customer group has a dominant reservation price for one color, the constraint on the price for red ($p_r \leqslant p_g + R_r^A - R_g^A$) ceases to be binding. In other words, there is no danger that the A group will transfer its demand from red cars to lower-quality cars when charged a price $p_r = R_r^A$. It is understandable, then, that producers try not only to segment their market but also to have each customer identify itself with one particular brand (or quality or type), so that they will order the qualities differently and will be willing to pay more for their preferred quality than the other customer groups.

Costs and socially optimal qualities

The introduction of nonzero costs can change the conclusions reached, both with respect to which product mix is socially optimal and with respect to which product selection is the most profitable. Consider optimality first and suppose, for concreteness, that each type of car is produced at the same constant marginal cost c. In addition, there are overhead costs associated with each type of color (quality): an overhead of K_g for (the design, marketing, and production of) gray cars, one of K_b for blue cars, and one of K_r for red cars.

The usual approach is to compute the social surplus for all possible product selections and to determine which selection dominates under which set of cost conditions. Thus we compare

for red only (sold to group A only): $N_A(R_r^A - c) - K_r$
for red only (sold to both groups): $N_A(R_r^A - c) + N_B(R_r^B - c) - K_r$

for red (to group A) plus blue (to B): $N_A(R_r^A - c) + N_B(R_b^B - c) - (K_r + K_b)$

for red (to group A) plus gray (to B): $N_A(R_r^A - c) + N_B(R_g^B - c) - (K_r + K_g)$

Selling red cars only to A-type customers only would be optimal, compared with selling red to A and blue to B, or selling red to A and gray to B, if

$$K_b + N_B c > N_B R_b^B \qquad (14.11a)$$

or

$$K_g + N_B c > N_B R_g^B \qquad (14.11b)$$

In Cases 4 and 5 above, the socially optimal mix was the red-plus-blue combination, because all costs were set equal to zero. We now discover that positive costs may reduce the optimal mix to one color offered to one customer group only. For the same reason, it may be optimal not to serve the customer group with the lower reservation price in Cases 1, 2, and 3.

On the other hand, selling red cars to both A-type and B-type customers is optimal, compared with the red–blue or red–gray combinations, if

$$K_b > N_B(R_b^B - R_r^B) \qquad (14.12a)$$

or

$$K_g > N_B(R_g^B - R_r^B) \qquad (14.12b)$$

respectively. These conditions are always satisfied, that is, whatever the value of K_b or K_g, when $R_r^B > R_b^B$ or $R_r^B > R_g^B$, as in cases 1, 2, and 3.

An alternative, but equivalent, approach is to consider each quality change separately and to treat it as a modification of the product's characteristics. This is the method used by Drèze and Hagen (1978) in their analysis of the choice of product quality by a number of firms who produce one differentiated commodity each and behave either monopolistically or "competitively."[10] The characteristics of a commodity are formally equivalent to (local or regional) public goods, so that quality change can be seen as a public-choice problem. Indeed, the public-good aspect of product quality is due to the facts that (a) the same range of choice is imposed on *all* consumers and (b) if one firm changes the quality of its commodity, this (common) range of choice will be modified.

The present section considers terms of quality, that is, a bundle of characteristics, rather than characteristics per se, and examines a single firm producing different qualities. Yet the public-good aspect of quality is the same as in the Drèze–Hagen model: The same range of choice is obviously imposed on all consumers by the firm (even if some consumers are not served at all), and any change in quality affects everybody's range of choice. Furthermore, the quality change can be treated as a change in characteristics in a particular direction, say, along the color axis.

Not surprisingly, then, the conditions for Pareto-optimal product quality appear as a natural extension of the "Samuelson conditions" for Pareto-optimal production of public goods: Quality should be increased until marginal social value equals marginal cost. Marginal social value is the sum of the individual evaluations of the marginal change in quality considered, whereas marginal cost refers to the cost of the same marginal change in quality.

Suppose the firm considers changing from the red–gray product mix to the red-only policy (with sales to both groups). This action amounts to a switch in quality for the B-type consumers only, who are now served with red rather than gray cars, whereas the A-type consumers continue to receive red cars, as before. Marginal social value is thus $N_B(R_r^B - R_g^B)$. The marginal cost is the difference between the cost of producing N red cars, that is, $K_r + Nc$, and the cost of producing N_A red and N_B gray cars, that is, $K_r + N_A c + K_g + N_B c$. Marginal cost of eliminating gray and shifting all consumers to red is here $-K_g$. The Samuelson condition says that gray should be transformed into red as long as $N_B(R_r^B - R_g^B) > -K_g$, which is exactly Inequality (14.12b). With the numbers given in Case 1–3, we see that gray should turn red as long as $K_g > -20$, that is, always.

The Drèze–Hagen firms, which produce only one quality each and behave either monopolistically or competitively, do not, in general, satisfy the Samuelson conditions. The same is true for a monopolist who can produce several qualities, as will become clear in the next section.

Costs and profits

Let us examine profitability under the same assumptions about costs, and consider first the red-only-to-A-only policy. This policy is more profitable than the red–blue or red–gray mix when

$$K_b + N_B c > (N_A + N_B) R_b^B - N_A R_b^A \qquad (14.13a)$$

or

$$K_g + N_B c > (N_A + N_B) R_g^B - N_A R_g^A \qquad (14.13b)$$

respectively, with (14.3) binding. These optimal-profit conditions are found by subtracting the costs from (14.6), and they are very different from (14.11a) and (14.11b), which reflect the social optimum.

Similarly, compare the red-only-to-A-plus-B policy with the red–blue and red–gray product mixes by subtracting costs from Inequality (14.7). The first is more profitable if

$$K_b > N_B(R_b^B - R_r^B) + N_A(R_b^B - R_b^A) + N_A(R_r^A - R_r^B) \qquad (14.14a)$$

or

$$K_g > N_B(R_g^B - R_r^B) + N_A(R_g^B - R_g^A) + N_A(R_r^A - R_r^B) \qquad (14.14b)$$

These results are to be compared with Inequalities (14.12a) and (14.12b). It does not suffice, here, that $R_r^B > R_b^B$ or $R_r^B > R_g^B$ for (14.14a) or (14.14b) to be satisfied always: Under these conditions, red-only-to-A-plus-B may *not* be the most profitable thing to do. Indeed, the right side of (14.4a) and (14.4b) may be positive if $R_r^A - R_r^B$ is positive and sufficiently large.

If (14.3) is not binding, then Inequalities (14.4a) and (14.4b) become

$$K_b > N_B(R_b^B - R_r^B) + N_A(R_r^A - R_r^B) \qquad (14.15a)$$

and

$$K_g > N_B(R_g^B - R_r^B) + N_A(R_r^A - R_r^B) \qquad (14.15b)$$

respectively, so that the profitability of selling red only (to A plus B) becomes even more difficult to achieve. The reason should be clear: Greater dispersion in the reservation prices creates larger opportunities for price discrimination and makes it more profitable to put several colors in the market.

Yet it remains true that, the higher the overhead cost associated with a quality change, the more likely it is for a monopolist to offer a single product and the less likely it is for price discrimination over quality to occur.

Welfare and product selection

I now focus on the pricing aspect of our problem and want to highlight the discriminatory aspects and the welfare implications of the prices at which a variety of qualities are sold.

The reader will have noticed that, in the discussion above, these prices are determined as soon as the product selection problem is solved. Indeed, once the firm has decided which qualities to put on the market, and therefore, which classes of customers to serve, there are n given qualities sold to n classes. As customers are supposed to buy, at most, one quality and, at most, one unit of that quality, a particular consumer group and a corresponding quality can be identified using the index i. Each group i buys quality q_i on the condition that no other quality gives a higher surplus, that is, that $(R_i^i - p_i)$ is higher than $(R_j^i - p_j)$, where R_j^i is the reservation price in group i for quality j, or

$$R_i^i - p_i \geqslant R_j^i - p_j \qquad (14.16)$$

for all i and j, $j \neq i$. Needless to say, this is a direct generalization of (14.3). Transfers of demand from one group to another are thus avoided.

Suppose further that qualities can be ordered along an objectively given increasing scale. For example, all consumers agree that quality $(i+1)$ is better than quality i, because they all have the same utility function and receive the same information. Differences in their reservation prices result only from differences in income. Then it must be that $R^i < R^{i+1}$ for all quality levels. Suppose, in addition, that quality is continuous and that $\partial R^i/\partial q_i < \partial R^{i+1}/\partial q_i$. Then we are in Case 1, and (14.16) is binding. Indeed, to maximize profits, the seller wants to extract as much surplus as possible from each group. The highest possible prices, given the n qualities and the n corresponding groups, are:

$$p_1 = R_1^1$$
$$p_2 = R_2^2 - R_1^2 + p_1$$
$$\vdots$$
$$p_i = R_i^i - R_{i-1}^i + p_{i-1}$$
$$\vdots$$
$$p_n = R_n^n - R_{n-1}^n + p_{n-1}$$

or

$$p_i = \sum_{j=1}^{i} (R_j^j - R_{j-1}^j) \tag{14.17}$$

with the understanding that $R_0^i = 0$ for all i. *Once the n qualities (classes) are given and the reservation prices entering (14.16) are known, all prices are determined.* This result is formally equivalent to Spence's (1980) characterization of quantity-dependent prices (see Chapter 10).

It is possible to derive the socially optimal and the profit-maximizing product selection conditions under this pricing rule and to compare these with marginal-cost pricing – following Spence (1980) – on the assumption that quality is continuous. Let $m(q_i)$ be the unit cost of producing products of quality q_i, so that total cost is $\sum_i N_i m(q_i)$. The profits of the firm are

$$\Pi = \sum_{i=1}^{n} N_i p_i - \sum_{i=1}^{n} N_i m(q_i)$$

and the social consumer surplus is

$$S = \sum_{i=1}^{n} N_i (R_i^i - p_i)$$

The general welfare problem amounts to maximizing

$$W = \lambda S + \Pi = \lambda \sum_{i=1}^{n} N_i R_i^i + (1 - \lambda) \sum_{i=1}^{n} N_i p_i - \sum_{i=1}^{n} N_i m(q_i)$$

where $0 \leq \lambda \leq 1$. When $\lambda = 1$, we have marginal-cost pricing. When $\lambda = 0$, we have the special case of profit maximization.

Define

$$M_i = \sum_{j=i}^{n} N_j, \qquad i = 1, \ldots, n$$

Using p_i as defined in (14.17), we can write W in terms of qualities alone as

$$W = \sum_{i=1}^{n} [N_i + (1 - \lambda)M_{i+1}]R_i^i - (1 - \lambda) \sum_{i=1}^{n-1} R_i^{i+1}M_{i+1} - \sum_{i=1}^{n} N_i m(q_i)$$

The optimal product selection is obtained by differentiating W with respect to q_i and setting the result equal to zero:

$$\frac{\partial R_i^i}{\partial q_i} = \left[\frac{N_i}{N_i + (1 - \lambda)M_{i+1}} \right] m'(q_i) + \left[\frac{(1 - \lambda)M_{i+1}}{N_i + (1 - \lambda)M_{i+1}} \right] \frac{\partial R_i^{i+1}}{\partial q_i} \tag{14.18}$$

When $\lambda = 1$, Equation (14.18) reduces to $\partial R_i^i / \partial q_i = m'(q_i)$. The marginal reservation price in group i is equal to the marginal cost of quality i, and we have the unconstrained optimum. When $0 < \lambda < 1$, marginal price is *equal to marginal cost only for the highest quality* (when $i = n$, so that $M_{i+1} = 0$). For all other groups the marginal price is a weighted average of the marginal cost and the marginal value placed on quality i by the *next* group higher up on the quality scale. The same is true when $\lambda = 0$, that is, when profits only are maximized, the only special feature being that $m'(q_i)$ has a smaller weight. In profit-maximizing product selection, the emphasis is on the transferability of demand rather than on marginal cost.

All in all, class n (the richest) keeps the highest surplus according to Equation (14.17) and receives the quality it would have received if quality n were priced at marginal cost, according to Equation (14.18). All other classes are worse off: Their marginal benefit is smaller than marginal cost, and the surplus they retain is lower. The poorest class has *no* surplus left.

If the preference orderings of classes i and $(i+1)$ are such that we cannot suppose $R^i < R^{i+1}$ for all quality levels, then (14.16) cannot be supposed to be binding, and Equations (14.17) and (14.18) do not necessarily hold. All we can say is that, by an appropriate product selection, it should be possible to choose classes and qualities such that the entire surplus is taken away from all chosen classes.

Whether (14.16) is binding or not, price discrimination arises as soon as and to the extent that

$$p_i - p_{i-1} \neq m(q_i) - m(q_{i-1})$$

The case where $(p_i - p_{i-1}) > m(q_i) - m(q_{i-1})$ may be said to imply "phantom quality" by analogy with "phantom freight" in spatial pricing (delivered prices increase over space by more than the unit cost of transportation). When $(p_i - p_{i-1}) < m(q_i) - m(q_{i-1})$, there is "quality absorption," a situation comparable to the "freight absorption" cases that are so frequent in spatial economics.

As the differences $(p_i - p_{i-1})$ are fully determined by the reservation prices and the constraints resulting from the demand side, there is no reason why they should correspond to $m(q_i) - m(q_{i-1})$. Price discrimination should thus be the rule.

CHAPTER 15

Quality uncertainty

The very existence of quality differences creates opportunities to price discriminate – as does the existence of spatial or temporal differentiation – as we saw in the preceding chapter. Furthermore, quality uncertainty creates additional opportunities that are worth highlighting briefly – as does uncertainty about terms of delivery, about entry of new firms or future demand, or about prices charged. It is essential, however, as before, to be careful about the side of the market on which the uncertainty occurs, that is, to note whether it is the seller's or the buyer's information that is imperfect.

In this final chapter, I first look at a market in which information about quality is assumed to be perfect, not only to have a starting point but also because most of standard economics is based on this assumption. I then move to another popular and polar case, in which information is asymmetric, because one side of the market has no way of knowing the quality before the purchase, whereas the seller is perfectly informed: This the "market for lemons." Finally, I am going to admit that information can improve, at a cost, on both sides of the market. The empirical relevance of this last approach, as compared with that of the preceding approaches, will be tested with reference to the observed behavior of physicians, since the quality of their services is particularly difficult to evaluate.

Efficient markets

Consider the abstract and, in my view, totally unrealistic example of an "ideal" efficient market for medical services in which all private information is transmitted freely through market prices, as worked out by Salop:

> Suppose physicians differ in the quality of medical services provided and that these differences may be quantified in dollar terms. For example, suppose the best doctors provide $4,000 worth of services per year, the worst provide $2,000, and the rest provide services in the $2,000–4,000 range. An efficient market would be one in which the relative prices of medical services of the various physicians are proportional to their relative values; that is, the $2,000 doctors ought to earn one-half the price of the $4,000 doctors.

237

> If the quality of medical services provided are easily observable by well-informed patients, then the market prices will reflect relative values in equilibrium. Otherwise, if some physicians offer a better buy than others, then they will gain patients at the expense of other doctors. As they gain patients and others lose patients, there will be an incentive to charge a price that reflects value more closely. This dynamic process of customer movements and price changes will continue until an equilibrium is reached in which prices do reflect values. [1978, pp. 4–5]

The explanatory power of this model with respect to the behavior of doctors and patients, as I observe it in my personal life, strikes me as particularly poor. In my experience, patients find it difficult to quantify physicians' services, especially at the time they have to choose a doctor, that is, when they are sick. (Quantification may be easier, once they have recovered.) And it is not clear to me that it is the better doctor who gains patients nor that the dynamic process to which Salop alluded leads to an equilibrium. Admittedly the model of an efficient market has some explanatory power, and reality must always be simplified in a theoretical analysis. What is particularly cumbersome, though, is the difficulty of using this model as a norm in markets where quality information is poor, because of the contradiction that follows.

Indeed, when asked what doctor a new uninformed patient – who just arrived in town, say – should use, the economist who believes in the efficiency of well-informed markets should answer: Pick any physician at random whose prices are compatible with your income and preferences, since prices reflect relative values. In other words, there is no need for everybody to search. Equilibrium prices will transmit the relevant information as a result of the search by the informed patients. However, if this is so, then *nobody* should, individually speaking, bother to gather information (the more so if gathering information is costly). But if nobody gathers information, then prices will not transmit information! This phenomenon Salop (1978, p. 5) calls the "central conundrum of the economics of information." It seems to me that it results from the application to imperfect markets of a logic that makes sense only for perfect markets. An alternative approach is welcome.

Lemons, physicians, and quacks

Consider the other polar case, in which one side of the market only is well informed. This case was first analyzed in Akerlof's seminal 1970 paper on the market for lemons. Given its popularity, I shall stick to the case of lemons and shall discuss its applicability to the market for physicians' services as a corollary. Akerlof describes the case as follows:

The example of used cars captures the essence of the problem. From time to time one hears either mention of or surprise at the large price difference between new cars and those which have just left the showroom. The usual lunch table justification for this phenomenon is the pure joy of owning a "new" car. We offer a different explanation. Suppose (for the sake of clarity rather than reality) that there are just four kinds of cars. There are new cars and used cars. There are good cars and bad cars (which in America are known as "lemons"). A new car may be a good car or a lemon, and of course the same is true of used cars.

The individuals in this market buy a new automobile without knowing whether the car they buy will be good or a lemon. But they do know that with probability q it is a good car and with probability $(1-q)$ it is a lemon; by assumption, q is the proportion of good cars produced and $(1-q)$ is the proportion of lemons.

After owning a specific car, however, for a length of time, the car owner can form a good idea of the quality of this machine; i.e., the owner assigns a new probability to the event that his car is a lemon. This estimate is more accurate than the original estimate. An asymmetry in available information has developed: for the sellers now have more knowledge about the quality of a car than the buyers. But good cars and bad cars must still sell at the same price – since it is impossible for a buyer to tell the difference between a good car and a bad car. It is apparent that a used car cannot have the same valuation as a new car – if it did have the same valuation, it would clearly be advantageous to trade a lemon at the price of new car, and buy another new car, at a higher probability q of being good and a lower probability of being bad. Thus the owner of a good machine must be locked in. Not only is it true that he cannot receive the true value of his car, but he cannot even obtain the expected value of a new car.

Gresham's law has made a modified reappearance. For most cars traded will be the "lemons," and good cars may not be traded at all. The "bad" cars tend to drive out the good (in much the same way that bad money drives out the good). But the analogy with Gresham's law is not quite complete: bad cars drive out the good because they sell at the same price as good cars; similarly, bad money drives out good because the exchange rate is even. But the bad cars sell at the same price as good cars since it is impossible for a buyer to tell the difference between a good and a bad car; only the seller knows. In Gresham's law, however, presumably both buyer and seller can tell the difference between good and bad money. So the analogy is instructive, but not complete. [1970, pp. 489-90]

There is an analogy between the market for used cars and the market for physicians' services, at least to the extent that bad information leads to the success of quacks. Indeed, quacks tend to be successful on the less informed segments of the markets: in poor neighborhoods, among people with a poor education, in the treatment of old people. There may also be an analogy with Gresham's law in the fact that qualified doctors "vanish" from the market in the following sense. During a prolonged stay in the United States, several medical doctors who were recommended to us refused to examine members of my family because we were visitors. Only well-known and registered customers had access to these doctor's offices, just as good used cars are sold among family members and acquaintances.

To illustrate the working of the market for lemons, Akerlof constructs the following extreme numerical example, in which no market for used cars exists at all, although there are several qualities available. Assume that the demand for used cars depends on the price p of the car and on the average quality μ of used cars traded, whereas the supply depends on the price. In equilibrium, the supply must equal the demand for the given average quality, which depends in turn on the price.

For algebraic results, specify the utility function of each of two groups of traders as follows. Group 1 has the utility function

$$U_1 = M + \sum_{i=1}^{n} q_i \tag{15.1}$$

where M is the consumption of goods other than cars, q_i is the quality of the ith used car, and n is the number of qualities. Group 1 also has N used cars with uniformly distributed quality q $(0 \leqslant q \leqslant 2)$. Group 2 has utility function

$$U_2 = M + \sum_{i=1}^{n} \frac{3}{2} q_i \tag{15.2}$$

but no (used) cars at all. The linearity of these two utility functions is unrealistic (it does not take the risk aspect of uncertainty into account and implies that each additional car [quality] consumed adds the same amount of utility) but has the advantage of leading to corner solutions, which are typical for the case under analysis.

Consider group 1. Its budget constraint is

$$M + pn = Y_1 \tag{15.3}$$

when the price of "other goods" M is set equal to one and Y_1 is the income (including that derived from the sale of used cars) of all type 1 traders. Their indifference field and budget constraint are depicted in Figure 15.1 (when $M=0$, $n=Y_1/p$).

The number of used cars demanded by group 1, that is, D_1, is obtained by maximizing the expectation of U_1 subject to Equation (15.3) or by maximizing

$$E(U_1) = E\left(M + \sum_{i=1}^{n} q_i\right) = M + \sum_{i=1}^{n} E(q_i)$$
$$= M + \mu n = Y_1 + (\mu - p)n \tag{15.4}$$

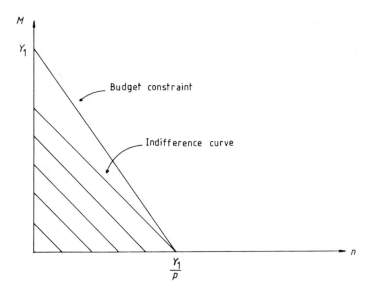

Figure 15.1. Consumer equilibrium under quality uncertainty.

since the expectation $E(q_i)$ is equal to μ for all used cars. This expected utility is linear in n and is therefore maximized if

$$D_1 = Y_1/p \qquad \text{when } \mu > p \tag{15.5a}$$

since Y_1/p is the largest possible value of n, that is, the corner solution, or

$$D_1 = 0 \qquad \text{when } \mu < p \tag{15.5b}$$

that is, the other corner solution (the smallest possible value of n). Then no market exists at all.

To find the supply of cars offered by type 1 traders, we must use the assumption that quality is distributed uniformly, as in Figure 15.2. The shaded area represents the probability that q is between zero and p. When $p=2$, this area is equal to one by convention, so that the vertical side of the rectangle, the uniform density, is equal to one-half. The supply of used cars by type 1 traders will thus be a proportion of stock equal to

$$S_1 = (p \cdot \tfrac{1}{2}) \cdot N = p \cdot \frac{N}{2} \tag{15.6}$$

and the average quality μ will be $S_1/N = p \cdot (N/2) \cdot (1/N) = p/2$, since group 2 has no cars to offer.

The demand of type 2 traders is determined in an analogous way as

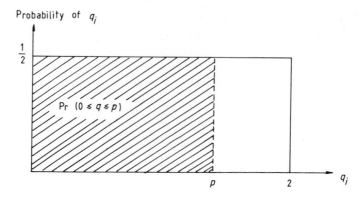

Figure 15.2. Distribution of quality between zero and two.

$$D_2 = Y_2/p \qquad \text{when} \quad \frac{3\mu}{2} > p \tag{15.7a}$$

and

$$D_2 = 0 \qquad \text{when} \quad \frac{3\mu}{2} < p \tag{15.7b}$$

Total demand for used cars is thus

$$D(p, \mu) = (Y_1 + Y_2)/p \qquad \text{if } p < \mu$$

$$D(p, \mu) = Y_2/p \qquad \text{if } \mu < p < \frac{3\mu}{2}$$

$$D(p, \mu) = 0 \qquad \text{if } p > \frac{3\mu}{2} \tag{15.8}$$

However, the average quality μ is equal to $p/2$, so that the condition $p > 3\mu/2$ is always satisfied: At no price will any trade take place at all!

This extreme example makes it clear that average quality is important. An increase in μ can make the market work again (in the example, as soon as μ is larger than $2p/3$). Knowing this fact, traders will make sure that average quality does not deteriorate: For example, medical doctors will try to make it illegal for anyone they consider a quack to offer services. In other words, only shortsighted traders would let a situation such as that described in Akerlof's numerical example develop. This is the point[1] made by Heal (1976a).

Intelligent traders will indeed react. Rather than withdraw from the market when they have better quality to offer, they will follow a number of strategies. First of all, sellers will set up an institutional framework in which quality goods stand a good chance of not being driven out, because intertemporal considerations will dominate. One policy is that just mentioned: Only well-trained medical students – as guaranteed by their doctor's degree – will be admitted to practice and will be permitted to call themselves doctors. (In product markets, brand names play the same role.) Simultaneously, buyers will look for signals to improve their information. They will use screening devices to separate the good from the bad. In important matters, such as problems of health and survival, they will actively search, even when searching is costly.

It is in such an environment that price discrimination, based on quality differences *and* differences in quality uncertainty, will develop.

Quality certification and price discrimination

To illustrate the role of quality certification in a market with asymmetric information about quality, we can construct the following example.[2]

Consider a firm that sells nine different qualities of the same commodity. This firm could be a car producer who puts nine different models on the market, or a used car dealer who happens to have nine types of car at hand, or a music shop selling nine brands of grand pianos. To focus on quality uncertainty, suppose the only quality differences are those due to differences in the probability of failure (probability that the new car will be produced on a Monday and will therefore be a source of trouble, probability that the used car will be a lemon or that the piano will have its soundboard broken). Suppose further that the seller knows these differences, whereas the buyers have no way of checking, so that they ignore the true probabilities of success (absence of failure) p_i, where i designates quality i, where $i = 1, \ldots, 9$.

These p_i are equal, in fact, to $i/10$. All the buyers know is the average probability of success of the seller's products, which is here $\bar{p} = 0.5$. (The strange number nine was chosen to obtain this average from a series of decreasing p_i's.)

In Akerlof's model, it was the average quality of used cars that determined their price. Here, the average probability of failure comes into play, together with the buyers' reservation price. If this reservation price is one, then price π, corrected for the cost of failure times its average probability, cannot be higher than one. Let the buyers place a value of minus one on failure (an unfavorable purchase). Then we have

$$\pi - (1 - 0.5)(-1) \leqslant 1$$

where $(1 - 0.5)$ is the average probability of failure, or

$$\pi + 0.5 \leqslant 1$$
$$\pi \leqslant 0.5$$

Sellers can obviously improve matters – rather than to stop the production or sale of above-average quality – by altering the buyers' assessment of the probabilities involved. Suppose they can convey the true probability of failure p_i for each quality i at some cost, namely the cost of quality certification (use of brand names, information about properties of the nine products, free rides, guarantees, etc.). In other words, and more technically, suppose they can alter the buyers' probability distribution so that its mean becomes p_i. Then they can charge higher prices for better qualities.

For quality 9,

$$\pi_9 - (1 - 0.9)(-1) \leqslant 1$$

or

$$\pi_9 \leqslant 0.9$$

and similarly, $\pi_8 \leqslant 0.8$, $\pi_7 \leqslant 0.7$, and so forth.

Quality certification is profitable as long as it costs no more than the difference between the price π_i and the price π based on the average probability of failure, or

$$0.9 - 0.5 = 0.4 \qquad \text{for quality 9}$$
$$0.8 - 0.5 = 0.3 \qquad \text{for quality 8}$$
$$0.7 - 0.5 = 0.2 \qquad \text{for quality 7}$$
$$0.6 - 0.5 = 0.1 \qquad \text{for quality 6}$$

Qualities equal or below 5 are not worth being certified. The seller will leave the buyers ignorant of the quality differences below 5: There is no incentive to reveal inferior quality. Yet the market works, and bad quality does *not* drive out good quality.

Notice that, in my terminology, the result is not price discrimination, as far as the price differences for above-average quality are concerned, if these duly reflect differences in uncertainties. The latter are elements of product differentiation leading to costs of certification. With cost differences truly reflected in price differences, nobody should complain. However, price discrimination would be present if products with probabilities of success varying between 0.5 and 0.1 were sold at the same price π, as will be the case in this model. It is also of some interest to notice that, once again, as in Chapter 14, it is the buyer of good quality who gets a fair deal, whereas the ignorance of the buyer of lower quality is not corrected and leads to discriminatory prices.

The example worked out above is of course unrealistic to the extent that all buyers are supposed to have the same reservation price. Suppose buyers can be separated into nine subsets with reservation prices equal to

$(i = 1, \ldots, g)$, respectively. And suppose the corresponding costs of failure are evaluated at $-i$, respectively. Then I find, by the same reasoning – with quality certification – the following prices:

$$\pi_g - (1 - 0.9)(-9) \leqslant 9$$

or

$$\pi_9 \leqslant 8.9$$
$$\pi_8 \leqslant 6.4$$
$$\pi_7 \leqslant 4.9$$
$$\pi_6 \leqslant 3.6$$
$$\pi_5 \leqslant 2.5$$
$$\pi_4 \leqslant 1.6$$
$$\pi_3 \leqslant 0.9$$
$$\pi_2 \leqslant 0.4$$
$$\pi_1 \leqslant 0.1$$

Now the cost of quality certification is always prohibitive for the two lowest qualities only. The possibility of posting different prices increases the quality range over which certification is profitable and (rather paradoxically) reduces the extent of price discrimination against the buyers of lower-quality goods.

All in all, the extent upon which more information on qualities leads to more or less price discrimination depends on the structure of the reservation prices as compared with the costs of quality certification. A next and much-debated question is to ask whether more information on prices affects the quality of the goods put on the market. The problem is particularly acute in the market for physicians' services, where price advertising is prohibited by professional codes in many countries, on the grounds that it would threaten the quality of service. (The same is true for a number of markets for professional services.) The argument is typically Akerlof's: Consumers are ignorant of sellers' true qualities, and therefore high-quality sellers will be driven from the market. In view of the possibility of quality certification available to the professions, this argument loses most of its weight, it seems to me. Could not these prohibitions of price information be means of facilitating price discrimination? This discrimination should not necessarily apply to low-quality services but could as well apply to the richer customers (some of whom might prefer to pay less, even if the quality of the service deteriorates, when better informed about prices). I shall turn to this type of price discrimination in medicine after discussing a possible move of the buyers that parallels quality certification by the seller.

Screening devices and "rat races"

To this point we have supposed that uninformed buyers could do nothing about their ignorance (after supposing, initially, that they *should* do nothing, individually, and should let the market somehow do its job). The time has come to note that they will attempt to infer the actual quality of prospective purchases by making an informed guess on the basis of available observable data.

Salop develops this idea in the following provocative way:

> For example, buyers may infer that low mileage cars owned by religious old ladies have not depreciated significantly. Red sportscars, former taxi-cabs and dealers named Nixon will be avoided. Average repair data from *Consumer Reports* may be consulted. Screening devices are surely imperfect solutions to the Lemons problem, since they rely on use of an average statistic; however, they can improve performance somewhat...
>
> Two types of screening devices may be distinguished. *Indices* are rules of thumb that sort on the basis of observable variables that directly bear on values. On average, former taxi-cabs have high depreciation rates; dealers named Nixon are thought to be unethical Rats (Rational Economic Men). On the other hand, *Self-selection Devices* sort on the basis of evidence revealed by the seller's own decision. King Solomon's threat to cut the baby in half caused each mother-claimant to reveal her true identity. A red sportscar is avoided not because red sportscars are inherently of lower value; rather the personality-type who prefers a red sportscar is thought to be the type who engages in reckless driving and performs insufficient maintenance. The decision to purchase a red sportscar reveals information regarding the owner and, hence, the quality of the car.
>
> For either type, if sellers are aware of buyers' use of these rules-of-thumb, they have an incentive to exploit the screening device to misrepresent the value of their product. At a cost, a red sportscar can be painted blue, the identity of a former taxi may be camouflaged, and a dealer can change his name from Nixon to Carter. [1978, p. 6]

The dynamics of screening devices have been studied in economics under the labels of signaling and self-selection. The so-called rat race is the commonly used example.[3]

In an efficient market for medical services, a consumer would learn immediately (or would know everything). In a real world market for medical services, a consumer can learn to evaluate a doctor's services through experience, using a screening device. Working hours could be such a device, if the consumer were to observe that those doctors who provide the highest quality are also those who work the longest hours.

The dynamics could then involve a chain reaction: Physicians who work longer hours gain at the expense of the others; in particular, hard-working incompetents gain new clients at the expense of lazy but competent doctors; as a result, every doctor will have to begin to work harder (at least at the margin) to offset or to exploit the screening device. Salop concludes that "doctors will begin to pursue a 'Rat Race' dynamics in which each physician works harder than he did before, discovers the other Rats catching up, and begins to work even harder. These dynamics may or may not settle down" (1978, p. 7).

There is clearly an element of truth in this type of reasoning. Yet the example strikes me as somewhat farfetched. It is true that buyers search actively and use whatever signal they have at hand. And sellers no doubt adjust to this behavior, trying to exploit the signal in their own advantage. But I see no reason why this process should become a race. It would be far more intelligent to use screening devices and signals as means toward market segmentation and thus toward price discrimination.

Search costs and third-degree price discrimination

Masson and Wu (1974) have developed a model that, to my taste, describes the price behavior of physicians in the most satisfactory way. By introducing search costs explicitly, it generates the result that price discrimination will be practiced by all physicians and explains the history and the recent trend of pricing behavior on the American market for physicians' services remarkably well.

Masson and Wu first show how information costs insulate physicians' individual markets from one another and thus lead to third-degree price discrimination by income. Next they incorporate the role of charity and conclude that both a profit motive and a charity motive are needed to explain the evidence regarding physician pricing accurately.

Consider a world in which, as a start, all physicians' services are homogeneous, in which no physicians price discriminate and such that the elasticity of demand would be no lower for the rich than for the poor if all prices were known by all consumers. We have to show that under imperfect information, the demand curve as seen by a single physician will be less elastic for the rich patients.

Assume that rich and poor patients will all face the same expected price distribution if they search further, and consider a physician who charges a relatively high price – the same for all patients – compared with other physicians' prices. The high price will drive proportionately more poorer customers away from this doctor, because the poor have lower search costs. (Similarly, a relatively low price would attract proportionately more poor patients.)

Let x_r designate the proportion of the rich population served by the same physician. Then, in Figure 15.3, at high price levels $E[x_r \mid p]$ is greater than $E[x_p \mid p]$, and at low levels $E[x_r \mid p]$ is less than $E[x_p \mid p]$.

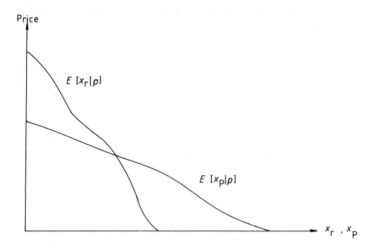

Figure 15.3. Expected demand curves for rich and poor patients.

In other words, even given identical demands for medical services per se and facing identical price distributions, the expected demand curve for the rich patients *as seen by a single doctor* is more inelastic than the corresponding curve for the poor patients.[4]

However, a physician is never alone. The above curves are in fact derived on the assumption that when this physician varies the price from the going level, the other physicians maintain their existing prices. These curves are thus analogous to the Chamberlin *dd* curve. One can also define another set of expected demand curves for a particular doctor, corresponding to Chamberlin's *DD* curve, along which all physicians have the same price, or rather along which the mean value of their prices rises or falls by the same amount (to keep to the assumption that there is a distribution of prices). Given these expected demands, how will our physician determine the allocation of his services to the two groups of patients and the prices charged to each of them?

For simplicity, Masson and Wu suppose that the physician's utility function is $u = y + \beta l$, where y is income and l is leisure. Then his expected utility is

$$E[u] = E[y + \beta l] \tag{15.9a}$$

or

$$E[u] = E\left[\sum_{i=1}^{n} N_i(p_i - c) + \beta \bar{L} - \beta \sum_{i=1}^{n} N_i h \right] \tag{15.9b}$$

where p_i is the price per patient in income group i, c is the direct cost per patient, $l = \bar{L} - h$, $\bar{L}$ is the total number of hours available, and h is the hours used per patient (independent of income group). We can rewrite (15.9b) as

$$E[u] = \sum_{i=1}^{n} E[N_i](p_i - c) + \beta \bar{L} - \beta \sum_{i=1}^{n} E[N_i]h \qquad (15.9c)$$

or as

$$E[u] = \sum_{i=1}^{n} E[N_i][p_i - (c + \beta h)] + \beta \bar{L} \qquad (15.9d)$$

The summation is now over $E[N_i]$, which is the expected value of the number of patients in income group i. (If we divide it by the total number of people in income group i, we get $E[x_i \mid p]$.) The physician's problem is thus the same as that faced by a discriminating monopolist, since both are maximizing a sum of profits in a number of separated markets, where each market has a demand curve ($E[x_i \mid p]$).

The answer should therefore be no surprise: The physician should equalize marginal revenues, in each market, to the unique marginal cost (here $c + \beta h$) and therefore among themselves. We must find the third-degree discrimination rule! Take the first derivative of (15.9d) with respect to p_i and set it equal to zero, remembering that $E[N_i]$ is a function of the price p_i:

$$(dE[N_i]/dp_i)p_i + E[N_i] - (c + \beta h)(dE[N_i]/dp_i) = 0$$

or

$$p_i + dp_i/dE[N_i] \cdot E[N_i] = c + \beta h$$

or

$$p_i\left(1 + \frac{1}{\epsilon_i}\right) = c + \beta h \qquad (15.10)$$

where $\epsilon_i = (dE[N_i]/dp_i)(p_i/E[N_i])$ is the elasticity of the expected demand curve for income group i. *Expected marginal revenue must be equal from one income group to the other.* Notice that marginal cost includes the term βh, which is the cost, in terms of utility, of the time spent per patient.

Needless to say, this discrimination rule implies that rich patients are charged higher prices than poor patients. However, it also implies that better information on prices would make price discrimination less profitable (expected demand curves more elastic), to the extent that a lack of information causes each individual physician's demand curves to be downward sloping.

If we now add the additional circumstance that physicians' services are in fact heterogeneous, then the expected demand curves will obviously appear as even less price elastic. Masson and Wu comment and conclude as follows:

> In addition, the rich patient's demand curve becomes even more inelastic as compared to the poor patient's demand curve. This further divergence is caused by an additional increase in the search costs for the rich. A poor patient may be more likely to change doctors on the basis of price information alone. The rich patient, however, will also be more likely to search for quality information before changing. Not only is quality much harder to assess, quality search also narrows the number of acceptable doctors; searching for both price and quality characteristics thus increases total search costs. For this reason, a rich person may search more than a poor person but remain less price responsive. In addition, the uncertainty associated with physicians' quality may also prevent the rich patient from changing doctors. Following an argument used by Arrow (1963), since a patient has experience with one doctor's quality but finds it very hard to assess another's, he may bear those ills rather than fly to others he knows not of.
>
> In summary, we hypothesize that because rich patients have a higher opportunity cost of time relative to the proportion of their income spent on physicians' services, because they are concerned about quality, and because there are search costs for both price and quality, the price elasticity of demand for physicians' services is less elastic for the rich patients than for the poor patients, any profit-maximizing physician will, ceteris paribus, charge rich patients higher prices than they charge the poor. But from this we find all profit-maximizing physicians doing so, and by a series of feedback effects, this result is strengthened even more. [1974, p. 69]

To account for the often-observed fact that many doctors do have charitable feelings and do provide services below cost and even free to certain poor patients, it suffices to add a parameter to the Masson–Wu model. Let this parameter γ_i measure a psychic return and be positive when the physician feels charitable to patients in the ith income group (and zero elsewhere). It has simply to be added to p_i, as an additional income, so that the discrimination rule becomes

$$p_i\left(1 + \frac{1}{\epsilon_i}\right) + \gamma_i = c + \beta h \tag{15.11}$$

The implication is that, if the doctor has a charitable feeling toward patients in income group i, the amount of medical service to group i will exceed the level at which the marginal (pecuniary) income is equal to marginal cost. Charity simply reinforces the price discrimination behavior by accentuating observed price differences. It can make price fall below marginal cost and thus allows the observed price elasticity of a physician's demand curve to fall below one – an otherwise puzzling result, as emphasized by Arrow (1963).

The Masson–Wu model explains not only the prevalence of price discrimination in the market for medical services but also its decline since the 1950s, especially among middle- and low-income classes. In the framework of the model, it suffices to note that (a) it becomes more and more difficult for doctors to assess the patient's income in those classes; (b) there is a marked reduction in search costs, for the patients, as a result of much improved information on medical treatments and charges in the general public; (c) many more alternative medical facilities are made available for the poor (with a concomitant decrease in γ_i).

Finally, it is clear to me that the Masson–Wu model can be used, without major changes, to explain the role of quality uncertainty in the pricing of consumption goods, especially consumer durables such as cars, refrigerators, dishwashers, television sets, and so on. The reader will find no difficulty in explaining why this type of uncertainty increases the reservation prices of the high-income classes for quality goods and makes price discrimination even more profitable than it appeared to be in previous chapters, under conditions of certainty about quality.

Notes

Preliminaries

1 This absence of homogeneity does not preclude the possibility, though, of defining aggregate demand curves for "commodities," i.e., for groups of differentiated products. For a discussion of this point, see Phlips (1964a) or, more recently, Lancaster (1979).
2 Similar definitions can be found in Davidson (1955, p. 23), Steiner (1957), Hirschleifer (1958), Ekelund and Hulett (1973) or Demsetz (1973), and other works.
3 Chamberlin did so with respect to sales of on-peak and off-peak electricity in a discussion of a paper by Steiner (1957, p. 590, n. 9).
4 See, e.g., Spulber (1979) and Norman (1981a, b) following Greenhut and Greenhut (1975). See Chapters 3 and 6 for an analysis of oligopolists who discriminate over space and over time, respectively.
5 Fixed costs must be such that these markets can be served and arbitrage can be prevented. It should be emphasized, perhaps, that fixed costs are *not* the motivating factor, contrary to the still popular idea of, say, J. M. Clark (1950).
6 See also Battalio and Ekelund (1972). The tendency of a discriminating seller to serve markets that would be excluded by a single-price seller also dominates possible output, reducing effects due to the curvature when demand curves are not linear.

ESSAY I SPACE

1 Business practices

1 See Commons (1924, pp. 505–8), Burns (1936, pp. 282–8), Möller (1943a, pp. 87–9), Mund (1948, pp. 366–9), Herlemann (1950, pp. 54–9), *Report on the Supply of Chemical Fertilizers* (1959, paras. 537 and 567), Phlips (1962a, pp. 201–18 and 265–8).
2 See the reports by the defunct British Price Commission.
3 It is called "franco-gare" or "franco-quai."
4 The best-known works include Clark (1938), Möller (1943a), Machlup (1949), Stigler (1949), Kaysen (1949), Wagner (1952), Harbers (1953), Beckerath (1930, pp. 199–200 and 263–4), Erb (1956), Erb and Rogge (1958), Imkamp (1958), Justman (1958), Allais (1958), Loescher (1959, chap. 1), and Scherer (1970, chap. 10).
5 A historical description of the operation of these systems is given by Zimmermann (1962, pp. 209–35).

6 A detailed analysis can be found in Stegemann (1968).
7 This system is generally discussed alongside the basing-point system: See main references given in footnote 4.
8 The concept of a natural market is analyzed by Fetter (1923–4), Hoover (1936–7), Hyson (1950), and Greenhut (1952).
9 This system was put forward by Kaysen (1949), Pegrum (1951), Stocking (1954, p. 188), and Loescher (1959, pp. 233–42).

2 The isolated firm

1 The adaptation is recent and is due to the work of Stevens and Rydell (1966), Greenhut and Ohta (1972), and Greenhut, Hwang, and Ohta (1975).
2 For a demonstration, see Greenhut and Ohta (1972). The conclusions to the contrary reached by Stevens and Rydell (1966) are erroneous.
3 To draw it, one must use the result that (net) marginal revenue is the same in all markets. Horizontal addition of the (net) marginal revenue curves automatically imposes this condition.

3 A group of firms

1 The following four sections are based on the 1975 article by Greenhut and Greenhut.
2 An econometric verification of this equation for the United States can be found in Greenhut, Greenhut, and Li (1980).
3 Greenhut and Greenhut (1975) show that the linear form of the spatial configuration of π is unrelated to the assumption of linear demand curves.
4 Only when all firms were located in the point in space – a most unrealistic assumption – did an increase in the number of firms lead to fob pricing at the limit.
5 Since the distribution of profits among colluding firms implies side payments and cheating is almost always profitable, explicit agreements must be legally enforceable to be operational. See J. W. Friedman (1977, pp. 26–8).
6 A fascinating discussion of tacit collusion can be found in Dewey (1979) and Smith (1981).
7 On quasi-agreements see Fellner (1960).
8 On the practical ways of detecting "cheating," see Stigler (1964).
9 See Harbers (1953).
10 See, e.g., Wagner (1952, p. 12).
11 See Adelman (1948 and 1949), Clark (1950), Mestmäcker (1955), Loescher (1959, pp. 26–9), Schmidt (1963), and Phlips (1964b). A contrary opinion on the role of perfect information is expressed by Demaria (1958, p. 33), Menze (1963), and others.
12 See Clark (1938) for the United States and Möller (1943a) and Beckerath (1930, pp. 199–200 and 263–4).
13 See Smithies (1941a, b).
14 See Smithies (1942, pp. 711–12).
15 See Stigler (1949).

16 Or they may adopt uniform delivered prices, in small regional markets where cross-hauls are negligible, since this policy gives the same output and profits when firms are free to determine the extent of their market areas, as shown in Chapter 2.

4   Welfare implications

1 This point is discussed more thoroughly by Koopmans (1957, chap. 1). Perhaps it is worth adding that by competitive equilibrium I do not necessarily mean pure and perfect competition. The existence of a noncollusive production oligopoly may be compatible with the concept, as demonstrated by Gabszewicz and Vial (1972).
2 The rest of this paragraph was inspired by Thisse (1975, pp. 69–75).
3 Takayama and Judge (1971) obtained similar results.
4 Holahan (1975) compares the unconstrained optima under discriminatory and fob-mill prices under similar assumptions. These assumptions contain the main features of the Greenhut–Ohta (1975) model.
5 See, e.g., Herlemann (1950, pp. 54–9) and Semler (1963, p. 345) on uniform delivered prices and Demaria (1958, pp. 81–2) and Fallon (1958, p. 231) on the basing-point system.
6 Spulber (1981a) considers a different case, where quantity-dependent prices are offered at the mill.
7 This area looks exactly like the lower envelope in Figure 10.7. Figure 10.8 also applies here, with p, $(p-\tau)$ and γ replaced by π_f, π_d, and V, respectively.
8 The difficulty, in practice, is to make sure that the price charged at the factory is equal to p_f and not close to π_0 (which would destroy the incentive to take delivery at the factory).
9 See, e.g., Schneider (1934 and 1938), Möller (1941, pp. 28–9; 1943a, b), Mund (1948, pp. 238–42), Sauermann (1951–2), Justman (1958), and Semler (1963).
10 For criticism of this concept, see, e.g., Clark (1950, pp. 416–20 and 459–60), Hahn (1952, pp. 97–8), Erb (1956, p. 67), Allais (1958, pp. 524–5), Byé (1950), Guitton (1958), Phlips (1962a, pp. 80–7).
11 See, e.g., Greenhut (1963, pp. 186–91).
12 Here I am taking over the argument by Stocking (1954, and particularly app. A), correcting the analysis of Isard and Capron (1949).

ESSAY II   TIME

5   Business practices

1 Blinder (1981) indicates that changes in inventories account for 37% of the variance of changes in the American GNP. The importance of inventory investment in business fluctuations is thus totally out of proportion to its size (only about 1% of GNP). Finished goods contribute 5.3%, and distributors' inventories contribute 46.9% to the variance (of deviations from trend) of total inventories.

2 Paul Olbrechts, from the Institut de Recherches Economiques et Sociales Université Catholique de Louvain (IRES-UCL), kindly produced Figure 5.1.

3 Empirical analyses of the relationship between the prices of natural resources and the rate of interest can be found in McRae (1978) and in Heal and Barrow (1979 and 1981).

4 On the prices of movies, see Whitney (1955). Reekie (1978) discusses the pricing of new drugs.

5 The following details and data are taken from Mitchell (1978, pp. 65–75), who also explains how marginal costs are defined and computed.

6 Storable commodities

1 See Samuelson (1957) on intertemporal price equilibria on competitive markets. An excellent introduction to the literature on futures markets is to be found in Goss and Yamey (1976). Weymar (1968) presents a remarkable empirical analysis of the cocoa market.

2 In fact, we shall see that this statement is not entirely correct: We shall have to distinguish between changes in demand and changes in costs.

3 Notice that future costs must also be evaluated today and must therefore be discounted. In the case where production is starting three months from today, say, whereas sales are to take place six months from now, the difference in the discounting of sales and production will truly reflect future storage costs (if these reduce to interest costs).

4 On this consistency problem, see Strotz (1956), Pollak (1968), Blackorby, Nissen, Primont, and Russell (1973), or, for a brief overview, Phlips (1974, pp. 245–9). The same problem arises when a consumer allocates his or her purchases over several time periods.

5 The expectation interval is what we would call the planning period, i.e., the period extending from $t = 0$ until $t = T$.

6 Robinson (1933, p. 181).

7 This parallelism was also perceived by Smithies (1939) and by F. and V. Lutz (1951, chap. 7), who summarized Smithies's and Shaw's ideas. Since the critique by Arrow, Karlin, and Scarf (1958) on a technicality – the incorrect handling of a nonnegativity constraint – the analysis was drowned in a gigantic flow of operations research papers on "the inventory problem" in which the price of the commodity is supposed given. The originality of the Smithies–Shaw approach is that price, output, and sales are determined *simultaneously*.

8 Imagine that AB intersects the marginal cost curve to the right of D. Then deferred sales would be larger than present production, which is of course impossible. So-called nonnegativity constraints must come into play (such as the condition that stocks cannot increase by more than production) and might affect all the outcomes, including total production. Mathematical techniques developed by Kuhn and Tucker allow us to handle these constraints but were not available in Shaw's days. A further discussion is given in the next section.

9 The next section shows how Smithies derived it in a continuous-time formulation.

10 Once again, we encounter the consistency problem. Today's programming techniques allow us to avoid these inconsistencies between plans made in week 1 for week 2 and decisions made in week 2, when future costs and demands are known with certainty.

11 This and the following sections are based on Phlips (1980).

12 It is of some interest to note that one way of solving Smithies's general problem (with nonnegativity constraints) correctly is to treat x and q as controls, to treat s as a state variable, and to maximize (6.1) with respect to x and q subject to the state equation $s'(t) = x - q$ and the inventory constraints (6.2) and $s(t) \geq 0$ for all $t \in (0, T)$. The latter constraint implies $s'(t) \geq 0$ over the interval where $s(t) = 0$. We can then write the Hamiltonian as $H = e^{-rt}(\pi q - cx) + (\mu + \nu)(x - q)$, where $\mu(t)$ is associated with the state equation and $\nu(t)$ is associated with $s(t)$. The equilibrium conditions are

$$\frac{\partial H}{\partial x} = \mu(t) + \nu(t) - e^{-rt}\left(c + x\frac{\partial c}{\partial x}\right) \geq 0$$

$$\frac{\partial H}{\partial q} = -\mu(t) - \nu(t) + e^{-rt}\left(\pi + q\frac{\partial p}{\partial q}\right) \geq 0$$

$$\mu(t) = \lambda = \nu(T)$$

$$\nu(t)s(t) = 0 \quad \text{and} \quad \nu(t)s'(t) = 0$$

$$\nu(0) = 0$$

where $\nu(t) \geq 0$ and λ is a constant because $\mu'(t) = 0$. Smithies's discrimination rule is thus valid in the case of an interior solution ($x > 0$ and $q > 0$) with $s > 0$. This seems to be a quite frequent situation. In other cases, his discrimination rule has to be corrected; e.g., when $x > 0$, $q > 0$ and $s = 0$, $\nu(t)$ is nonzero and is to be added to λ.

13 Mathematical details can be found in Phlips and Phlips (1981).

14 Recent work on the microfoundations of macroeconomics has renewed the theoretical interest in the phenomenon of price rigidities (see, e.g., Böhm 1978, Drèze 1975, and Malinvaud 1976). Curiously enough, this literature is starting from the assumption of given rigidities, without really trying to explain the phenomenon. The rationalizations suggested refer to nonoptimizing behavior or to the industrial organization literature (folklore?), whereas it should be clear that these rigidities should be analyzed as resulting from optimizing behavior, if only because of their pervasiveness.

15 As pointed out by Telser (1972, pp. 132-42) and Hause (1977).

16 Compare with Equation (3.5).

17 I include here my own, e.g., Phlips (1973), admittedly!

18 Another type of intertemporal price discrimination might result from pricing differently before and after entry, as discussed in Spulber (1981b). In Spulber's approach, the ad hoc assumption that entry depends on the current price (my Assumption 3) is abandoned.

19 These data were explained in greater detail and were reproduced in the appendix to chapter 2 in Phlips (1971) and were also used in my 1973 reply to Ross in the *Journal of Industrial Economics*.

20 This construction uses the information given in the appendix to chapter 3 in Phlips (1971).

21 In interpreting these regression results, the reader should recall that the estimating equation (6.8) is just another way of writing Equation (6.6). The latter implies $p = \delta \bar{k}$, with $\delta = m\eta/(1 + m\eta)$. Notice that $\delta > 1$ because η is negative. It should be clear, then, that δ is not to be confused with the regression coefficient of the cost variable. The presence of the demand variable in the regressions reflects the fact that the influence of costs on prices (δ) is a function of the elasticity of demand.

22 The objective of the test is not to estimate m and γ. After all, m is normally known for each industry in the sample (although that happens not to be the case for the data used here). And the degree of cooperation could be derived, in principle, from historical case studies. (If the objective had been to estimate m and γ, it would have been necessary to impose the constraint that the third coefficient in Equation (6.23) is equal to the second coefficient times γ and thus to use a nonlinear estimation method.) What our test does suggest, though, is that, whenever m and γ are known for a particular industry, these numbers can be used to evaluate the impact of changes in demand ($\gamma/[m+\gamma]$) and in variable unit costs of production ($m/[m+\gamma]$) on the industry's price.

23 For more mathematical details, see Phlips and Thisse (1981). Discounting is ignored, since the time horizon is supposed to be small (at most a year).

24 It was introduced to explain "inverse carrying charges," implying that net storage costs may be negative and the futures (therefore) below the spot price. See Kaldor (1939) and Working (1948).

25 This is equal to C_T, since $C'_{iT} = 0$.

26 The final and intermediate price could differ by distribution costs (*other* than storage costs), which are ignored here. That is why the intermediate price is typically equal to the final price minus a distributor's margin.

7 New commodities, exhaustible resources, and intertemporal welfare

1 On the fiftieth anniversary of the publication of Hotelling's paper, Devarajan and Fisher (1981) wrote a quite accessible review in the light of the many contributions that have emerged since the early 1970s.

2 See Equation (6.3) and set $\partial \pi / \partial q$ equal to zero. Or see Pyatt (1978) or Phlips and Thisse (1981).

3 The oligopoly case was studied only very recently and will be discussed in the next section.

4 Similar distinctions must be made when exploration costs are brought into the picture, as in Stewart (1979a) and Eswaran and Lewis (1980).

5 See Stiglitz (1976), Khalatbari (1977), and especially Dasgupta and Heal (1979, chap. 11). Solow and Wan (1976) and Kemp and Long (1980) discuss the effects of rising extraction costs.

6 I use the dynamic programming method explained in Phlips and Thisse (1981).

7 A similar analysis can be found in Dasgupta and Heal (1979, pp. 336–40). It is easy to show that the noncooperative solution tends to the competitive solution as the number of competitors becomes large.

8 Parallel analyses of the role of OPEC can be found in Schmalensee (1976), Cremer and Weitzman (1976), Hnyilicza and Pindyck (1976), and Gilbert (1978).

9 For an analysis of price discrimination between users of a natural resource, with the help of vertical integration, see Carlton and Perloff (1981).

10 Once the cartel's sales fall to zero, the (discounted) marginal revenue must never exceed the marginal revenue in any period of positive sales.

11 If the firms outside the cartel did not behave competitively, but as oligopolists, then price would of course rise at less than the rate of interest already before π^*.

12 Newbery (1981) discusses intertemporal consistency of the cartel's policy.

13 However, when a resource is both exhaustible *and* durable, its price might decline first and follow Hotelling's rule only when depletion grows closer. This is the point made by Levhari and Pindyck (1981).

14 I am not saying that this type of price discrimination is always the most profitable policy to follow. For some income distributions, it might be profitable to concentrate all sales on one single date; see Stokey (1979 and 1981). I *am* saying that the passage of time is a sufficient element of product differentiation to make price discrimination possible.

15 This analysis is inspired directly by Spence (1977, p. 9, n. 6).

16 See Spence (1977, pp. 9–10). Differentiation with respect to y gives a second condition that allows us to determine the level of $\pi(t)$.

17 Stokey (1979 and 1981) provides an analysis of this problem in continuous time.

18 In other words, class i should purchase in period $(t = T - i + 1)$.

19 These ladies are also better informed. For an analysis of "sales" in the framework of the economics of imperfect information, see Varian (1980). See also Chapter 12 for a simple exposition of the model of the "noisy monopolist" due to Salop (1977).

8 Nonstorable commodities

1 See Boiteux (1951).

2 This single-price constraint might be due to the simple fact that the company's distribution system might have meters capable of measuring the amount consumed but not the time of day (or week or month) at which the commodity is consumed. For a formal analysis of the single-price constraint, see Mohring (1970).

3 In other words, demands of the separate periods upon capacity are complementary, not competitive. That is why demands will have to be added vertically. A similar situation arises in the case of public goods in the theory of public expenditure. See Samuelson (1955).

4 These conclusions are altered if storing of the product over the off-peak period is feasible: Peak price would be lower and off-peak price would be higher, as shown by Nguyen (1976). Storage facilities do exist, e.g., for water, gas, and coal.

5 This Steiner calls the "firm peak case."

6 This is Steiner's "shifting peak case."
7 On this point, see Marchand (1974) and Kay (1979).

9   Business practices

1 This section is largely based on P. De Neef's 1979 thesis. Tariffs for several other countries can be found in Mitchell, Manning, and Acton (1978).
2 See Turvey (1968). Mitchell (1978) discusses the optimal two-part tariff for local telephone service in similar terms.
3 This committee coordinates total capacity, system interconnection, accounting methods, and tariffs. It comprises government, utilities, and trade-union representatives. Its annual reports are the best source of information on the Belgian electricity industry.
4 *United States* v. *Northern Pacific Railway and Northwestern Improvement Co.,* 142 F. Supp. 679 (W.D. Wa. 1956); *Northern Pacific Railway and Northwestern Improvement Co.* v. *United States,* 356 U.S.1 (1958).
5 See the discussion, in Chapter 3, of price competition and imperfect information.
6 *International Salt Co.* v. *United States,* 332, U.S. 392 (1947).
7 371 U.S. 38,52 (1962).
8 This point was noticed by Telser (1965).

10   Two-part tariffs and quantity-dependent prices

1 See Spulber (1979) for an analysis of the conditions under which a unique noncooperative equilibrium exists for a group of firms that practice first-degree price discrimination.
2 We shall follow Oi's 1971 seminal paper rather closely in the next three sections. For a recent extension and generalization of Oi's analysis, see Schmalensee (1980).
3 Let $\psi(p)$ be a constant utility demand curve, with $u_0 = u(0, Y)$. Then

$$T^* = \int_p^\infty \psi(p)\,dp = \int_\infty^p - \psi(p)\,dp$$

so that

$$dT^*/dp = -\psi(p) = -q.$$

4 Distributional aspects can be and have been taken into account. Feldstein (1972), e.g., finds that, for normal goods, the price p must be proportional to and higher than marginal cost. The inefficiency loss due to not charging marginal cost is outweighed by the gains in distributional equity.
5 Oi (1971) also discusses the curious case where it behooves the monopolist to set price below marginal cost.
6 Gabor (1955) was the first to show that two blocks suffice to extract the entire surplus.

7 A nonlinear price schedule is analogous to an income tax schedule. In the optimal tax problem, the government has to distinguish among individuals in order to tax them according to their ability to pay. Mirrlees (1971) provided the analytical breakthrough in the taxation problem and inspired the literature on nonlinear prices.

8 Notice that schedule A is "nonlinear," although it is represented by a straight line. The dependence of average price on quantity is a consequence of the presence of a nonzero intercept.

9 Recent analyses of nonlinear prices can be found in Spence (1977), Willig (1978), Roberts (1979), Spence (1980), Ordover and Panzar (1980), and Mirman and Sibley (1980). I shall follow Spence (1980) and Willig (1978). Brown and Heal (1980) consider a general equilibrium framework. Faulhaber and Panzar (1977) show that schedule C is the limiting case of a schedule of several declining block tariffs (such as schedule B) in the sense that aggregate consumer welfare can be increased by expanding any finite set of optimal two-part tariffs from which a continuum of consumers is permitted to choose.

10 See also Chapters 7 and 14.

11 A simple way to check that this statement is correct is to write Equation (10.10) in detail for $n=1$, $n=2$, $n=3$, etc.

12 Remember the discussion, in Chapter 9, of the circumstances of this move.

11 Multiproduct pricing

1 A generalization to multiple-product nonlinear pricing can be found in Spence (1980).

2 A similar analysis, using third-degree price discrimination (since customers are supposed to have demand *curves*), can be found in Paroush (1978) and Paroush and Peles (1981).

3 If $p_1 = 10$ and $p_2 = 90$, profits are $(10-20)\cdot 4 + (90-30) = -40 + 60 = 20$, etc. With $p_1 = 60$ and $p_2 = 90$, profits are $(60-20)\cdot 2 + (90-30) = 80 + 60 = 140$.

4 For details, see Adams and Yellen (1976).

5 See Bowman (1957), Burstein (1960), Telser (1965 and 1979), Demsetz (1973), and Hansen and Roberts (1980). Hilton (1958) and Ferguson (1965) discuss the economics of a number of antitrust cases.

6 It may also be more profitable when reservation prices for the *bundle* are relatively uniform, as in the case of block booking.

7 In matrix notation, Equations (11.1) become $p_B = Ap$, where p_B is $i \times 1$, A is $\{a_{ij}\}$ and p is $j \times 1$, whereas Equations (11.2) are written as $q_B = b - Bp_B$, with B diagonal. Let $\mathbf{q}$ be the vector of quantities of the products. Then $\mathbf{q} = A'q_B = A'b - A'Bp_B = A'b - A'BAp$. The unit cost of q_B^i is $c_B^i = \sum_j a_{ij}c_j$, or $C_B = AC$.

8 A result due to Vernon and Graham (1971), Schmalensee (1973), Hay (1973), Warren-Boulton (1974), and Perry (1978).

9 See the interesting discussion of potential cost savings in Williamson (1971).

12 Imperfect information

1 See table 16 of the EEC's Eighth Report on Competition Policy, Brussels, April 1979. Of 503 products on the Dutch market, e.g., 166 had a dispersion

between 10% and 40%, 89 had a dispersion larger than 40%, and 248 had less than 10% dispersion. Dispersion was measured as the difference between the maximum and the minimum price, divided by the maximum price. For non-homogeneous goods, see also Figures 13.2 to 13.4. Further empirical work can be found in Jung (1960), Marvel (1976), and Pratt, Wise, and Zeckhauser (1979).

2 I am following the nice presentation given in Deaton and Muellbauer (1980, pp. 410-11).

3 By definition, the expected value is the integral of $[1 - F_x(x)]$, where $F_x(x)$ is the distribution function. Here, it amounts to taking the integral of $\{1 - 1 + [1 - F(m)]^n = [1 - F(m)]^n\}$.

4 Nelson (1970) analyzes the case where quality information is gathered by experience rather than by search, because experience is less expensive. Experience implies evaluating quality by actual purchase rather than by search. Nelson also derives the implications of this phenomenon for the competitive structure of markets for quality goods.

5 Telser (1973) explores the properties of reasonable rules of thumb.

6 The reader should consult Salop (1977) for a more rigorous discussion of the problem and of the solution. The costate variable is $\lambda(c)$ while $\pi(c)$ is the state variable. The cost of production is ignored, for simplicity.

7 A linear demand curve that shifts upward becomes less price elastic at any given price. A positive γ has this effect.

8 Otherwise - i.e., if only the price of the insurance (the premium) were determined - the buyer would have an interest in burning his or her house as soon as the contract had been signed!

9 $V = (1 - p) \cup (W_1) + p \cup (W_2)$. Customers are supposed to be risk averse, so that $\cup'' < 0$, and the indifference curve is convex to the origin.

10 Namely, $-dW_1/dW_2 = \cup'(W_1)(1 - p)/\cup'(W_2)p$.

11 Marginal utilities of income are the same: Only the accident probabilities differ between the two groups. Hence $MRS^H/MRS^L = p^L/(1 - p^L) \cdot (1 - p^H)/p^H$.

13 Business practices

1 This section is largely based on Pilati's 1979 thesis.

2 Volkswagen advertisement in the Belgian newspaper *Le soir* of March 10, 1979.

3 Unfortunately, these prices refer to different producers, whereas our reasoning applies only to different qualities and varieties put on the market by the *same* producer.

4 See Masson and Wu (1974), pp. 74-8, for references to empirical studies on the historical evolution of physicians' pricing behavior.

14 Product selection

1 The best way to model switches from one variety (brand) to another variety (brand) of the same commodity is probably to assume that indifference curves between varieties are linear, as argued in Phlips (1964a).

2   Hotelling's assumptions were made explicit by Lerner and Singer (1937).
3   This assumption was relaxed by Smithies (1941a).
4   The more important references include Lerner and Singer (1937), Lewis
    (1945), Stern (1972), Eaton and Lipsey (1975), Shaked (1975), Spence (1976),
    Lancaster (1979), Salop (1979), and Lane (1980). Heal (1980) went as far as to
    suppose that Hotelling's firms fix constant delivered prices and concluded
    that this type of price discrimination can lead to socially optimal market areas.
    See also the special Sept.–Dec. 1982 issue of the *Journal of Industrial Eco-
    nomics,* "Spatial Competition and the Theory of the Differentiated Markets."
5   This and the following sections are taken from Phlips and Schuler (1981).
6   Vertical product differentiation is analyzed in the framework of monopolistic
    competition, without explicit reference to price discrimination, in Gabszewicz
    and Thisse (1979 and 1980) and Shaked and Sutton (1982).
7   Except, possibly, for the inspiring graphic analysis presented by Clemens
    (1950–1).
8   In their discussion of joint optimization over quality and price, Dorfman and
    Steiner mention (1954, p. 833) that if groups of consumers differ in their re-
    sponsiveness to quality changes and/or price changes, there will be a range of
    qualities offered in order to exploit these differences. They conclude, without
    further elaboration, that the analogy to discriminating monopoly is apparent.
9   The theorem says: "Under increasing returns to scale, monopoly control of a
    market sector will lead to a lesser degree of product differentiation over that
    sector than is socially optimal."
10 Behavior is said to be "competitive" when the firms act as if prices were in-
    sensitive to their quantity decisions but know how their quality choices affect
    the price at which a given output can be sold and choose quality so as to maxi-
    mize profits at a given output.

15   Quality uncertainty

1 Technically speaking, Akerlof's is an instantaneous noncooperative Nash equilibrium. In a game that is repeated infinitely many times, i.e., a "supergame,"
   chances that bad products will drive out good fall as the weight that traders give
   to future benefits rises.
2 This material is adapted from Viscusi (1978).
3 See Akerlof (1976) and Spence (1973).
4 Note that if rich patients face a price distribution with a higher mean, then the
   $E[x_r \mid p]$ curve would shift outward, so that the difference in elasticities would
   be even more pronounced.

References

Abramovitz, M. (1948). *The Role of Inventories in Business Cycles.* Occasional Paper 26. New York: National Bureau of Economic Research, May.

Adams, W. J., and J. Yellen (1976). "Commodity Bundling and the Burden of Monopoly." *Quarterly Journal of Economics 90:* 475–98.

Adelman, M. A. (1948). "Effective Competition and the Anti-Trust Laws." *Harvard Law Review 61:* 1289–350.

—— (1949). "The Large Firm and Its Suppliers." *Review of Economics and Statistics 31:* 113–18.

Akerlof, G. A. (1970). "The Market for 'Lemons': Quality, Uncertainty, and the Market Mechanism." *Quarterly Journal of Economics 84:* 488–500.

—— (1976). "The Economics of Caste and of the Rat Race and other Woeful Tales." *Quarterly Journal of Economics 90:* 599–617.

Allais, M. (1958). "Le système des prix et la concurrence dans le marché commun de la C.E.C.A." In *Actes officiels du congrès international d'études sur la Communauté Européenne du Charbon et de l'Acier,* vol. 6, 143–210. Milan: Dott A. Giuffrè.

Allen, G. C. (1959). "Note of Dissent." In *Report on the Supply of Chemical Fertilizers,* 229–30. London: Monopolies Commission.

Andersen, P. (1974). "Public Utility Pricing in the Case of Oscillating Demand." *Swedish Journal of Economics 76:* 402–14.

Andrews, P. W. S. (1949). *Manufacturing Business.* London: Macmillan.

—— (1951). "A Further Inquiry into the Effects of Rates of Interest." In T. Wilson and P. W. S. Andrews, eds., *Oxford Studies in the Price Mechanism,* 51–67. Oxford: Oxford University Press.

Arrow, K. . (1963). "Uncertainty and the Welfare Economics of Medical Care." *American Economic Review 53:* 941–73.

Arrow, K. J., S. Karlin, and H. Scarf (1958). *Studies in the Mathematical Theory of Inventory and Production.* Stanford: Stanford University Press.

Auerbach, A., and A. Pellechio (1978). "The Two-Part Tariff and Voluntary Market Participation." *Quarterly Journal of Economics 92:* 571–87.

Bailey, M. J. (1954). "Price and Output Determination by a Firm Selling Related Products." *American Economic Review 44:* 82–93.

Battalio, R. C., and R. B. Ekelund (1972). "Output Change under Third Degree Price Discrimination." *Southern Economic Journal 39:* 285–90.

Baumol, W. J., and D. F. Bradford (1970). "Optimal Departures from Marginal Cost Pricing." *American Economic Review 60:* 265–83.

Beckerath, H. von (1930). *Der moderne Industrialismus.* Jena: Gustav Fischer.

Beckmann, M. J. (1968). *Location Theory.* New York: Harper.

—— (1971). "Equilibrium versus Optimum: Spacing of Firms and Patterns of Market Areas." *Northeast Regional Science Review 1:* 1–20.

—— (1972). "Spatial Cournot Oligopoly." *Papers of the Regional Science Association 28:* 37–47.

—— (1976). "Spatial Price Policies Revisited." *Bell Journal of Economics 7* (autumn): 619–30.

Beguin, H., and J.-F. Thisse (1981). "Space and Time in Geography: An Axiomatic Approach." In D. Griffith, ed., *Dynamic Spatial Models,* 20–35. Alphen: NATO-ASI, Sijthoff-Noordhoff.

Blackorby, C., D. Nissen, D. Primont, and R. Russell (1973). "Consistent Intertemporal Decision Making." *Review of Economic Studies 40:* 239–48.

Blackstone, E. A. (1975). "Restrictive Practices in the Marketing of Electrofax Copying Machines and Supplies: the SCM Corporation Case." *Journal of Industrial Economics 23:* 189–202.

Blair, R. D., and D. L. Kaserman (1978). "Vertical Integration, Tying, and Antitrust Policy." *American Economic Review 68:* 397–402.

Blinder, A. S. (1981). "Inventories and the Structure of Macro Models." *American Economic Review 7:* (May): 11–16.

Bliss, C. J. (1975). *Capital Theory and the Distribution of Income.* Amsterdam: North Holland.

Böhm, V. (1978). "Disequilibrium Dynamics in a Simple Macroeconomic Model." *Journal of Economic Theory 17:* 179–99.

Boiteux, M. (1949). "La tarification des demandes en pointe." *Revue générale de l'électricité 58:* 321–40.

(1951). "La tarification au coût marginal et les demandes aléatoires." *Cahiers du séminaire d'econométrie 1:* 56–69.

(1960). "Peak Load Pricing." *Journal of Business 33* (April): 157–79.

Böventer, E. von (1962). *Theorie des raümlichen Gleichgewichts.* Tübingen: J. C. B. Mohr (Paul Siebeck).

Bowman, W. S., Jr. (1957). "Tying Agreements and the Leverage Problem." *Yale Law Journal 67:* 19–36.

Brennan, M. J. (1958). "The Supply of Storage." *American Economic Review 48:* 50–72.

Brown, D. J., and G. M. Heal (1980). "Two-Part Tariffs, Marginal Cost Pricing, and Increasing Returns in a General Equilibrium Framework." *Journal of Public Economics 13:* 25–49.

Brown, G., Jr., and M. B. Johnson (1969). "Public Utility Pricing and Output under Risk." *American Economic Review 59:* 119–28.

Buchanan, J. M. (1952-3). "The Theory of Monopolistic Quantity Discounts." *Review of Economic Studies 20:* 199–208.

Burns, A. R. (1936). *The Decline of Competition.* New York: McGraw-Hill.

Burstein, M. L. (1960a). "The Economics of Tie-in Sales." *Review of Economics and Statistics 42:* 68–73.

(1960b). "A Theory of Full-Line Forcing." *Northwestern University Law Review 55:* 62–95.

Byé, M. (1950). "Unions douanières et données nationales." *Economie appliquée 3:* 121–57.

Capozza, D. R., and R. Van Order (1977). "Pricing under Spatial Competition and Spatial Monopoly." *Econometrica 45:* 1329–38.

Carlton, D. (1977). "Pricing with Stochastic Demand." *American Economic Review 67:* 1006–10.

Carlton, D. W., and J. M. Perloff (1981). "Price Discrimination, Vertical Integration, and Divestiture in Natural Resource Markets." *Resources and Energy 3:* 1–11.

Chiang, R., and C. S. Spatt (1982). "Imperfect Price Discrimination and Welfare." *Review of Economic Studies 49:* 155–81.

Chow, G. C. (1967). "Technological Change and the Demand for Computers." *American Economic Review 57:* 1117–30.

Clark, J. M. (1938). "Basing Point Methods of Price Quoting." *Canadian Journal of Economics and Political Science 4:* 477–89.

(1950). *Studies in the Economics of Overhead Costs.* Chicago: University of Chicago Press.

Clemens, E. W. (1941). "Price Discrimination in Decreasing Cost Industries." *American Economic Review 31:* 794–802.

(1945). "Incremental Cost Pricing and Discriminatory Pricing." *Journal of Land and Public Utility Economics 21:* 68–70.

(1950–1). "Price Discrimination and the Multi-product Firm." *Review of Economic Studies 19:* 1–11.

Coase, R. H. (1946). "The Marginal Cost Controversy." *Economica 13:* 169–82.

(1947). "The Marginal Cost Controversy: Some Further Comments." *Economica 14:* 150–3.

(1960). "The Problem of Social Cost." *Journal of Law and Economics 3:* 1–44.

(1972). "Durability and Monopoly," *Journal of Law and Economics 15:* 143–9.

Commons, J. R. (1924). "Delivered Price Practice in the Steel Market." *American Economic Review 14:* 505–19.

Cremer, J., and M. Weitzman (1976). "O.P.E.C. and the Monopoly Price of World Oil." *European Economic Review 8:* 155–64.

Crew, M. A., and P. R. Kleindorfer (1976). "Peak Load Pricing with a Diverse Technology." *Bell Journal of Economics 7* (Spring): 207–31.

(1978). "Reliability and Public Utility Pricing." *American Economic Review 68:* 31–40.

Cummings, F. J., and W. E. Ruhter (1979). "The *Northern Pacific* Case." *Journal of Law and Economics 22:* 329–50.

Dasgupta, P. S., and G. M. Heal (1979). *Economic Theory and Exhaustible Resources.* Cambridge: Cambridge University Press; Welwyn: J. Nisbet.

Davidson, R. K. (1955). *Price Discrimination in Selling Gas and Electricity.* Baltimore: Johns Hopkins University Press.

Dean, J. (1949). *Managerial Economics.* Englewood Cliffs: Prentice-Hall.

Deaton, A., and J. Muellbauer (1980). *Economics and Consumer Behavior.* Cambridge: Cambridge University Press.

Debreu, G. (1959). *Theory of Value.* New York: Wiley.

de Chazeau, M. G. (1938). "Public Policy and Discriminatory Prices of Steel: A Reply to Professor Fetter." *Journal of Political Economy 46* (1938): 537–66.

Demaria, G. (1958). "Le système des prix et la concurrence dans le marché commun." In *Actes officiels du congrès international d'études sur la Communauté Européenne du Charbon et de l'Acier,* vol. 6. Milan: Dott. A. Giuffrè.

Demsetz, H. (1968). "The Cost of Transacting." *Quarterly Journal of Economics 82:* 33–53.

(1970). "The Private Production of Public Goods." *Journal of Law and Economics 13:* 293–306.

(1973). "Joint Supply and Price Discrimination." *Journal of Law and Economics 16:* 389–415.

De Neef, P. (1979). "Two-Part Tariffs and Nonlinear Prices." Mimeographed. Louvain-la-Neuve: Université Catholique de Louvain.

Devarajan, S., and A. C. Fisher (1981). "Hotelling's 'Economics of Exhaustible Resources': Fifty Years Later." *Journal of Economic Literature 19:* 65–73.

Dewey, D. (1955). "A Reappraisal of F.O.B. Pricing and Freight Absorption." *Southern Economic Journal 22* (July): 48–54.

(1979). "Information, Entry, and Welfare: The Case for Collusion." *American Economic Review 69:* 587–94.

Diamond, P., and M. Rothschild, eds. (1978). *Uncertainty in Economics: Readings and Exercises.* New York: Academic Press.

Dorfman, R., and P. O. Steiner (1954). "Optimal Advertising and Optimal Quality." *American Economic Review 44* (December): 826–36.

Drèze, J. H. (1964). "Some Postwar Contributions of French Economists to Theory and Public Policy." *American Economic Review 54* (June), supp.: 1–64.

(1975). "Existence of an Exchange Equilibrium under Price Rigidities." *International Economic Review 16:* 301–20.

(1979). "Demand Estimation, Risk Aversion, and Sticky Prices." *Economics Letters 4:* 1–6.

Drèze, J. H., and K. P. Hagen (1978). "Choice of Product Quality: Equilibrium and Efficiency." *Econometrica 46* (May): 493–513.

Dupuit, J. (1844). ["On the Measurement of the Utility of Public Works."] *Annales des ponts et chaussées,* 2d ser., *7.* Reprinted in *International Economic Papers* (London: Macmillan, 1952).

(1849). ["On Tolls and Transport Charges."] *Annales des ponts et chaussées,* 2d ser. *17.* Reprinted in *International Economic Papers* (London: Macmillan, 1962).

(1933). *De l'utilité et sa mesure: Écrits choisis et republiés.* Ed. M. De Bernardi. Turin: La Riforma Sociale.

Eaton, B. C., and R. G. Lipsey (1975). "The Principles of Minimum Differentiation Reconsidered: Some New Developments in the Theory of Spatial Competition." *Review of Economic Studies 42:* 27–50.

Eckstein, O., and D. Wyss (1972). "Industry Price Equations." In *The Econometrics of Price Determination.* Washington, D.C.: Board of Governors of the Federal Reserve System.

Edgeworth, F. Y. (1912). "A Contribution to the Theory of Railway Rates." *Economic Journal 22:* 198–218.

Edwards, E. O. (1950). "The Analysis of Output under Discrimination." *Econometrica 18:* 168–72.

Ekelund, R. B. (1970). "Price Discrimination and Product Differentiation in Economic Theory: An Early Analysis." *Quarterly Journal of Economics 84:* 268–78.

Ekelund, R. B., and J. R. Hulett (1973). "Joint Supply, The Taussig–Pigou Controversy, and the Competitive Provision of Public Goods." *Journal of Law and Economics 16:* 369–87.

Enke, S. (1951). "Equilibrium among Spatially Separated Markets: Solution by Electric Analogue." *Econometrica 19:* 40–7.

Erb, G. (1956). "Das Diskriminierungsproblem in der Montan-Union." Ph.D. dissertation. Bonn: Bonn University.

Erb, G., and P. Rogge (1958). *Preispolitik im teilintegrierten Markt.* Tübingen: J. C. B. Mohr (Paul Siebeck).

Eswaran, M., and T. R. Lewis (1980). "A Note on Market Structure and the Search for Exhaustible Resources." *Economics Letters 6:* 75–80.

Fallon, D. (1958). "Les règles du Traité de la C.E.C.A. en matière de cotation des prix et d'alignement et leur justification." In *Actes officiels du congrès international d'études sur la Communauté Européenne du Charbon et de l'Acier,* vol. 6, 223–31. Milan: Dott. A. Giuffrè.

Faulhaber, G. R. (1975). "Cross-subsidization: Pricing in Public Enterprises." *American Economic Review 65:* 966–77.

Faulhaber, G. R., and J. C. Panzar (1977). "Optimal Two-Part Tariffs with Self-Selection." Economic Discussion Paper 74. Murray Hill, N.J.: Bell Laboratories.

Feldstein, M. (1972). "Equity and Efficiency in Public Sector Pricing: The Optimal Two-Part Tariff." *Quarterly Journal of Economics 86:* 175–87.

Fellner, W. (1960). *Competition among the few.* New York: Kelley.

Ferguson, J. M. (1965). "Tying Arrangements and Reciprocity: An Economic Analysis." *Law and Contemporary Problems 30:* 552–80.

Fetter, F. A. (1923–4). "The Economic Law of Market Areas, Note." *Quarterly Journal of Economics 38:* 520–9.

(1931). *The Masquerade of Monopoly.* Reprint ed. Fairfield, N.J.: Kelley.

Finn, T. J. (1974). "The Quantity of Output in Simple Monopoly and Discriminating Monopoly." *Southern Economic Journal 41:* 239–43.

Fourastié, J. (1959). *Documents pour l'histoire et la théorie des prix.* Paris: Colin.

(1969). *L'évolution des prix à long terme.* Paris: PUF.

Fox, K. A. (1953). "A Spatial Equilibrium Model of the Livestock Feed Economy in the U.S.A." *Econometrica 21:* 547–66.

Fox, K. A., and R. C. Täuber (1955). "Spatial Equilibrium Models of the Livestock Feed Economy." *American Economic Review 45:* 584–608.

Friedman, D. D. (1979). "In Defense of the Long-haul/Short-haul Discrimination." *Bell Journal of Economics 10:* 706–8.

Friedman, J. W. (1977). *Oligopoly and the Theory of Games.* Amsterdam: North Holland.

Gabor, A. (1955). "A Note on Block Tariffs." *Review of Economic Studies 23:* 32–41.

Gabszewicz, J. J. (1980). "A Note on Product Variety under Monopoly and Duopoly." Mimeographed. Louvain-la-Neuve: CORE, Université Catholique de Louvain.

Gabszewicz, J. J., and J.-F. Thisse (1979). "Price Competition, Quality, and Income Disparities." *Journal of Economic Theory 20:* 340–59.

(1980). "Entry (and Exit) in a Differentiated Industry." *Journal of Economic Theory 22:* 327–38.

Gabszewicz, J. J., and J. J. Vial (1972). "Oligopoly 'à la Cournot' in a General Equilibrium Analysis." *Journal of Economic Theory 4:* 381–400.

Gannon, C. A. (1973). "Optimization of Market Share in Spatial Competition." *Southern Economic Journal 40:* 66–79.

Gilbert, R. J. (1978). "Dominant Firm Pricing in a Market for an Exhaustible Resource." *Bell Journal of Economics 8* (autumn): 385–95.

Godley, W., and W. D. Nordhaus (1972). "Pricing in the Trade Cycle." *Economic Journal 82:* 853–82.

Goldman, M., H. Leland, and D. Sibley (1977). "Optimal Nonuniform Prices." Economic Discussion Paper 100. Murray Hill, N.J.: Bell Laboratories, May.

Goss, B., and B. S. Yamey (1976). *The Economics of Future Trading.* London: Macmillan.

Gould, J. R. (1977). "Price Discrimination and Vertical Control: A Note." *Journal of Political Economy 85:* 1063–71.

Gray, L. C. (1914). "Rent under the Assumption of Exhaustibility." *Quarterly Journal of Economics 28:* 466–89.

Greenhut, M. L. (1952). "The Size and Shape of the Market Area of a Firm." *Southern Economic Journal 19:* 37–50.

(1960). "Size of Markets vs. Transport Costs in Industrial Location: Surveys and Theory." *Journal of Industrial Economics 8:* 172–84.

(1963). *Microeconomics and the Space Economy.* Chicago: Scott Foresman.

(1970). *Theory of the Firm in Economic Space.* New York: Meredith.

(1980). "Spatial Pricing in U.S.A., West Germany, and Japan." *Economica 48:* 79–86.

Greenhut, J., and M. L. Greenhut (1975). "Spatial Price Discrimination, Competition, and Locational Effects." *Economica 42:* 401–19.

(1977). "Nonlinearity of Delivered Price Schedules and Predatory Pricing." *Econometrica 45* (November): 1871–75.

Greenhut, J., M. L. Greenhut, and S.-Y. Li (1980). "Spatial Pricing Patterns in the United States." *Quarterly Journal of Economics 94* (March): 329–50.

Greenhut, M. L., M. Hwang, and H. Ohta (1974). "Price Discrimination by Regulated Motor Carriers: Comment." *American Economic Review 64:* 780–4.

(1975). "Observations on the Shape and Relevance of the Spatial Demand Function." *Econometrica 43:* 669–82.

Greenhut, M. L., and H. Ohta (1972). "Monopoly Output under Alternative Spatial Pricing Techniques." *American Economic Review 62* (September): 705–13.

(1973). "Spatial Configurations and Competitive Equilibrium." *Weltwirtschaftliches Archiv 109* 87–104.

(1975). *Theory of Spatial Pricing and Market Areas.* Durham: Duke University Press.

(1976). "Joan Robinson's Criterion for Deciding Whether Market Discrimination Reduces Output." *Economic Journal 86:* 96–7.

Gronberg, T., and J. Meyer (1981). "Competitive Equilibria in Uniform Delivered Pricing Models." *American Economic Review 71:* 758–63.

Guasch, J. L., and J. Sobel (1979). *Product Selection, Market Structure, and Heterogeneity of Quality Valuations.* Discussion Paper 79–34. San Diego: University of California.

(1980). "Monopoly and Product Selection." *Economics Letters 5:* 81–3.

Guitton, H. (1958). "L'Europe et la théorie économique." *Revue d'économie politique:* 324–39.

Hahn, C. H. (1953). *Der Schumanplan: Eine Untersuchung im besonderen Hinblick auf die deutsch-französische Stahlindustrie.* Ph.D. dissertation. Munich.

Hall, R. L., and C. J. Hitch (1951). "Price Theory and Business Behaviour." In T. Wilson and P. W. S. Andrews, eds., *Oxford Studies in the Price Mechanism,* 107–38. Oxford: Oxford University Press.

Hansen, R. S., and R. B. Roberts (1980). "Metered Tying Arrangements, Allocative Efficiency, and Price Discrimination." *Southern Economic Journal 47:* 73–83.

Harbers, C. C. (1953). *Frachtbasis-systeme.* Ph.D. dissertation. Frankfurt: Frankfurt University.

Hause, J. C. (1977). "The Measurement of Concentrated Industrial Structure and the Size Distribution of Firms." *Annals of Economic and Social Measurement 6* (winter): 73–107.

Hay, G. A. (1970). "Production, Price, and Inventory Theory." *American Economic Review 60:* 531–45.

(1972). "The Dynamics of Firm Behavior under Alternative Cost Structures." *American Economic Review 62:* 403–13.

(1973). "An Economic Analysis of Vertical Integration." *Industrial Organization Review 1:* 188–98.

Heal, G. (1975). "Economic Aspects of Natural Resource Depletion." In D. W. Pearce and J. Rose, eds., *The Economics of Depletion,* 118–39. London: Macmillan.

(1976a). "Do Bad Products Drive Out Good?" *Quarterly Journal of Economics 90:* 499–502.

(1976b). "The Relationship between Price and Extraction Cost for a Resource with a Backstop Technology." *Bell Journal of Economics 7* (autumn): 371–8.

(1980). "Spatial Structure in the Retail Trade: A Study in Product Differentiation with Increasing Return." *Bell Journal of Economics 11:* 565–83.

Heal, G., and M. Barrow (1979). "The Influence of Interest Rates on Metal Price Movements." *Review of Economic Studies 47:* 161–81.

(1981). "Empirical Investigation of the Long-term Movements of Resource Prices: A Preliminary Report." *Economics Letters 7:* 95–103.

Herlemann, H. H. (1950). *Die Versorgung der westdeutschen Landwirtschaft mit Mineraldünger.* Kieler Studien. Kiel: Weltwirtschaftliches Institut.

Hicks, J. R. (1936). *Value and Capital.* Oxford: Oxford University Press.

Hilton, G. W. (1958). "Tying Sales and Full-Line Forcing." *Weltwirtschaftliches Archiv:* 265–76.

Hirschleifer, J. (1958). "Peak Loads and Efficient Pricing: Comment." *Quarterly Journal of Economics 72:* 451–62.

(1973). "Where Are We in the Theory of Information?" *American Economic Review 63* (May): 31–39.

Hnyilicza, E., and R. S. Pindyck (1976). "Pricing Policies for a Two-Part Exhaustible Resource Cartel: The Case of OPEC." *European Economic Review 8:* 139–54.

Hoel, M. (1978). "Resource Extraction, Substitute Production, and Monopoly." *Journal of Economic Theory 19:* 28–37.

Holahan, W. L. (1975). "The Welfare Effects of Spatial Price Discrimination." *American Economic Review 65:* 498–503.

Hoover, E. M. (1936–7). "Spatial Price Discrimination." *Review of Economic Studies 4:* 182–91.

Hotelling, H. (1929). "Stability in Competition." *Economic Journal 39:* 41–57.

——— (1931). "The Economics of Exhaustible Resources." *Journal of Political Economy 39:* 137–75.

Houthakker, H. S. (1951). "Electricity Tariffs in Theory and Practice." *Economic Journal 61:* 1–25.

——— (1952–3). "Compensated Changes in Quantities and Qualities Consumed." *Review of Economic Studies 19* no. 50: 155–64.

Hyson, C. D., and W. P. Hyson (1950). "The Economic Law of Market Areas." *Quarterly Journal of Economics 64:* 319–27.

Imkamp, M. J. J. A. (1958). *Prijsdiscriminatie in Amerika en in het E.G.K.S.-verdrag.* The Hague.

Isard, W., and W. W. Capron (1949). "The Future Locational Pattern of Iron and Steel Production in the United States." *Journal of Political Economy 67:* 118–31.

Jacquemin, A., and J. Thisse (1972). "Recent Applications of Optimal Control Theory to Industrial Organization." In K. Cowling, ed., *Market Structure and Corporate Behavior.* London: Gray-Mills.

Jung, A. F. (1960). "Price Variations among Automobile Dealers in Metropolitan Chicago." *Journal of Business 83:* 31–42.

Justman, J. P. L. (1958). *Concurrentieregime en prijsvorming: Internationale aspecten.* Preadvies II. The Hague: Vereniging voor de Staathuishoudkunde.

Kaldor, N. (1939). "Speculation and Economic Stability." *Review of Economic Studies 7:* 1–27.

——— (1976). "Inflation and Recession in the World Economy." *Economic Journal 86:* 703–14.

Kamien, M. I., and N. L. Schwartz (1971). "Limit Pricing and Uncertain Entry." *Econometrica 39:* 441–54.

Katz, E., and Z. M. Berrebi (1980). "On the Price Discriminating Labour Cooperative." *Economics Letters 6:* 99–102.

Kawasaki, S., J. McMillan, and K. F. Zimmerman (1981). "Inventories and Price Inflexibility." Mimeographed. Mannheim: Mannheim University.

Kay, J. A. (1979). "Uncertainty, Congestion, and Peak Load Pricing." *Review of Economic studies 46:* 601–11.

Kaysen, C. (1949). "Basing-Point Pricing and Public Policy." *Quarterly Journal of Economics 63:* 289–314.

Kemp, M. C., and N. V. Long (1980). "On Two Folk Theorems Concerning the Extraction of Exhaustible Resources." *Econometrica 48:* 663–73.

Kessel, R. A. (1958). "Price Discrimination in Medicine." *Journal of Law and Economics 1:* 20–53.

Khalatbari, F. (1977). "Market Imperfections and Optimal Rate of Depletion of an Exhaustible Resource." *Economica 44:* 409–14.

King, M. (1978). "Corporate Policy, Uncertainty, and the Stock Market." In G. Schwödiauer, ed., *Equilibrium and Disequilibrium in Economic Theory,* 315–36. Dordrecht: Reidel.

Kirman, A. P., and M. J. Sobel (1974). "Dynamic Oligopoly with Inventories." *Econometrica 42:* 279–87.

Koopmans, T. C. (1957). *Three Essays on the State of Economic Science.* New York: McGraw-Hill.

Lancaster, K. (1975). "Socially Optimal Product Differentiation." *American Economic Review 65:* 567–85.

(1979). *Variety, Equity, and Efficiency.* New York: Columbia University Press.

Lane, W. J. (1980). "Product Differentiation in a Market with Endogenous Sequential Entry." *Bell Journal of Economics 11* (spring): 237–60.

Leland, H. (1979). "Quacks, Lemons, and Licensing: A Theory of Minimum Quality Standard." *Journal of Political Economy 87:* 1328–46.

Leland, H. E. (1977). "Quality Choice and Competition." *American Economic Review 67:* 127–35.

Leland, H. E., and R. Meyer (1976). "Monopoly Pricing Structures with Imperfect Information." *Bell Journal of Economics 7* (autumn): 449–62.

Lerner, A. P., and H. W. Singer (1937). "Some Notes on Duopoly and Spatial Competition." *Journal of Political Economy 45:* 145–86.

Levhari, D., and R. S. Pindyck (1981). "The Pricing of Durable Exhaustible Resources." *Quarterly Journal of Economics 96:* 365–78.

Lewis, W. A. (1945). "Competition in Retail Trade." *Economica 12:* 202–34.

Littlechild, S. (1975). "Two-part Tariffs and Consumption Externalities." *Bell Journal of Economics 6* (autumn): 661–70.

Loescher, S. M. (1959). *Imperfect Collusion in the Cement Industry.* Cambridge, Mass.: Harvard University Press.

Lutz, F., and V. Lutz (1951). *The Theory of Investment of the Firm.* Princeton: Princeton University Press.

Machlup, F. (1949). *The Basing-Point System.* Philadelphia: Blakiston.

Machlup, F., and M. Taber (1960). "Bilateral Monopoly, Successive Monopoly, and Vertical Integration." *Economica 27:* 101–19.

McRae, J. J. (1978). "On the Stability of Non-replenishable Resource Prices." *Canadian Journal of Economics 11:* 287–9.

Malinvaud, E. (1953). "Capital Accumulation and Efficient Allocation of Resources." *Econometrica 21:* 233–68.

(1976). *The Theory of Unemployment Reconsidered.* Yrjö Johnsson Lectures. Oxford: Blackwell Publisher.

Marchand, M. G. (1974). "Pricing Power Supplied on an Interruptible Basis." *European Economic Review 5:* 263–74.

Marengo, L. (1955). "The Basing-Point Decisions and the Steel Industry." *American Economic Review 45:* 509–22.

Maroni, Y. R. (1947). "Discrimination under Market Independence." *Quarterly Journal of Economics 61:* 95–117.

Marvel, H. P. (1976). "The Economics of Information and Gasoline Price Behavior: An Empirical Analysis." *Journal of Political Economy 84:* 1033–60.

Masson, R. T., and S. Wu (1974). "Price Discrimination for Physicians' Services." *Journal of Human Resources 9:* 63–79.

Maynes, E. S. (1976). "The Concept and Measurement of Product Quality." In N. Terleckyj, ed., *Household Production and Consumption,* 529–60. New York: National Bureau of Economic Research.

Meade, J. E. (1974). "The Optimal Balance between Economies of Scale and Variety of Products: An Illustrative Model." *Economica 41:* 359–67.

Meade, J. E., and P. W. S. Andrews (1951). "Summary of Replies to Questions on Effects of Interest Rates." In T. Wilson and P. W. S. Andrews, eds., *Oxford Studies in the Price Mechanism,* 27–30. Oxford: Oxford University Press.

Menze, H. (1963). "Markttransparenz in Theorie und Wettbewerbsrecht." *Wirtschaft und Wettbewerb 13:* 578–90.

Mestmäcker, E. J. (1955). "Offene Preise, Diskriminierungen, und Wettbewerbsbeschränkungen in der Montanunion." *Wirtschaft und Wettbewerb 5.*

Meyer, R. A. (1975). "Monopoly Pricing and Capacity Choice under Uncertainty." *American Economic Review 65:* 326–37.

——— (1979). "Optimal Nonlinear Pricing Structures: An Application to Energy Pricing." *Applied Economics 11:* 241–54.

Mills, E. S. (1962). *Price, Output, and Inventory Policy.* New York: Wiley.

Mirman, L. J., and D. Sibley (1980). "Optimal Nonlinear Prices for Multiproduct Monopolies." *Bell Journal of Economics 11* (autumn): 659–70.

Mirrlees, J. M. (1971). "An Exploration in the Theory of Optimum Income Taxation." *Review of Economic Studies 38:* 175–208.

Mitchell, B. M. (1978). "Optimal Pricing of Local Telephone Service." *American Economic Review 68:* 517–37.

Mitchell, B. M., W. G. Manning, Jr., and J. P. Acton (1978). *Peak Load Pricing: European Lessons for U.S. Energy Policy.* Cambridge, Mass.: Ballinger.

Mohring, H. (1970). "The Peak Load Problem with Increasing Returns and Pricing Constraints." *American Economic Review 60:* 693–705.

Möller, H. (1941). *Kalkulation, Absatzpolitik, und Preisbildung.* Vienna.

——— (1943a). "Die Formen der regionalen Preisdifferenzierung." *Weltwirtschaftliches Archiv 57:* 81–112.

——— (1943b). "Grundlagen einer Theorie der regionalen Preisdifferenzierung." *Weltwirtschaftliches Archiv 57:* 335–91.

Mougeot, M. (1975). *Théorie et politique économiques régionales.* Paris.

Mund, V. A. (1948). *Open Markets.* New York.

Mussa, R., and S. Rosen (1978). "Monopoly and Product Quality." *Journal of Economic Theory 18:* 301–17.

Negishi, T. (1960). "Welfare Economics and Existence of an Equilibrium for a Competitive Economy." *Metro-economica 12:* 92–97.

Nelson, P. (1970). "Information and Consumer Behavior." *Journal of Political Economy 78:* 311–29.

Newbery, D. M. G. (1981). "Oil Prices, Cartels, and the Problem of Dynamic Consistency." *Economic Journal 91:* 617–46.

Nordhaus, W. D. (1973). "The Allocation of Energy Resources." *Papers on Economic Activity, 3.* Washington, D.C.: Brookings Institution.

——— (1976). "Inflation Theory and Policy." *American Economic Review 64* (May): 59–64.

Ng, Y., and W. Weisser (1974). "Optimal Pricing with a Budget Constraint – The Case of the Two-Part Tariff." *Review of Economic Studies 41:* 337–45.

Nguyen, D. T. (1976). "The Problems of Peak Loads and Inventories." *Bell Journal of Economics 7* (spring): 242–8.

Norman, G. (1981a). "Spatial Competition and Spatial Price Discrimination." *Review of Economic Studies 48:* 97–111.

——— (1981b). "Spatial Pricing with Differentiated Products." Discussion Paper. Reading, England: University of Reading.

Ohta, H. (1981). "The Price Effects of Spatial Competition." *Review of Economic Studies 48:* 317–25.

Oi, W. Y. (1971). "A Disneyland Dilemma: Two-Part Tariffs for a Mickey Mouse Monopoly." *Quarterly Journal of Economics 85:* 77–90.

Olson, J. (1972). "Price Discrimination by Regulated Motor Carriers." *American Economic Review 62:* 395–402.

Ordover, J. A., and J. C. Panzar (1980). "On the Nonexistence of Pareto Superior Outlay Schedules." *Bell Journal of Economics 11* (spring): 351–54.

——— (1981). "On the Nonlinear Pricing of Inputs." Mimeograph.

Padoa Schioppa, F. (1981). "Cross-sectional and Intertemporal Price Variability." Discussion Paper 8115. Louvain-la-Neuve: CORE, Université Catholique de Louvain.

Panzar, J. C. (1976). "A Neoclassical Approach to Peak Load Pricing." *Bell Journal of Economics 7* (autumn): 521–30.

Panzar, J. C., and D. S. Sibley (1978). "Public Utility Pricing under Risk: The Case of Self-Rationing." *American Economic Review 68:* 888–95.

Paroush, J. (1978). "On Quality Discrimination." *Southern Economic Journal 45:* 592–97.

Paroush, J., and Y. C. Peles (1981). "A Combined Monopoly and Optimal Packaging." *European Economic Review 15:* 373–83.

Pegrum, D. F. (1951). "The Present Status of Geographic Pricing." *Journal of Marketing 15:* 425–35.

Perry, M. K. (1978). "Price Discrimination and Forward Integration." *Bell Journal of Economics 9* (spring): 209–17.

   (1980). "Forward Integration by Alcoa: 1888–1930." *Journal of Industrial Economics 29:* 37–53.

Peterman, J. L. (1979). "The *International Salt* Case." *Journal of Law and Economics 22:* 351–64.

Phlips, L. (1962a). *De l'intégration des marchés.* Louvain: Nauwelaerts.

   (1962b). "Common Markets: Towards a Theory of Market Integration." *Journal of Industrial Economics 10:* 81–92.

   (1964a). "Demand Curves and Product Differentiation." *Kyklos 17:* 408–18.

   (1964b). "Markttransparenz in Theorie und Wirklichkeit." *Wirtschaft und Wettbewerb 14:* 205–11.

   (1971). *Effects of Industrial Concentration: A Cross-Section Analysis for the Common Market.* Amsterdam: North Holland.

   (1973). "Illusions in Testing for Administered Prices: A Reply." *Journal of Industrial Economics 21:* 196–99.

   (1974). *Applied Consumption Analysis.* Amsterdam: North Holland.

   (1976). *Spatial Pricing and Competition.* Studies of the Commission of the European Communities, Competition: Approximation of Legislation Series, No. 29. Brussels: Commission of the EEC.

   (1980). "Intertemporal Price Discrimination and Sticky Prices." *Quarterly Journal of Economics 94* (May): 525–42.

Phlips, L., and R. E. Schuler (1981). "Product Selection and Price Discrimination." Discussion Paper 8126. Louvain-la-Nueve: CORE, Université Catholique de Louvain.

Phlips, L., and J.-F. Thisse (1981). "Pricing, Distribution, and the Supply of Storage." *European Economic Review 15:* 225–43.

   (Forthcoming). "Spatial Competition and the Theory of Differentiated Markets: An Introduction." *Journal of Industrial Economics.*

Phlips, P. J., and L. Phlips (1981). "Price Variability, Changes in Demand, and the Rate of Interest." *Economics Letters 7:* 7–10.

Pigou, A. C. (1912). *Wealth and Welfare.* London: Macmillan.

   (1920). *The Economics of Welfare.* 4th ed. London: Macmillan.

Pilati, P. (1979). "Prolifération des marques: Barrière à l'entrée." Mimeographed. Louvain-la-Neuve: Université Catholique de Louvain.

Pindyck, R. S. (1978a). "The Optimal Exploration and Production of Nonrenewable Resources." *Journal of Political Economy 86:* 841–61.

   (1978b). "Gains to Producers from the Cartelization of Exhaustible Resources." *Review of Economics and Statistics 60:* 238–51.

   (1980). "Uncertainty and Exhaustible Resource Markets." *Journal of Political Economy 88:* 1203–25.

Pollak, R. A. (1968). "Consistent Planning." *Review of Economic Studies 35:* 201–8.

Pratt, J. W., D. A. Wise, and R. Zeckhauser (1979). "Price Differences in Almost Competitive Markets." *Quarterly Journal of Economics 93* (May): 189–211.

Prescott, E., and M. Visscher (1977). "Sequential Location among Firms with Foresight." *Bell Journal of Economics 8* (autumn): 378–93.

Pyatt, G. (1978). "Marginal Costs, Prices, and Storage." *Economic Journal 88* (December): 749–62.

Reekie, W. D. (1978). "Price and Quality Competition in the United States Drug Industry." *Journal of Industrial Economics 26:* 223–37.

Report on the Supply of Chemical Fertilizers. London: Monopolies Commission, 1959.

Robert, A. (1958). "Speech delivered 6 June 1957 at the Stresa Conference." *Actes officiels du congrès international d'études sur la Communauté Européenne du Charbon et de l'Acier,* vol. 6, 594–9. Milan: Dott. A. Giuffrè.

Roberts, K. (1979). "Welfare Considerations of Nonlinear Pricing." *Economic Journal 89:* 66–83.

Robinson, J. (1933). *The Economics of Imperfect Competition.* London: Macmillan.

Rosen, S. (1974). "Hedonic Prices and Implicit Markets: Product Differentiation in Pure Competition." *Journal of Political Economy 82:* 34–55.

Ross, H. W. (1973). "Illusions in Testing for Administered Prices." *Journal of Industrial Economics 21:* 187–95.

Rothschild, M. (1973). "Models of Market Organization with Imperfect Information: A Survey." *Journal of Political Economy 81:* 1283–308.

(1974). "Searching for the Lowest Price When the Distribution of Prices Is Unknown." *Journal of Political Economy 82:* 689–711.

Rothschild, M., and J. Stiglitz (1976). "Equilibrium in Competitive Insurance Markets: An Essay on the Economics of Imperfect Information." *Quarterly Journal of Economics 90:* 629–50.

Rowlatt, P. A. (1976). "A Micro-Model of Inflation." *Economica 43:* 255–66.

Ruffin, R. J., and D. E. Leigh (1973). "Charity, Competition, and the Pricing of Doctors' Services." *Journal of Human Resources 8:* 212–22.

Salant, S. (1976). "Exhaustible Resources and Industrial Structure: A Nash–Cournot Approach to the World Oil Market." *Journal of Political Economy 84:* 1079–93.

Salop, S. (1977). "The Noisy Monopolist: Imperfect Information, Price Dispersion, and Price Discrimination." *Review of Economic Studies 44:* 393–406.

(1978). "Parables of Information Transmission in Markets." In A. A. Mitchell, ed., *The Effect of Information on Consumer and Market Behavior,* 3–12. Proceedings Series. Chicago: American Marketing Association.

(1979). "Monopolistic Competition with Outside Goods." *Bell Journal of Economics 10* (spring): 141–56.

Samuelson, P. A. (1952). "Spatial Price Equilibrium and Linear Programming." *American Economic Review 42:* 283–303.

(1954). "The Pure Theory of Public Expenditure." *Review of Economics and Statistics 36:* 387–9.

(1955). "Diagrammatic Exposition of a Theory of Public Expenditure." *Review of Economics and Statistics 37:* 350–6.

(1957). "Intertemporal Price Equilibrium: A Prologue to the Theory of Speculation." *Weltwirtschaftsliches Archiv 79:* 181–221.

Sauermann, H. (1951). "Wirtschaftliche Integration Europas." *Kölner Zeitschrift für Soziologie 4:* 305–10.

Sayers, R. S. (1951). "The Rate of Interest as a Weapon of Economic Policy." In T. Wilson and P. W. S. Andrews, eds., *Oxford Studies in the Price Mechanism,* 1–16. Oxford: Oxford University Press.

Scherer, F. M. (1970). *Industrial Market Structure and Economic Peformance.* Chicago: Rand McNally.

Schmalensee, R. (1973). "A Note on the Theory of Vertical Integration." *Journal of Political Economy 81:* 442-9.

———— (1976). "Resource Exploitation Theory and the Behavior of the Oil Cartel." *European Economic Review 7: 257-79.*

———— (1980). *Monopolistic Two-Part Pricing Arrangements.* Working Paper 1105-80. Rev. ed. Cambridge, Mass.: Massachusetts Institute of Technology, October.

———— (1981). "Output and Welfare Implications of Monopolistic Third-Degree Price Discrimination." *American Economic Review 71:* 242-7.

Schmidt, I. (1963). "Markttransparenz als Voraussetzung für Wettbewerbsbeschränkungen." *Wirtschaft und Wettbewerb 14:* 97-106.

Schneider, E. (1934). "Preisbildung und Preispolitik unter Berücksichtigung der geographischen Verteilung von Erzeugern und Verbrauchern." *Schmollers Jahrbuch 58,* no. 3.

———— (1938). "Zur Konkurrenz und Preisbildung auf vollkommenen und unvollkommenen Märkten." *Weltwirtschaftliches Archiv 48,* pt. 2: 399-419.

Schuler, R. E. (1973). "Air Quality Improvement and Long-Run Urban Form." *Regional Science Association Papers 31:* 133-48.

———— (1979). "The Long Run Limits to Growth: Renewable Resources, Endogenous Population, and Technological Change." *Journal of Economic Theory 21:* 166-85.

Schuler, R. E., and W. L. Holahan (1978). "Competition vs. Vertical Integration of Transportation and Production in a Spatial Economy." *Papers of the Regional Science Association 41:* 209-25.

Segelmann, F., and E. Niederleithinger (1967). "Frankostationspreis- und Frachtbassissysteme der Syndikate nach dem Gesetz gegen Wettbewerbsbeschränkungen." *Wirtschaft und Wettbewerb 27:* 453-86.

Semler, R. (1963). "Zementkartelle in Vergangenheit und Gegenwart." In *Kartelle in der Wirklichkeit: Festschrift für Max Metzner.* Cologne: Carl Heymanns.

Shaked, A. (1975). "Nonexistence of Equilibrium for the 2-Dimensional 3-Firm Location Problem." *Review of Economic Studies 42:* 51-6.

Shaked, A., and J. Sutton (1982). "The Self-Regulating Profession." *Review of Economic Studies 48:* 217-34.

Shaw, E. S. (1940). "Elements of a Theory of Inventory." *Journal of Political Economy 48:* 465-85.

Sherman, R., and M. Visscher (1977). "Public Utility Price and Capacity in the Case of Oscillating Demand." *Scandinavian Journal of Economics 79:* 41-53.

———— (1978). "Second Best Pricing with Stochastic Demand." *American Economic Review 68:* 41-53.

———— (1979). "Persistent Multiple Prices for Oscillating Demand." *Scandinavian Journal of Economics 81:* 494-504.

Sheshinski, E. (1976). "Price, Quality, and Quantity Regulation in Monopoly Situations." *Economica 43:* 127-37.

Smith, R. L., II (1981). "Efficiency Gains from Strategic Investment." *Journal of Industrial Economics 30:* 1-24.

Smithies, A. (1939). "The Maximization of Profits over Time with Changing Cost and Demand Functions." *Econometrica 7:* 312-18.

———— (1941a). "Optimum Location in Spatial Competition." *Journal of Political Economy 49:* 423-39.

———— (1941b). "Monopolistic Price Policy in a Spatial Market." *Econometrica 9:* 63-73.

———— (1942). "Aspects of the Basing-Point System." *American Economic Review 32:* 702-26.

Solow, R. M. (1974). "The Economics of Resources or the Resources of Economics." *American Economic Review 64:* 1-14.

Solow, R. M., and F. Y. Wan (1976). "Extraction Costs in the Theory of Exhaustible Resources." *Bell Journal of Economics 7* (autumn): 359-70.

Spence, M. (1973). *Market Signalling*. Cambridge, Mass.: Harvard University Press.

    (1975). "Monopoly, Quality, and Regulation." *Bell Journal of Economics 6* (autumn): 417-29.

    (1976). "Product Selection, Fixed Costs, and Monopolistic Competition." *Review of Economic Studies 43:* 217-35.

    (1977). "Nonlinear Prices and Welfare." *Journal of Public Economics 8:* 1-18.

    (1978). "Tacit Co-ordination and Imperfect Information." *Canadian Journal of Economics 11:* 490-505.

    (1980). "Multi-Product Quantity-Dependent Prices and Profitability Constraints." *Review of Economic Studies 47:* 821-41.

Spulber, D. F. (1979). "Non-cooperative Equilibrium with Price Discriminating Firms." *Economics Letters 4:* 221-7.

    (1981a). "Spatial Nonlinear Pricing." *American Economic Review 71:* 923-33.

    (1981b). "Capacity, Output, and Sequential Entry." *American Economic Review 71:* 503-14.

Stegemann, K. (1967). "Drei Funktionen eines Frachtgrundlagensystems in Artikel 60 des Montanvertrages." *Kyklos 20:* 642-81.

    (1968). "Three Functions of Basing-Point Pricing and Article 60 of the E.C.S.C. Treaty." *Antitrust Bulletin* (summer): 395-432.

Steiner, P. O. (1957). "Peak Loads and Efficient Pricing." *Quarterly Journal of Economics 71:* 585-610.

    (1958). Reply to Hirschleifer. *Quarterly Journal of Economics 72:* 467.

Stern, N. (1972). "The Optimal Size of Market Areas." *Journal of Economic Theory 4:* 154-73.

Stevens, B. H., and C. P. Rydell (1966). "Spatial Demand Theory and Monopoly Price Policy." *Papers of the Regional Science Association 17:* 195-204.

Stewart, M. (1979a). "Market Structure and the Search for Exhaustible Resources." *Economics Letters 2:* 85-90.

Stewart, M. B. (1979b). "Monopoly and the Choice of Product Characteristics." *Economics Letters 2:* 79-84.

Stigler, G. J. (1949). "A Theory of Delivered Price Systems." *American Economic Review 39:* 1143-59.

    (1951). "The Division of Labor Is Limited by the Extent of the Market." *Journal of Political Economy 59* (June): 185-93.

    (1961). "The Economics of Information." *Journal of Political Economy 69:* 213-85.

    (1962). "Administered Prices and Oligopolistic Inflation." *Journal of Business 35.*

    (1964). "A Theory of Oligopoly." *Journal of Political Economy 72.*

    (1968). "A Note on Block Booking." In *The Organization of Industry.* Homewood, Ill.: Irwin.

Stiglitz, J. (1976). "Monopoly and the Rate of Extraction of Exhaustible Resources." *American Economic Review 66:* 655-61.

    (1977). "Monopoly, Non-linear Pricing, and Imperfect Information: The Insurance Market." *Review of Economic Studies 44:* 407-30.

Stokey, N. L. (1979). "Intertemporal Price Discrimination." *Quarterly Journal of Economics 93:* 355-71.

    (1981). "Rational Expectations and Durable Goods Pricing." *Bell Journal of Economics 12* (spring): 112-28.

Stocking, G. W. (1954). *Basing-Point Pricing and Regional Development.* Chapel Hill.

Strotz, R. H. (1956). "Myopia and Inconsistency in Dynamic Utility Maximization." *Review of Economic Studies 23:* 165-80.

Takayama, T., and G. Judge (1971). *Spatial and Temporal Price and Allocation Models.* Amsterdam: North Holland.

276   **References**

Taussig, F. W. (1891). "A Contribution to the Theory of Railway Rates." *Quarterly Journal of Economics 5:* 438ff.

(1933). "The Theory of Railway Rates Once More." *Quarterly Journal of Economics 47:* 337ff.

Taylor, L. D. (1975). "The Demand for Electricity: A Survey." *Bell Journal of Economics* 6 (spring): 74–110.

Telser, L. G. (1965). "Abusive Trade Practices: An Economic Analysis." *Law and Contemporary Problems 30:* 488–505.

(1972). *Competition, Collusion, and Game Theory.* Chicago: Aldine-Atherton.

(1973). "Searching for the Lowest Price." *American Economic Review 63* (papers and proceedings): 41–9.

(1979). "A Theory of Monopoly of Complementary Goods." *Journal of Business 52:* 211–30.

Thisse, J. (1975). "Contribution à la théorie microéconomique spatiale." Ph.D. dissertation. Liège University.

Turvey, R. (1968). *Optimal Pricing and Investment in Electricity Supply.* London: George Allen and Unwin.

(1970). "Public Utility Pricing and Output under Risk: Comment." *American Economic Review 60:* 485–6.

Varian, H. R. (1980). "A Model of Sales." *American Economic Review 70:* 651–9.

Vernon, J. M., and D. A. Graham (1971). "Profitability of Monopolization by Vertical Integration." *Journal of Political Economy 79:* 924–5.

Viscusi, W. K. P. (1978). "A Note on 'Lemons' Markets with Quality Certification." *Bell Journal of Economics 9* (spring): 277–9.

Visscher, M. (1973). "Welfare-maximizing Price and Output with Stochastic Demand." *American Economic Review 63:* 224–9.

Wagner, H. (1952). *Eigenart und Problematik der Frachtgrundlagen.* Ph.D dissertation. Mannheim: Mannheim University.

Walras, L. (1875/1980). "The State and the Railways." Trans. P. Holmes. *Journal of Public Economics 13:* 81–100. Originally published 1875.

Warren-Boulton, F. R. (1974). "Vertical Control with Variable Proportions." *Journal of Political Economy 82:* 783–802.

Wenders, T. J. (1976). "Peak Load Pricing in the Electric Utility Industry." *Bell Journal of Economics 7* (spring): 232–41.

Weymar, F. H. (1968). *The Dynamics of the World Cocoa Market.* Cambridge, Mass.: M.I.T. Press.

White, L. J. (1977). "Market Structure and Product Varieties." *American Economic Review 67:* 179–82.

Whitney, S. N. (1955). "Vertical Disintegration in the Motion Picture Industry." *American Economic Review 45:* 491–8.

Williamson, O. E. (1966). "Peak-Load Pricing and Optimal Capacity under Indivisibility Constraints." *American Economic Review 56:* 810–27.

(1971). "The Vertical Integration of Production: Market Failure Considerations." *American Economic Review 61:* 112–23.

(1974). "Peak Load Pricing: Some Further Remarks." *Bell Journal of Economics and Management Science 5:* 223–8.

Willig, R. (1976). "Consumer's Surplus without Apology." *American Economic Review 66:* 589–97.

(1978). "Pareto-superior Nonlinear Outlay Schedules." *Bell Journal of Economics 9* (spring): 56–69.

Wilson, T., and P. W. S. Andrews, eds. (1951). *Oxford Studies in the Price Mechanism.* Oxford: Oxford University Press (Clarendon Press).

Witlox, H. (1960). "Compositie rond de commerciële voorkeursbehandeling: Prijsdiffer-tiatie of prijsdiscriminatie." *Maandschrift Economie 24,* no. 8: 457–75.

Worcester, D. A., Jr. (1948). "Justifiable Price 'Discrimination' under Conditions of Nat-ural Monopoly." *American Economic Review 38:* 382–8.

Working, H. (1948). "The Theory of Inverse Carrying Charge in Futures Markets." *Jour-nal of Farm Economics 30:* 1–28.

Wright, J. F. (1965). "Some Reflections on the Place of Discrimination in the Theory of Monopolistic Competition." *Oxford Economic Papers 17:* 175–87.

Yamey, B. (1974). "Monopolistic Price Discrimination and Economic Welfare." *Journal of Law and Economics 17:* 377–80.

Zimmerman, E. (1962). *Die Preisdiskriminierung im Recht der Europäischen Gemeinschaft für Kohle und Stahl.* Frankfurt.

Zusman, P. (1967). "A Theoretical Basis for Determination of Grading and Sorting Schemes." *Journal of Farm Economics 49:* 89–106.

Index